THE

CONSPIRACY

COLLECTION

By Christopher D Spivey

CONTENT

	Introduction	4
1	LAND OF HOPE AND GLORY – DON'T MAKE ME LAUGH	6
2	SHUT UP HILLARY	13
3	Osborne hammers home, what could well be the final nail in Britain's coffin	16
4	WHY THE JUSTICE SYSTEM FAVOURS PAEDOPHILES	23
5	UFO's - Fact, Fiction or the countdown to WW3?	30
6	ARRESTED? NOT ON YOUR LIFE	43
7	THE BBC MAKE A 'PROPER' CHARLIE OUT OF 911	48
8	Remembering 7/7 on 9/11	63
9	Welcome to Hateland, have a nice day	72
10	Invasion of the Baby snatchers	80
11	Disgraced Peer apologises - Exactly for what is anyone's guess	94
12	Putting a stop to the car insurance racket	97
13	The Cancer Con	102
14	Playthings For The Powerful	122
15	Houston...We got a problem	140
16	9/11: Never Forgive. Never Forget	144
17	There's Something In The Air	159
18	I Don't Like It, It's Quiet... Too Quiet	173
19	God bless all the little children	189
20	Living In The Material World	193
21	Terrorism: A modern day fairy tale	202
22	MONEY MADE EASY	219
23	Never in the field of human conflict was so much owed by so many to so few - Winston Churchill... He wasn't fucking lying, dontcha know	239
24	Drills of the Dead: Maine Prepares for Zombie Attack	252
25	Facebook: The Devil's Playground For Social Misfits	255
26	Fukushima	272
27	It's never Harry's fault, is it?	288
28	The True Axis Of Evil: 9/11 remembered	295

Introduction

When I first started writing back in the summer of 2011 - originally for the Sovereign Independent Newspaper and then for my website: chrisspivey.org - I was angry... Very fucking angry.

But I am getting ahead of myself. You see, sometime in the year 2000 my perception of how the world really works began to change and after the World Trade Center "terrorist attack" there really was no turning back.

That is because the world we live in is not real... It is all smoke and mirrors. Indeed, everything that we are taught from birth is a lie - a lie to keep us in our place. Nothing ever in fact changes, the rich get richer and the poor get poorer, but it doesn't have to be that way because the truth is, the world is ours.

Unfortunately, the one percenters AKA the Satanic Monster Elite do not want us to know that fact... They live in constant fear that their evil plans will become known to the world's population and if that should ever happen then their house of cards will collapse quicker than the WTC twin towers did... An event that they orchestrated themselves.

Sadly, I now fear that the mass awakening will come too late to save the human race, which the Satanic Monster Elite are hell bent on destroying and as such, I am no longer angry... Just resigned and disappointed.

Nevertheless, that is not to say that I have given up. I will never ever do that because to do so I would be failing in my role as a parent & grandparent and as the saying goes: *It ain't over until the fat lady sings.*

Which brings me to the point of this book. You see, what follows are a number of articles that I wrote along the way as I began to see the world for what it really is. These articles are no longer in the public domain simply because they are no longer relevant to my website - they were just taking up space.

However, to get to my level of understanding of how the world really works, you too will need to go through the same learning curve as I did… And believe me, that is not ego talking - that is just a fact. Therefore, I am re-publishing those articles in the hope that you too will awaken to the evil that surrounds you.

In turn, you will notice that nothing has changed for the better over the years. In fact things have got decidedly worse...

Christopher D Spivey. 15th of October 2018.

Chapter 1
LAND OF HOPE AND GLORY –
DON'T MAKE ME LAUGH

*This article was first released on my website on December 31st 2011 after originally being published in the Sovereign Independent Newspaper and takes a look at the British cconomy and how the unemployed are being made scapegoats for governments failings... A fact that is still true today...

Let's face it, there are two and only two reasons why the world is in the mess it is in today. Those two reasons are Corruption and Greed. Everything, from the world's economy teetering on the brink of collapse, through to the unrest in the Middle East, right down to the starving in Africa all stem from the money scam employed by the greedy international bankers and the corrupt politicians that they control.

The money scam – *creating money through debt with added interest* – ensures that a country's national debt will keep rising until the interest payments on that debt are so high that the repayment can't be met; resulting in the collapse of a country's economy.

This is what we are seeing happening now in many countries and in an effort to stave off the inevitable collapse, puppet politicians everywhere are making drastic and sweeping cuts right across the board - the likes of which have never been seen before. The UK I'm afraid is no exception.

In fact I think that it's fairly safe to say that we haven't had it this tough here in England since rationing was stopped in 1954 and that includes the days of Edward Heath (*A despicable perverted, totally corrupt man*) and his 3 day week.

Course, to be fair, I'm too young to remember that period in the early 1970's but I do know that back then the majority of homes got by on one income. Nowadays, a working class family depends on the wife also bringing home a wage. And without wanting to dwell on this fact too much, there can be no doubt that the absence of a 'stay at home mum' has seen a decline in the traditional family unit, leading to a marked down turn in the moral thinking of our young.

Typically, those most affected by the spending cuts are those who can least afford it. Amongst that number are the working class, the unemployed, the elderly and the sick since it doesn't do to upset those slightly higher up the social scale as these are people more likely to rock the status quo should their comfortable lives be affected.

However, while those who are managing fairly well at the moment remain by and large unaffected by what's going on around them, they too could soon be in for a rude of wakening according to Roger Hayes of the British Constitution Group. Speaking last month Roger revealed that the Government were making plans to extend the so called 'Carbon tax' so as it applies to everybody. This will be levied on the size of your car, the size of your house, the number of holidays you take a year, in fact on just about any luxury you can think of. Furthermore the tax is based on the completely false pretence that Carbon Dioxide is destroying the planet.

Meanwhile the National Health Service, already in its death throes, has been told it has to make a further £15-20 Billion in 'efficiency cuts' by the year 2015. These cuts will be made at the expense of Doctors, Nurses and essential auxiliary jobs.

The public service union, UNISON claimed in March of this year that 54,000 jobs had already gone with an estimated 4000 more going every month. Nevertheless, despite the NHS paying over the odds for drugs to the tune of an estimated £500-600 million per year, it can't expect any help from the billions of pounds the pharmaceutical industry makes in yearly profits. Indeed, with the NHS paying out somewhere around £700-800 Million a year in compensation for its negligence, a person really is taking his life in his hands when going into hospital.

We are told that Local and County Councils have also been savaged by cuts to their budgets. While that may be so in terms of getting our dustbins emptied or the closure of special needs schools and even the turning off of street lighting, Local Councils appear intent on clawing the money back in terms of increased parking fees. Alright, that may be a bit tongue in cheek, but have you seen how much it costs to park your car these days?

And talking of street lighting, the Economy crisis hasn't put the Government off looking into the possibility of replacing existing street lights with ones that house spy cameras and listening in devices. Come to think of it, it might be just as easy for you to read George Orwell's novel '1984' rather than try to predict what the future holds.

As for the Police force who the Government say are going to lose up to 20% of their yearly budget, I say don't make me laugh. While it's true, the force could lose some admin staff, I can't see this overly affecting them. To further cut costs any Police officers that leave or take redundancy will no doubt be replaced with cheaper CSO's who are gradually being given the same power as their police colleagues anyway.

The cuts certainly are not affecting the 'Bully boy' Riot Squads who appear to be swelling in numbers. Then there is the question of their spy planes. According to a report in Saturday's Telegraph, the Police have a fleet of Spy Planes each costing at least £3 million and similar to those used by MI5.

The planes which are capable of listening in on a specific mobile phone conversation are still in use despite costing "hundreds of thousands of pounds" to keep operational. The planes which are based at an airfield in Farnborough, Hampshire are operated separately from the Mets air support unit, which has 3 helicopters and costs the taxpayer around a further £3 million a year to run.

It is indeed an outrage that the government stands by and lets OAP's die of hypothermia due to rising fuel costs, while at the same time the energy providers make vast sums of money in profits. Meanwhile others hit particularly hard by the cuts are the unemployed.
On the face of it, it's easy to imagine that the reason behind this is the need to cut the cost of the £200 billion paid out every year in benefits. This is simply propaganda on behalf of the Government. Ultimately, it is true that the taxpayer covers a good percentage of this vast sum of money but then again haven't they always done?

There is a fairy story, undoubtedly encouraged by the Government that the unemployed are lazy spongers who sit on their backsides all day getting drunk and taking drugs while those in employment work their socks off to pay for this fun. This simply is not true although I'm not saying that there aren't those who play the system.

However, the real reason that the jobless are stigmatised as being lazy freeloaders is because to the Government - every person out of work is a lost asset on the Slave treadmill. Granted there does appear to be a lot of school leavers out of work but they can't claim benefits until they are 18. Even then, many don't bother because of the rigmarole involved in claiming in return for a pittance.

Not that there are any jobs for them anyway, except low paid menial dead end jobs. Furthermore, the Government has to take responsibility for these kids after engineering a dumbing down policy in education which has resulted in a whole generation of semi literate unemployable youths.

As for those unemployed and eligible to claim Job Seekers Allowance (JSA), I find it hard to believe that anyone with a full set of brain cells can even begin to think that they are *having it off* at the workers expense. For a start, most of those claiming JSA have paid National Insurance, which covers them for unemployment, yet the only jobs available are menial minimum wage jobs.

I for one would not expect a fully qualified Carpenter or Bricklayer to take a job cleaning McDonald's toilets only to find that he was better off claiming his £67.50 per week JSA. That is to say £67.50 per week if you are single and over 25. If you're under 25 that figure is reduced to £53.45.

Married couples or those in a civil partnership are even worse off receiving just £105.95 per week. I personally spend £90 a week on cigarettes which means if I was claiming JSA I would be left with minus £22.50 to buy my food and pay my bills. Work that one out. Hardly what I would call living the life of Riley.

And in return for this pittance, those out of work, no doubt already low on self esteem, have to be prepared to be vilified by the general public and interrogated once a fortnight by some holier than thou Muppet sat behind a jobcentre desk. Therefore anyone who believes a person on JSA is sitting around drunk as a skunk or high as a kite all day is no more than a state controlled robot.

However, despite the attached stigma, in reality it isn't the unemployed who are responsible for the massive £200 billion yearly benefits bill. Those on JSA only account for a measly £5 billion of the total bill. There are an estimated 60 million taxpayers in this country therefore even if the taxpayer was paying for all the money paid to the unemployed - which they are not - then their contribution would only be £1.59 per week. To further put that £5 billion in context; of the £11.8 billion paid out a year in family allowance benefit, £4.3 billion of it goes to families who really, really don't need it. But as I said earlier, the government don't dare upset the middle classes, upwards.

If the truth be known, by far the biggest chunk of the yearly benefits bill is paid out in pensions. Once again, the vast majority of pensioners have worked hard all their lives, paid their National insurance contributions and therefore they are only receiving what they are entitled to and in my opinion far less than they deserve.

Another point worth remembering is that all money paid out in benefits is paid back straight away into the system, stimulating the economy with a large chunk going straight back to the government. Don't ever fall for the Political Party line about the "*Something for Nothing culture*". The vast majority of people with that mentality go into Politics.

And as a footnote to the benefit myth, David Cameron has just announced further hardship for those on benefits. At the moment those on benefits who are given a court fine can only be made to pay the fine off at £5 per week maximum. Under Cameron's new proposals this is set to be raised to £25 per week. Can you imagine how much this is going to impact on already hard pressed families? And while it's all well and good to sit there in your nice comfortable chair and chirp out the old claptrap line: "*Well they shouldn't of broken the law in the first place*" it's worth remembering that poverty leaves people no option except to take risks.

Furthermore, don't be fooled into thinking that no one is so hard up that they have to resort to crime. You only have to look at the record number of people now having to go cap in hand to food 'banks' to realise that.

There is one final point that's worth mentioning and that is how out of touch with reality the puppets in government are. You see, at a time when a record number of people are losing their houses and others have to resort to food banks to stave off starvation, David Cameron has committed Britain into paying a further increase in the billions of pounds that the country already hands over in foreign aid.

This move is set to cost every family in the land £500 per year. At the same time and notwithstanding the already inflated salaries these parasites in government pay themselves, they see nothing wrong in dipping in to our money for such luxuries as redecorating their second homes.

God forbid should they ever feel a pang of guilt for their and their predecessor's corruption and mismanagement. Not only have these self serving, egotistical buffoons succeeded in taking the Mick out of us, they have also done a smashing job of taking the Great out of Britain.

Chapter 2
SHUT UP HILLARY

Again, this article was first released in the Sovereign Independent newspaper and as you will clearly see from the content, nothing ever changes and with a few subtle name changes, could in fact have been released today...

America took hypocrisy to a new level yesterday (6/12/11) When US Secretary of State, Hillary Clinton publicly condemned the Russian parliament over allegations of widespread vote rigging following the country's weekend election.

Course, had the American government been beyond reproach in regard to their own elections and war monger Clinton's remarks not had an ulterior motive behind them, then she would have been justified in her criticism of the rejuvenated superpower. However, nothing could be further from the truth.

You see, with a barely concealed smirk on her face, smug Clinton told a packed press conference that she was concerned by what she termed as stuffed ballot boxes and manipulated voter lists in the Russian vote.

The arrogance of this power crazed women apparently knows no bounds. Talk about the kettle calling the pot black. What Clinton seems to have conveniently forgotten is that George W Bush, the man who followed her husband into the White House, did so under very controversial circumstances following allegations of vote rigging.

However unlike the apathetic American public who sat back and let their dubiously elected new President almost single handedly destroy the American Bill of Rights, outraged Russian citizens took to the streets en masse to protest at the crooked ballot. Over 400 arrests were made as violent clashes between police and protesters continued for the second night running.

With relations between the two superpowers already strained by barely concealed American threats to invade Iran and Pakistan, a person could be forgiven for thinking that diplomacy would have been the order of the day. Instead, Clinton's remarks only succeeded in further antagonising the Kremlin.

A statement from the Russian foreign ministry labelled Clinton's comments as being *"unacceptable"*. The statement then went on to say;"*Regrettably, Washington sticks to outdated stereotypes and labels without even attempting to understand what is happening in our electorate. We hope that in the future the US side will refrain from such hostile attacks that run counter to the overall positive development of our bilateral relations*".

Predictably, wherever the US pokes its unwanted snout, Europe is never far behind. Eager to jump on the hypocrite band wagon, the European Union's foreign policy chief, Catherine Ashton released a statement expressing serious concern about media bias and the harassment of independent monitoring during the election. Is she for real?

Indeed, I think that it's safe to say that the Globalist controlled Western mainstream Media holds the monopoly on bias. And at the end of the day at least Russia held an election, crooked or not, unlike the European capital Brussels which is home to the unelected MEP.

Ms Ashton's statement read: "*Reports of procedural violations, such as lack of media impartiality, lack of separation between party and state, and the harassments of independent monitoring attempts, are however of serious concern*". In response to Clinton's and Ashton's baiting, Russian president Dmitry Medvedev warned the West not to criticise Russia's political system adding that it was none of their business.

Course, it doesn't take an experienced political analyst to work out why America and Europe are using every available opportunity they can to antagonise the Russians. China too for that matter.

After all, the American war machine is clearly up and running and determined to bring about a world war. The UK in particular appear to be just as keen. That just leaves the question as to how much provocation China and Russia are prepared to stand for before potentially millions, if not billions of us are wiped of the face of the Earth.

Not that the loss of life will cause the psychopathic Clinton and Ashton to lose any sleep from the safety of their underground bunkers.

Chapter 3
Osborne hammers home, what could well be the final nail in Britain's coffin

Again, this article was first published in the Sovereign Independent Newspaper in 2011 and highlighted how people were dying as a result of poverty in Britain… A fact that still holds true today. Interestingly, the then Chancellor, the Right Obnoxious George Osborne - living the life of Riley at our expense - told the country to expect another 5 - 6 years of hardship. Yet seven years later, things are worse than ever...

In a tragedy just waiting to happen, Army veteran Mark Mullins and his new bride Helen killed themselves in a suicide pact earlier this month. With only £57 a week to live on the couple chose death over the living hell they were forced to endure day in day out in modern day England.

Despite living in only one room of their terraced house in order to save on heating costs the couple were forced to keep what little fresh food they had in plastic bags outside because they couldn't afford a fridge. Finally, after living hand to mouth for 18 months the couple took their own lives rather than face the 12 mile weekly walk to collect a food parcel from their nearest Coventry soup kitchen.

Unbelievable as it may seem Mark and Helen Mullins were far from alone in the daily struggle to survive. New figures just released suggest that there is now in excess of 100,000 people in Britain who are dependent on food parcels. Such is the demand for these free food hampers now that new 'food banks' are opening up and down the country at the rate of one a week.

The truth is, these days people can very easily find themselves moving very quickly from relative prosperity to abject poverty. Those who only a few short years ago were advised that they could not go wrong by investing in bricks and mortar have been particularly hard hit.

Indeed, many banks were only too willing to hand out mortgages to would be home owners, often above and beyond the means of what people could comfortably afford to re pay. It is now those very same banks who, according to the homeless charity '**Shelter'**, are being granted repossession orders at the rate of one every two minutes on many of the properties that they themselves agreed mortgages for.

Course most of you reading this will already know that banks create money for loans and mortgages out of thin air. This none existent money is then lent to a house buyer with added interest, using the very real, newly acquired house as surety for the non existent loan. It is therefore nothing short of criminal that these banks, having granted these mortgages, have now engineered this latest financial crisis, resulting in many of their borrowers losing their jobs. This obviously leaves these now unemployed borrowers unable to make the mortgage repayments, thus allowing the banks to repossess their homes. From homelessness to soup kitchen now becomes little more than a small step away.

At a time of crisis, people naturally look to their government to sort out the mess. After all that's why we elect them. Step up to the podium then, Chancellor of the Exchequer George Osborne, the British government's 2011 Bilderberg Representative. Should we be worried by that fact? Oh yes, but nevertheless, surely Georgie boy will save us all? Errr…Well no he won't actually, despite whatever he might say to the contrary.

In fact, far from being optimistic, Osborne has announced the need for more cuts in services. He then follows this bad news up by telling us that things are going to be really tough for at least the next 5 or 6 years. So bad in fact that a lot more of us can expect to lose our jobs.

Not exactly the best announcement to make if you need people to start spending again, but hey, at least he has a plan.

With David Cameron sat trying to look very stern, no doubt in order to stop himself insanely giggling, Osborne forlornly announced to a sombre House of Commons that it was now necessary to borrow £11 Billion more than he had anticipated, on our behalf , in order to keep the country afloat.

What a brilliant plan! Well it is if you happen to be one of the elite Central Bankers who were no doubt by now jubilantly punching the air as Georgie boy hammered home another nail in Britain's coffin.

In fact Who would've thought that the way to get out of crippling debt would be to borrow more money that we can't afford to pay back, to add to the trillions of pounds we already owe and can't afford to pay back, just so as Georgie boy can invest it in an economy that by his own admission is going to be dire for at least the next 5 years.

Course, maybe now would have been a good time for the man entrusted with our finances to explain to the nation why he needs to borrow an extra £11 Billion over and above the god knows how many £ billions he intended to borrow in the first place, while at the same time agreeing to nearly double our contributions to the IMF in order to prop up a currency that we opted out of and that has little chance of surviving the present financial crisis.

This doubled figure represents a payment of £19.7 Billion and that isn't taking into account the £13 Billion we have already pumped into the Euro zone in the form of loans. You couldn't make this up if you tried, don't cha know.

Course David Cameron would have you believe that the blame for the inevitable financial meltdown lies elsewhere. The Rothschild controlled Prime Minister will tell you that it's the likes of those pesky Public Sector workers who have the audacity to go on strike just because they have been told that they have to pay more and work longer in order to receive less on their pensions.

And according to Cameron this one day strike will cost the country £500 Million. That is £500 Million the country cannot afford to lose unless of course he decides we can afford to lose it by giving us all a day off to celebrate the wedding of the world's wealthiest woman's Grandson. Which is only fair really since we paid for it?

All this leads me to wonder at what point do we wake up and say enough is enough? It's blatantly obvious that not only are we all being taken for mugs financially, our government is hell bent on helping the USA start WW3. Yet the prospect of us all getting nuked appears to be unimportant to the apathetic British population who just shrug their shoulders and go back to watching *'Britain's got talent'*...

On the 27th of February, the Telegraph newspaper posted the following article:

In a stark warning ahead of next month's Budget, the Chancellor said there was little the Coalition could do to stimulate the economy.

Mr Osborne made it clear that due to the parlous state of the public finances the best hope for economic growth was to encourage businesses to flourish and hire more workers.
"The British Government has run out of money because all the money was spent in the good years," the Chancellor said. "The money and the investment and the jobs need to come from the private sector."

Mr Osborne's bleak assessment echoes that of Liam Byrne, the former chief secretary to the Treasury, who bluntly joked that Labour had left Britain broke when he exited the Government in 2010.

He left David Laws, his successor, a one-line note saying: "Dear Chief Secretary, I'm afraid to tell you there's no money left".
Mr Osborne is under severe pressure to boost growth, amid signs the economy is slipping back into a recession.

The Institute of Fiscal Studies has urged him to consider emergency tax cuts in the Budget to reduce the risk of a prolonged economic slump.

But the Chancellor yesterday said he would stand firm on his effort to balance the books by refusing to borrow money. "Any tax cut would have to be paid for," Mr Osborne told Sky News. "In other words there would have to be a tax rise somewhere else or a spending reduction.

"In other words what we are not going to do in this Budget is borrow more money to either increase spending or cut taxes."

The strongest suggestion of help for squeezed family budgets came from the Chancellor's claim that he was "very seriously and carefully" considering plans to help lower earners by raising the personal allowance for income tax, a proposal that has been championed by Nick Clegg, the Deputy Prime Minister.

But he implied there would be no more help for motorists struggling with record petrol prices this spring. "I have taken action already this year to avoid increases in fuel duty which were planned by the last Labour government," he said.

The Chancellor's tough words were echoed by Liberal Democrat Jeremy Browne, the foreign minister, who warned that Britain faced "accelerated decline" without measures to tackle its debt and increase competitiveness.

In an article published today in The Daily Telegraph, he writes that Britain's market share in the world used to be "dominant" but was now "in freefall" compared with the soaring economies of Asia and South America. "This situation has been becoming more acute for years," he adds. "It is now staring us in the face. So we need to take action."

Mr Browne writes that reform of pensions, welfare and defence is essential to stop the departments "collapsing under the weight of their own debt". "Just because the spending was sometimes on worthy causes does not in itself mean it was affordable," he says.

"Doing nothing when your prospects are at risk of declining is not the safe option. More of the same may be superficially more popular in the short-term but that does not make it right."

Amid warnings that Britain urgently needed to adopt a more pro-business outlook, senior Conservatives have urged the Government to get rid of the 50 pence top rate of tax.

Figures from the Treasury last week suggested the policy was not raising the expected amount of revenue and was threatening to drive leading business people and entrepreneurs away from Britain. Dr Liam Fox, the former Conservative Defence Secretary, yesterday argued for the top tax rate to be scrapped, but added that cutting taxes on employment was even more important.

"I would have thought the priority was getting the costs of employers down and therefore I would rather have seen any reductions in taxation on employers' taxation rather than personal taxation," he told the BBC's Sunday Politics show.

Any efforts to scrap the rate this parliament would face severe opposition from within the Coalition.

Simon Hughes, Liberal Democrat deputy leader, said yesterday that keeping the current 50p rate was "the right thing to do". He told the BBC: "I represent people in a pretty solid working-class community. What they're concerned about is what happens to ordinary people out of work and where they get jobs."

Last night, Labour argued Mr Osborne needed to take a more proactive stance on boosting growth by increasing public spending.

Chris Leslie MP, the shadow Treasury minister, said it was wrong of the Chancellor to argue that Britain was broke and to rely on business alone to create economic growth.

"George Osborne can't complacently wash his hands and claim the lack of jobs and growth in the economy is nothing to do with him," he said.

"He needs to realise that government has a vital role to play in creating an environment where the private sector can grow and create jobs."

Harriet Harman, Labour's deputy leader, urged Mr Osborne to cut VAT.

Meanwhile, the Chancellor made it clear he was resisting pressure to hand over up to another £17.5billion in taxpayers' money to help bail out struggling European Union countries.

He said Europe had not "shown the colour of its money" by taking measures to help itself tackle its debt problems.

Until that happens, Britain will not give any extra funds to the International Monetary Fund.

The Chancellor was speaking as finance ministers from the world's 20 most powerful economies met in Mexico.

Mr Osborne said: "While at this G20 conference there are a lot of things to discuss; I don't think you're going to see any extra resources committed (to the IMF) here because eurozone countries have not committed additional resources themselves, and I think that quid pro quo will be clearly established here in Mexico City."

Chapter 4
WHY THE JUSTICE SYSTEM FAVOURS PAEDOPHILES

This was the first major article that I wrote for the Sovereign Independent Newspaper and deals with elite paedophiles.

How many times have you read in the news about someone being sent to prison and thought to yourself 'Blimey that sentence is a bit harsh'?

A good example is the two young men given 4yr jail terms last month for trying to organise riots on Facebook. Now obviously the Government defend those sentences by saying that the jail terms reflect the sense of public outrage caused by the riots and that they wish to send out a clear message that this kind of behaviour will not be tolerated.

Course, we all know the Government dont give a toss about the public, be they outraged or not. However, they do indeed want to send out a clear message that this type of behaviour will not be tolerated in fact there is clear evidence emerging that the police purposely stood back and let the riots get out of hand.

One of the reasons for this inaction became clear when it was announced that as a result of the riots there is now in place a 30 day ban on all walking protests. After all, what is a riot if not a protest that has got out of hand? However, the Government have for years been looking at ways to remove the people's right to demonstrate and protest and handing out such heavy prison terms for relative misdemeanors cannot help but rest heavy on the minds of those thinking about protesting in the future.However, i digress...

Now, when expressing this view, that some punishments dished out by the law courts seem harsh, how many times have we gone on to say that the justice system is a joke or deeply flawed? This sentiment is usually backed up by us using the often derisory sentences dished out to paedophiles and child killers as a comparison.

An excellent example to highlight this two tier sentencing is a case that concluded in July , barely a month prior to the Two young men receiving their 4 yr prison terms for their internet capers.

This Case in July also involved crimes committed solely on the internet. However, unlike the investigation into the two young men which took the whole of a week to crack, this July case involved four men and took 7 years for the investigation to reach its conclusion.The two extremes in comparison don't end there however. For where as the two young men were convicted of trying to organise riots which only the police took any real notice of, these four men were convicted of heading an international child pornography ring,distributing millions of obscene images which thousands of paedophiles in 40 different countries world wide took very much notice of.

Neither did the two young men profit from their 'crime' whereas the four paedophiles netted £2.2 million between them. But where as the two young men received prison sentences of 4 yrs,It was a very different story for the four Paedophiles.Their sentencing was as follows:

Ian Frost and his civil partner Paul Rowland were each sentenced at Lincolnshire Crown Court to 33 months imprisonment.

Frost's brother Paul was jailed for 15 months and the fourth man Ian Sambridge was given a 12 month sentence, suspended for 2 yrs and 240 hrs of community service.

So on the face of things our justice system does appear to be deeply flawed. But is it? As a further consequence arising from the 7 year child porn ring investigation an undisclosed number of paedophiles were removed from positions of trust. These included Doctors, Teachers, Youth workers and Policemen. And this is where you get to the crux of the matter. For the higher up the social scale you go, the evidence points to the more acceptable paedophilia becomes.

Within 'high society' there are literally 1000's of Paedophiles,from judges, celebrities, politicians right through to the social elite and ex US presidents. Indeed, History is full of examples of this fact.

For example, back in the 1960's where the notorious East London gangster twins, Ronnie and Reggie Kray began providing Lord Robert Boothby with under age 'rent boys' and then used this involvement to blackmail him.

Course, that sealed the twin's fate. You see, after the press got wind of Boothby's involvement with the Krays, a massive cover up ensued which included considerable help from the then Prime Minister, Harold Wilson and the MP Tom Driberg.

The fact that both Wilson and Driberg were fully paid up members of the Labour party, while Boothby was a true blue tory, appeared not to matter. The outcome of this cover up saw Boothby walk away wrongly vindicated and considerably richer, while the twins were later sentenced to life imprisonment with a minimum 30 yr tariff.

Yet in a society where a life sentence can mean as little as 12 years in prison the fact that Reggie Kray served 33 yrs before being released on compassionate grounds and all for the murder of a small time villain shows it does not pay to upset the ruling class.

The trial itself was a travesty of justice with the Judge, Lord Melford Stevenson blatantly biased in favour of the prosecution and presiding over a case that involved two separate, unconnected murders despite some of the defendants on trial only being involved in one of them.

Moreover, both ex US Presidents, George Bush senior and Gerald Ford have been publicly denounced - in print and on film - as being paedophiles. The Bush family are of course multi Billionaires thanks largely to the wholly corrupt Prescott Bush, Father & Grandfather to ex Presidents, George Bush Snr and George W Bush.

All three of the Bush family members, Prescott, George Sr and George Jnr belonged to Yale University's elite secret society, '**Skull & Bones**'. The Skull & Bones initiation is said to include perverse homosexual sex acts.

Mind you, the fact that George Herbert Bush has shied away from taking legal action against his accusers speaks volumes. I mean, if there was no truth to the claims that he is a paedophile, Bush could easily afford to employ the finest legal minds in the world to silence his accusers. However, he chooses not to do so.

On the other hand, I feel positive that those who accuse him would love him to take legal action against them. And then there is Project MK Ultra.

Project MK Ultra was the code name given to an illegal, secret, mind control program run by the CIA in the 1950's & 60's. Indeed, there is much verbal testimony that a large part of this horrific program involved scrambling the minds of children using such means as having other children brutally murdered in front of them.

The children would then have their brains reprogrammed. Many of these children were either kidnapped off the street or sold to the project by orphanages. Once in the project the Children were treated like animals , locked in cages and used as sexual playthings for the rich and famous.

Many of the Doctors employed to carry out these mind control experiments were Nazi war criminals recruited from the WW2 German death camps where they had been carrying out horrific experiments on children under the Third Reich's Eugenics program.

Cathy O'Brien was one of the many children sold into the MK Ultra project. She was eventually rescued by the then CIA agent, Mark Phillips and together they have written a best selling book and give lecture tours on the horrors that went on at MK Ultra.

In fact, Cathy has publicly named Gerald Ford and many more Prominent American Politicians as people who had sex with her and other captive children. In 1973 the CIA ordered all files on the MK Ultra project be destroyed. It is also worth noting that George Bush Sr was made Head of the CIA in 1976.

Furthermore, In the 1960's ,The former Radio 1 DJ Alan 'Fluff' Freeman owned a large corner shop on the Lea Bridge Rd in London. This shop has recently been reported as a place where

'Fluff' held kinky parties attended by the likes of confirmed bachelor ,Sir Jimmy Savile , Jonathan King, the once jailed paedophile broadcaster & former pop star and Brian Epstein, who was at the time the Homosexual manager of the Beatles.

At these parties, young boys specially brought over from several children's homes would be plied with drugs and alcohol. However these parties were forced to come to an end when Police chiefs got wind that the MP & Ex Liberal Party leader Jeremy Thorpe was attending them along with several other prominent MP's.
Thorpe, a well known Homosexual had a taste for young street boys and Teenage runaways were often brought to him. During his later Court trial for the attempted murder of Male model Norman Scott, Thorpe threatened to expose the perversions of many of his fellow MP's. This had the desired effect on his trial and he was promptly found not guilty, bringing a whole new meaning to the saying; *'Getting off scot free'*.

Another MP with much to lose was Edward Heath, Prime Minister of England from 1970-74. Heath was a frequent visitor to the Haute Garrene children's care home on Jersey. He would quite often take young boys from the home away on 'sailing ' weekends on his Yacht, 'The Morning Cloud', which his bodyguards rechristened '*The Morning Sickness*'.

On no less than four occasions, Heath was warned by the Metropolitan police chief not to loiter in public toilets, where he would attempt to pick up young boys. Nevertheless, Heath fell foul to blackmail and Under threat of exposure he was forced to take Britain into the Common Market under very unfavourable conditions.

Peter Mandelson, AKA the Prince of Darkness and one time secretary of state for Northern Ireland is a particularly unsavoury character even by British Politician standards. Cherie Blair once famously referred to him as one of the most corrupt people in politics and thats coming from the wife of ex Prime Minister Tony Blair.

Mandelson, affectionately given the nickname Mandy was twice forced to resign from the cabinet but rejoined the government in 2008 after being made a life Peer by the Queen. What that says for the British Monarchy is open to interpretation .

Nevertheless, now back in favour, Mandy along with George Osborne attended the 2010 meeting of the Bilderberg group. However Mandelson's French Hospital records are alleged to contain details of internal injuries caused by the perverted, well known homosexual sex act involving the use of small furry animals.

Course, the list of scandals and cover ups involving paedophilia amongst the social elite is never ending. Michael Jackson and the emerging evidence of his involvement in the 'Illuminati' for instance is a whole article in itself.

In truth, the examples that I have given you are the mere tip of the iceberg. In fact, armed with this information you could be forgiven for coming to the conclusion that our justice system isn't so much flawed, as more likely embroiled in corruption and accepting of moral depravity.

Chapter 5
UFO's - Fact, Fiction or the countdown to WW3 ?

I originally wrote this article for the Sovereign Independent Newspaper, but it didn't make print because of their policy of not publishing material to do with UFO's. Mind you, the Irish based newspaper also had a policy of not publishing material criticising the Catholic Church.

Course, while many of you might initially agree that the newspapers policy on UFO's is a correct one, I would urge you to keep an open mind on the matter. Moreover, many researchers - myself included - believe that the Monster Elite are planning on launching a [fake] attack on the world supposedly carried out by aliens in a bid to bring about the New World Order.

And whilst that may sound far-fetched, let me tell you that the Monster's certainly have the capability to carry the hoax off and I would suggest to you, that we are being primed to think about the possibility of the unthinkable happening by means of the unprecedented amount of reporting on UFO activity by the Elite controlled mass media…

Quite why the subject of UFO's is taken so light heartedly by the general public is a mystery to me. You see, to my mind the concept of Aliens from another planet is nowhere near as far fetched as the existence of God in the conventional sense of the word. Yet religion is massive.

Indeed, Ghosts are another phenomenon that people are willing to buy into, yet there is infinite more data and evidence to suggest that UFOs exist. Anyone who doubts that fact needs to ask themselves the question, why do our Governments take the subject of UFO's so seriously, with sightings classified "Top Secret" and subject to the 30 year disclosure law. Furthermore to suggest that space travel over any real distance is impossible is just nonsense.

I mean, if we on earth don't already possess that kind of technology, then we are certainly very close to it. Proof of this was shown in a demonstration of Quantum levitation (the physics principle of flying saucers) recently given by a student from the *Superconductivity Group School of Physics and Astronomy*, Tel-Aviv University.

However, anyone who has studied the history behind the New World Order (NWO) could be forgiven for thinking that it is no coincidence that this type of technology has come out of Israel.

Evidence of the existence of UFO's date back to prehistoric times, with the depiction of flying saucers carved into cave walls. Indeed a credible theory exists that the Caucasian race are the descendants of Extraterrestrial beings. Furthermore, there are many well respected people who believe that the world is actually controlled by extraterrestrials.
And while this may sound like madness, until you have listened to the likes of Maxwell Jordon and David Icke lecture on the subject or read their research into the matter, then you would be wise to reserve judgement. Certainly, David Icke's explanation of the so called 'missing link' is as plausible as any other i have heard.

UFO reports fall primarily into the following Three categories:
A CLOSE ENCOUNTER OF THE 1st KIND, is a sighting of one or more UFO's.
A CLOSE ENCOUNTER OF THE 2nd KIND, is observing a UFO with evidence of its existence, such as Crop Circles, electrical interference, Evidence of a landing.
A CLOSE ENCOUNTER OF THE 3rd KIND, is making contact with the driver, so to speak.

Now, prior to the 19th century there was only one recorded instance of a 'Close Encounter' which occurred in Nuremberg, Germany on the 14th of April 1561. There were no more documented sightings from that point on until the 4th of August 1883 when Mexican Astronomer Jose Bonilla photographed some 300 UFO's in the night sky which subsequently turned out to be high flying Geese. Nevertheless, Mexico is considered to be a 'Hot Spot' for UFO activity.

On the 24th of October 1886 the US consul of Venezuela in Maracaibo reported that a bright object, accompanied with a humming noise, appeared during thunderstorm over a hut near Maracaibo, causing its occupants to display symptoms similar to radiation poisoning. Nine days later the trees surrounding the hut withered and died.

This incident was followed by the first documented report of a close encounter of the 3rd kind. This report came on the 17th of April 1897 from Aurora, Texas and alleges that a UFO had crashed and that an Alien had been buried in a local cemetery.

Moving on to the 20th century, there were around a hundred further documented cases, many witnessed by 100's of unconnected people.

Surprisingly enough, or not as the case may be, one of these documented sightings was reported by Ex US President Jimmy Carter in 1969. A further two sightings which were backed up by video evidence came from the Space Shuttles 'Discovery' and 'Columbia' in 1991 and 1996 respectively. This century alone, there has already been 49 documented encounters. Once again this figure includes an encounter, backed by video taken from on board the Space Shuttle 'Discovery'.

However, finding out the true extent of UFO related information is nigh on impossible. The United States Government agency, NASA, like most Government agencies, is shrouded in secrecy and is a minefield of outright lies and disinformation.

Needless to say, it is a cast iron certainty that most countries Governments know more than they are letting on. However one recent story to surface is that told by former NASA Data manager, Ken Johnston, who worked for NASA's Lunar Receiving Laboratory during the Apollo missions. Mr Johnston's contract was terminated after he accused his bosses of withholding important evidence that the moon was once inhabited by Extraterrestrials.

He alleges that Astronauts discovered evidence of an ancient city and the remains of "Amazingly advanced machinery". Mr Johnston's claim is further backed up by photographic evidence, which he says he was ordered to destroy but didn't (See Photo 1).

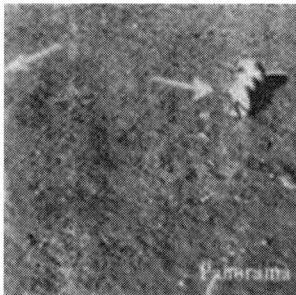

Others, such as ex NASA employee, Donna Hare have accused the agency of releasing photos that have been deliberately smudged or doctored so as to hide this sort of evidence. This fact ties in with other allegations made over the past 40 years by other scientists, Engineers and technicians who accuse NASA of 'Cover ups' and obscuring data.

These allegations range from hiding information pertaining to the strange artefacts found on the Moon's surface through to denying the evidence of life on Mars, allegedly reported back from the Viking Lander during the mid 1970's. This begs the question, why Mars?

I mean we never say life on Jupiter. We talk about Martians but never Mercurians. David Icke's book 'The Biggest secret' explores this question in depth and provides an excellent answer for its basis.

In December 1972, Apollo 17 astronaut Eugene Cernan spent about 75 hours on the Moon. Amongst the many photographs Cernan took are some that appear to be of a Robots Head complete with eye sockets, a nose, metallic cheekbones and a red line painted above what would be the top lip. The head was found along with other strange objects in an impact crater, which suggests that a UFO had made a crash landing (see photo 2).

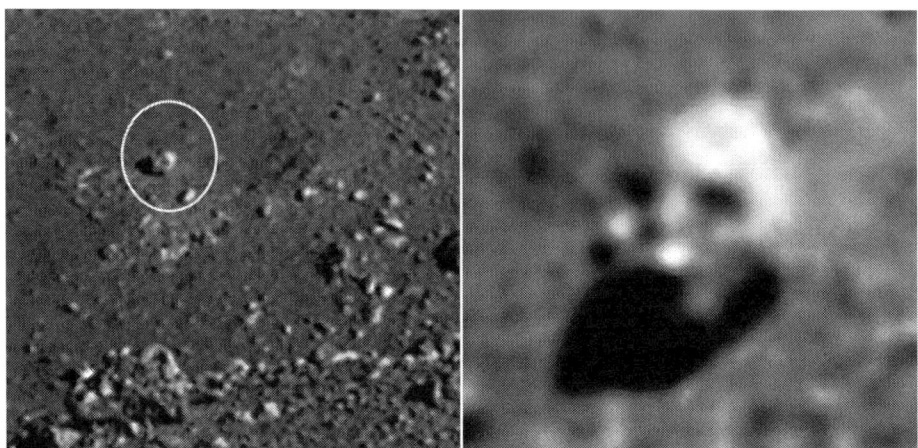

Further photographic evidence which points to the moon being inhabited is that taken of the so called **'Aristarchus Crater'**. This crater shows up as the brightest visible spot on the moon when viewed from the earth.

The crater periodically changes colour, sometimes producing a blue or red glow. This colour glow has given credence to a theory that there could be some sort of a power device, possibly a fusion reactor, in the crater. Certainly in photographs you can clearly see a road leading to a brightly lit entrance tunnel on the edge of the crater. Unsurprisingly however, Official NASA photos of the 'Aristarchus Crater' show it only as a bright white smudge.

Then there is the Photographic evidence sent back to Earth from the Soviet launched, unmanned space probe, Luna 9 which landed on the Moon on the 3rd of February 1966. These photos show what appears to be a large craft or vehicle whose shape resembles that of an ocean liner. This massive object comes to a point at one end and has an elevated section on top. A cable or tube appears to extend from the rear of the object toward the surface (See photo 3). Contact with the Luna 9 was mysteriously lost on February 6, 1966 just three days after landing.

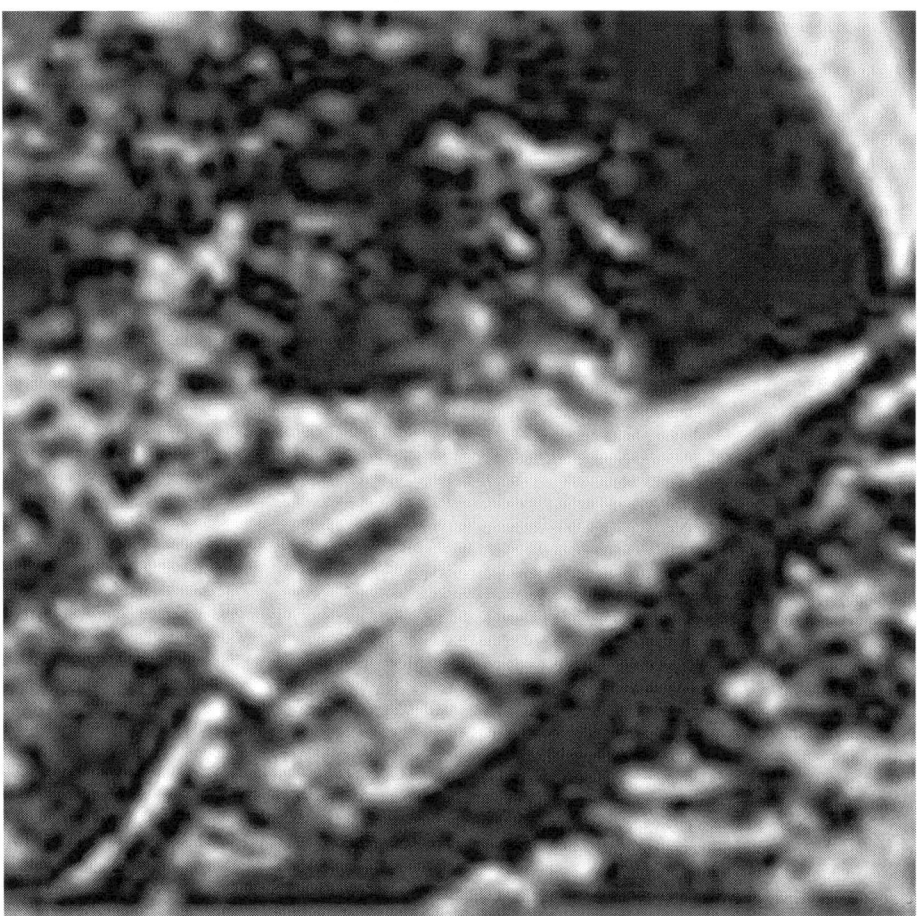

Now, amongst the mass of video evidence taken of UFOs there is one that shows footage of a UFO allegedly being shot at by The USA's 'Star Wars' space defence system. While it is true to say that videos can be doctored the immediate, acute angled, direction change this UFO makes is exactly the same as that made by a UFO that I witnessed personally one cold winter night while walking my dogs over the park.

Of the more recent UFO sightings there are two incidents in particular that can't be ignored. The first of these incidents happened in Russia on the 1st of March 2011 and was witnessed by 1000's of people who live in the Irkutsk region of Siberia. Reports described the UFO as being a large object hurtling towards the earth, while alternating in colour between Pink and Blue.

Is it coincidence then, that the Aristarchus Crater appears to glow Red and Blue? Witnesses, many of whom inundated the emergency services with phone calls, went on to describe a massive explosion as the UFO crashed into the ground. A large area around the impact site was quickly sealed off and deemed classified by the Military.

The second of these incidents took place in China (Another UFO hotspot) on the 20th of August 2011 and was also witnessed by 1000's of people. Amongst these was the pilot of China's Southern Airlines, flight CZ6554 who's radio call led to planes being diverted away from Chongqing's airport.

The pilot estimated the "*enormous spherical glowing heavenly body*" as being at an altitude of 10,700 meters. He added that it grew in size from small to large and appeared to be several hundred times larger than the moon. The Chinese Government in particular take the question of UFO's extremely seriously.

This fact was evidenced in a report printed in the Russian daily newspaper, **'Izvestia'** earlier this month. The report stated that China has a record number of UFO scientific and community-based organizations and whose actions are protected by the Government financed National Society of Extraterrestrial Studies, founded 25 years ago.

Indeed, many Chinese scientists believe that Extraterrestrials are living freely amongst us, a theory supported by a retired Chinese foreign ministry official, Sun Shili, who is now president of the Beijing UFO Research Society. Course, anyone familiar with David Ickes and Jordan Maxwell's research will know that they also whole heartedly believe this to be true.

My own experience with a UFO came about while walking my Dogs over the park sometime in late November 2010. I do this every night of the week between 3-4AM come rain or shine, the same as i have done for the past 3 years.

Up until the early hours of that November morning, I had often seen things in the night sky. However these could just have easily been shooting stars or space debris rather than UFO's. Nevertheless, on the night in question there is no doubt in my mind as to what i saw. It was a bitterly cold, crystal clear night just before the start of the big snow we had last year.

I had walked about a quarter of the way round the park when I first saw the UFO. It was of a circular disc type shape, almost translucent in makeup and yellow, blending into a light green colour at the centre. It was moving incredibly fast and looked as though it had flames trailing behind it.

Either the same one or one identical to it appeared again as I was leaving the park. This time as i looked up the disc shaped object was almost directly above my head in proximity. Whether it had been hovering or just moving slowly as I caught sight of it, i can't say, but as I looked up the disc accelerated forward extremely quickly. This forward motion lasted no more than a second or two before the disc changed direction, without slowing, at a perfect 90 degree angle. Having completed this, seemingly impossible change of direction, it vanished after another second or two.

However there were no flames trailing behind this disc, which leads me to believe that the first UFO was possibly lower. From the park I rushed the 5 minute walk home and quickly explained what i'd seen to my now ex-wife. I then suggested that we go back up to the park to see if the UFO would appear again.

Where I live is quite a built up area and the park is the only place that gives you an uninterrupted view of the night sky. We had been back in the park no more than 2 or 3 minutes when we both saw what can only be described as an extremely fast moving yellow streak.

At this point I should explain that I live very close to an Airport. I say this because over the past 3 years or so I have pretty much got the flight paths sussed of Planes taking off and coming into land. This fact makes what happened next stranger still.

You see, a few minutes after spotting the yellow streak, a fairly low flying, extremely quiet plane flew overhead. It had appeared from the east and was heading in a straight line west in the same direction as the first disc that I saw.

However, since the airport lies to the south of the park, it was obvious that the plane had neither come from the airport or was preparing to land there. The majority of planes leaving or arriving at the airport circle the park in an anticlockwise direction. Occasionally they will come into land from the north flying very low and noisily across the park as they make their descent.

This plane was followed no more than a minute later by another from the same direction but slightly adjacent to where the first had been. Again this plane was low, slow flying and very quiet. These two planes were the first of a succession of at least 8 more, all coming from the same easterly direction and all heading west and all slightly adjacent to each other.

Later that day I put what I had seen in a Facebook status expecting an avalanche of smart ass comments. Instead a long time friend of mine who lives roughly four or five miles away and who walks his dog in nearby fields told me he had previously witnessed an almost identical turn of events.

Although I have seen many strange things in the night sky since, none have come close to what I witnessed that November night. Neither since have I seen anything remotely like the formation of aeroplanes flying overhead.

However the significance of those planes cannot be underestimated for if they were in some way connected to the discs it begs the question: Were the planes tracking alien UFO's or were they monitoring something even more sinister? I say this because there is another theory surrounding UFO's that is not as far fetched as it may first sound.

This theory has been around for a while now and is rapidly growing in the number of people buying into it. To those not familiar with the centuries old NWO agenda this theory will sound like nonsense. Indeed, only when you fully understand the way the people behind this agenda have manipulated the world up to now will this theory make sense.

The scenario that this theory is based around is that the Earth will come under attack from Extraterrestrials. Once this attack on Earth is launched, we, the people are going to be told that it is necessary for all the heads of state in the world to combine their armies into one fighting force in order to repel the alien invaders.

Obviously, this means that there is going to have to be a top man and as such an unelected World-President will be put in place thus completing the agenda. Now, I appreciate that all this may sound far fetched to most people, but once you become aware of the way this elite brotherhood works, the clues pointing to this WW3 scenario are easy to recognize.

Some would even say that the illuminati controlled Hollywood has been preparing us for years by releasing blockbuster movies such as **'Independence day'**.

Moreover, on the 26th of September 2010 the Telegraph reported that the UN were considering appointing a "Space Ambassador" to act as first point of contact for Aliens trying to make contact with Earth. The person most likely to be assigned that task is 58 yr old , astrophysicist, Mazlan Othman who is currently head of the UN's little known, Office for Outer Space Affairs.

It is also a cast iron guarantee that anyone purporting to be a whistleblower who is given a stage by the equally, illuminati controlled mainstream media, is doing so with their backing. A typical example of this was the live TV coverage that CNN afforded a disclosure conference in Washington DC on September 27th 2010.

The conference was chaired by author and researcher Robert Hastings and made up of a panel of Seven, retired, senior ranking USAF personnel. The 'official' purpose of the conference was so as these 7 men could blow the whistle on classified information pertaining to their encounters with UFO's.

Most of these encounters reportedly took place at Top Secret Nuclear Missile Bases and in most instances resulted in the Nuclear warheads being disabled. The seven whistle blowers were named as:
ROBERT JAMISON- USAF Nuclear Missile targeting officer (ret)
CHARLES HALT-USAF Colonel (ret)
JEROME NELSON-USAF Nuclear Missile launch officer (ret)
PATRICK McDONOUGH-USAF Nuclear Missile site geodetic surveyor (ret)
BRUCE FENSTERMACHER-USAF Nuclear Missile launch officer (ret)
ROBERT SALAS-USAF Nuclear Missile launch officer (ret)
DWYNNE ARNESON-USAF Communications Centre Officer-in-charge (ret).

The fact that this conference was televised live on CNN, a well known outlet for illuminati propaganda, arouses suspicion from the start. That aside, I find it hard to believe that these extremely Conservative, high ranking USAF personnel, retired or not, would betray their Government in such a way. Even the timing of the conference was significant, coming at the time of an unprecedented rise in reported UFO activity.

All this leads me to believe that what I witnessed last November could very well of been some kind of Government trial. The fact that less than 10 miles from my home, and located in the direction that the planes came from are 2 military installations, plays a part in my belief.

These installations are supposedly for bomb testing, but who's to say what goes on down there. Neither can the airport be dismissed as having had no part to play. However, what convinces me more than anything that these UFOs were not as they seem is the type of plane involved.

You see, to my mind, had these UFOs been from outer space, then surely jet fighters would have been more appropriate?

So, what is the conclusion? At the end of the day only time will tell. However, from a personal point of view, I totally believe that the Illuminati have laid the foundations and have the technology to allow them to launch a false flag invasion of the earth. In all likelihood, the reason for the significant increase in UFO related stories, reported by the mainstream media of late is more to do with a form of mind control, rather than a coincidence.

For instance ,when the American government wanted to rape Afghanistan and Iraq, the media went into overdrive promoting the threat of terrorism. In the same way, we are now being conditioned into believing that the possibility of us making contact with aliens is increasingly imminent. Certainly, by launching such an invasion the illuminati would be able to achieve their goal of a one world government.

It would also afford them the opportunity to murder millions of innocent people in accordance with their population reduction agenda. Having said that, these people haven't spent hundreds of years gaining a stranglehold on the world just to put all their eggs in one basket. They have various other ways open to them in order to usher in the NWO and at the moment it appears to me that they are more likely to try and achieve this by deliberately collapsing the global economy.

As to the question of UFOs being Fact or Fiction? Well that is a matter for you to decide. I will however sign off with a few facts and a basic description of the Universe.

You see, it is said that there are more stars in the universe than there are grains of sand that go to make up all of the worlds beaches. Hats off to whoever did the counting, but even if that fact is untrue, there are still a mind blowing number of them. So, consider this. Most stars are thought to be ringed by planets, in the same way that the Sun (Earth's star) is ringed by the 9 commonly known planets.

These are Mercury, Venus, Earth, Mars, Jupiter, Saturn, Uranus, Neptune and Pluto. In turn these planets are orbited by a Moon or Moons. The Sun is just one star amongst 100 Billion that go to make up our Galaxy called the Milky Way which is a relatively small Galaxy, when compared to say the Andromeda Galaxy which is estimated to be made up of 300 Billion stars, with each star potentially orbited by an indeterminate number of planets.

The Universe in turn, is in itself made up of untold trillions of Galaxies. Therefore, anyone arrogant enough to believe that our small planet is the only planet capable of sustaining life forms far more advanced than what we are, really hasn't been paying attention."Beam me up Scotty".

Chapter 6
ARRESTED? NOT ON YOUR LIFE

Another Sovereign Independent Newspaper article of mine which focuses on the rise of police brutality in the UK.

Once upon a time,a clip around the ear from your friendly neighbourhood copper was the accepted 'norm' amongst young men who were up to a bit of skulduggery.

Furthermore any villain from 'back in the day' will tell you that once the 'rozzers' had you back at the 'nick', the odd slap was part and parcel of a police interview. In fact, everyone knew this type of police behaviour went on and by and large it was accepted. Accepted not only by those up to no good and who classed it as an occupational hazard. But also accepted by your average law abiding citizen who viewed it as a means of 'serves you right'.

However, during the mid 1970's sweeping police reforms were brought in and this form of police brutality was no longer considered acceptable...
Fast forward to 2011 and how those bygone days are missed. No longer will giving a 6ft 4in tall Policeman a bit of lip earn you a clip around the ear. For to do so these days will result in you being brutally bundled to the ground by at least 5 or 6 policemen dressed in full combat gear.

And woe betide you if you struggle or protest at the fact that you have 5 or 6 sets of knees digging into your back and legs while your face is being buried in the tarmac and your arms are being forced up your back at almost impossible angles.

To do so will result in the offending knees disappearing to be very quickly being replaced by a prolonged blast of pepper spray in your face… If you are lucky. If you're not you'll find your body subjected to 50,000 agonising volts of electricity discharged from a 'non lethal' - or so we are led to believe - taser.

At best this will leave you a quivering wreck on the pavement. Course,things are even worse these days for your average career criminal. For them, there is a very real chance that they may not even make it back to the nick at all.

Indeed, it is an extremely disturbing statistic that since 1998, at least 333 people in Britain have died while being arrested or while in police custody.

More worryingly still is not one single police officer has ever been convicted for any of these deaths despite compelling evidence in most cases that they did not occur from natural causes.

Unsurprisingly, although no doubt loathe to admit it, the police complaints authority have revealed that a disproportionate number of these deaths were of people from an Ethnic minority.

Alarmingly, in an 8 day period following the shooting to death of alleged gangster, Mark Duggan , the event blamed by the mainstream media as the cause of last months riots, no less than 3 other men have died at the hands of the police.

All 3 of these men had been either tasered, pepper sprayed or both. The use of tasers by the UK police on its citizens is now so widespread that Amnesty international has expressed concern on the matter. The events surrounding the death of one of these 3 men are as follows.

On the 24th of August, police in the Widnes area of Cheshire were called to the home of 25 yr old Amateur rugby player, Jake Michael. Despite Mr Michael being the person to make the 999 call, which he did so having received a threat on his life, Officers, for reasons not yet clear, tried to arrest him for affray.

When he resisted he was pepper sprayed in the face. Despite being blinded by the spray, Mr Michael managed to shrug of the police officers and make a dash for it. However, he only managed to run about 30 yards before he was brought down under the weight of at least 11 police officers.

After being taken to the local police station a police spokesman said Mr Michael became unwell and as a result was taken to hospital by ambulance. He died 2 hours later.

Mr Michael's neighbour, Ann Blease a 40yr old mother of 3 witnessed the arrest. In describing Mr Michael as an extremely popular and very well liked man, she said some of the 11 arresting officers appeared to be deliberately kneeing Mr Michael in the head and giving him 'digs' in the side.

She added that the others - one of them a female officer - were either kicking him or hitting him with their truncheons. Mrs Blease was adamant that this brutality lasted up to 15 minutes and took place despite Mr Michael having his hands handcuffed behind his back and him no longer resisting arrest.

Another of the 3 men to die in this 8 day period has been named as 27 year old Dale Burns. Mr Burns, a keen bodybuilder from Barrow-in-Furness, Cumbria became the first man in Britain to die from police taser after officers shot him 3 times with the powerful 50,000 volt gun.

Mr Burns had also been sprayed with Pepper Spray after officers had been called to his bedsit home on the 16th of August following reports of a disturbance.

The 3rd victim is named as 53 year old Phillip Hulmes from Over Hulton near Bolton who died on August 23rd. Mr Hulmes died after police shot him with tasers after breaking into his home, ironically to stop him committing suicide.

With regard to the death of Mark Duggan, the Metropolitan police have already been forced to admit that they have misled the public over the events that led to his death. While the investigation is still on going, it's a fact that early news reports on the incident suggested that there was a shoot out between Mr Duggan and armed police officers.

It was reported that along with the death of Mr Duggan , a police marksman was shot and only saved by the fact the bullet hit his radio first. However not only does it transpire that Mr Duggan never fired his gun, there is no evidence at the moment to suggest that he had even drawn the weapon. This means that if a Police Marksman was shot, then it was by one of his fellow officers as is the case with the radio which was actually in a police car when it was hit by a stray police bullet.

There can be little doubt that the British police are now being recruited for their aggression rather than their integrity. They are poorly trained in the written aspects of the law and quite often neither know or care of the difference between lawful and legal.

They no longer wear smart tunics and pass the time of day with the public. Instead they roam in pairs, dressed in combat gear almost daring you to make eye contact with them.

Even their cars are no longer 'good guy' white. Today their cars are increasingly 'bad guy' black. Indeed, it is easy to say that if you stay within the law then the police won't bother you. However it takes very little for someone to become the focus of police attention these days especially young men in packs of 3 or more.

Unfortunately unless your a complete mouse it also doesn't take long for their aggressive, rude intrusion into your private business to get your back up. To show a police officer the merest flicker of annoyance is to invite trouble upon yourself and to be forcibly arrested these days is to literally take your life in your hands

Chapter 7
THE BBC MAKE A 'PROPER' CHARLIE OUT OF 911

In November 2011 the BBC broadcast a program that was supposedly designed to change the minds of a coachload of 9/11 sceptics. One of those sceptics was the well known activist, Charlie Veitch and totally destroyed any credibility that the pillock had.
I covered that program for the Sovereign Independent newspaper.

Once again the BBC has gone into propaganda mode with their broadcast last night (7/11/11) of a programme entitled 911:Conspiracy Road Trip. Indeed, I find it amazing that some people are still willing to give up a percentage of their 'hard earned' to purchase a TV licence in order for a supposedly impartial organisation such as the BBC to finance such blatantly biased claptrap.

That the Beeb chose comedian Andrew Maxwell to front this insult to the victims of 911 was however quite appropriate.You see, the whole programme was a joke from start to finish although to be fair the programme initially looked as though it might be impartial, having included Charlie Veitch as one of the five road trippers.

However, for reasons known only to himself, Veitch, a fairly well known, one time outspoken Government critic has well and truly shafted those who followed his work. Not that he appeared at ease rolling over for his new role as a dog waiting to have his tummy tickled by his new master.

Could he have had the frighteners put on him? I mean that is hardly far fetched when you consider that the infamous Gangland enforcer, come actor, John Bindon was scared into keeping silent the details of his relationship with Princess Margaret.

Destitute towards the end of his life, Bindon could have made a small fortune from selling his story. However, years earlier, a single car ride with the shadowy men in suits ensured Bindon took the details of his affair with the Queen's sister to the grave with him.

There is of course no disputing the fact that Veitch was unconstitutionally detained and taken into custody by the authorities the day before Prince William got married. But even if he wasn't, it's certainly strange that someone deemed such a potential threat to the smooth running of the Royal wedding has within a couple of months suddenly become a sheep.

Was he warned about the possible consequences should he continue to be a thorn in the side of the powers that be? Was he offered large incentives to roll over? Charlie, was certainly a shadow of his former self. In fact for a man who used to take to the London streets and rant through a megaphone he was certainly uncharacteristically quiet throughout the programme.
Charlie Veitch aside, it was obvious the direction that this programme was going to take from the moment Irish comedian, Andrew Maxwell let it be known that the trippers were questioning the independent investigation report into 911.

Course, the White House was originally opposed to having a commission set up to investigate the events of 911 in the first place. However, when it became obvious that to not have an official investigation would be tantamount to admitting involvement, the Bush administration appointed veteran political puppet master Henry Kissinger to head the commission.

When Kissingers appointment was vehemently opposed Phillip Zelikow a Bush supporter with close ties to Condaleeza Rice was given the job. Begrudgingly the American Govt then handed over $14 million for the investigation to go ahead.

Nevertheless, to put that figure into perspective, $40 million was handed over to investigate the Bill Clinton- Monica Lewinsky affair. And of course, both President Bush and Vice President Dick Cheney were under pressure to give evidence for the investigation.

However both men agreed to do so only on the strict understanding that they (1) Would only give evidence together as opposed to doing so alone. (2) None of what they said was to be recorded.(3) Neither of them would be required to give their evidence or answer questions under oath.

Now, for anyone who has read the 911 Commission Report the glaring flaws and omitted facts throughout the paper are all too evident. It is in fact quite obvious that the evidence has been used to fit the conclusion rather than reach a conclusion.

Where the evidence pointed to something else as the cause; for instance the reason for the collapse of WTC building 7, the subject has simply been ignored and left out of the report.
For a detailed account into how this so called independent report is little more than a work of fiction,you should read '**The New Pearl Harbour**' by David Ray Griffin.

Nevertheless, back to last night's programme and the first 'conspiracy theory ' addressed by Andrew Maxwell was that of the one put forward by a woman introduced to the viewer simply as Charlotte.

Charlotte's gripe about the official version of events was that she failed to see how the hijackers, given their limited flight expertise could steer the massive 757 aeroplanes into the twin towers.

Well Charlotte, I can answer that. You see, assuming for argument's sake that the planes were actually being flown by Mohammed Atta and his motley crew (and there is a mountain of evidence to suggest otherwise) they would have been subjected to some good humoured teasing back at base, had they missed.

After all they only had to keep their eyes peeled for the two tall buildings sticking out way above the other buildings in New York City.

However, as if to read my mind the BBC wanted to to prove how feasible it would be for an inexperienced pilot to park a plane in the towers. In order to do so, one of the trippers was taken up in a Cessna light aircraft and allowed to take the controls. This apparently proved that someone who has never flown before could manage the task.

To add more credence to this revelation the flying instructor then told the awed trippers that it is in fact harder to fly a Cessna than it is a Jumbo Jet. However what the programme neglected to mention was that no one other than Charlotte has ever said the hijackers, if indeed there ever were any, could not steer a plane or that they were incapable of hitting the tall shiny things standing way above anything else on the New York skyline.

Especially while seated at the controls of an aeroplane with a 125 ft wingspan. However, where the doubt into the Hijackers flying expertise comes into question is with regards to the Pentagon. You see, it is now proven beyond doubt that the flying manoeuvre needed to take place in order for the plane to hit the Pentagon where it did, is way beyond the capabilities of the most experienced of pilots. More importantly still, it is beyond the manoeuvrability of a 757. Giving mind to this information, I suppose it is fair to say that, that is one in the eye for Charlotte. However, that is all it is fair to say.

Next up came Emily. Her conspiracy theory revolved around airport security. A student and active member of the 911 truth movement - though which 9/11 truth movement is anybody's guess - Emily finds it hard to believe that the Hijackers were not caught with their box cutters trying to board the planes.

She further maintained that the American Government had been given intelligence that the attacks were going to take place and as such the Hijackers were purposely allowed to board the planes unchallenged.

Now, of all the possible, supposed conspiracy theories surrounding 911, it is absolutely pointless to give airtime to this one. You see, once again anyone who is half clued up on the events that occurred that day would shy away from bringing the existence of the hijackers into play.

After all, Emily's argument is a no win situation for a person who doubts the official version of events. The fact that the official version of events says Hijackers boarded the planes with box cutters proves or disproves nothing. On the one hand, prior to 911 airport security was lax. Even more so for internal flights which all the alleged hijacked planes were scheduled to make. Therefore it would of been very easy to get these little knives aboard with or without the govts help.

And even after security was taken to an unprecedented level post 911, a journalist from the Sun Newspaper was able to get a knife on board a plane due to make an international flight.
Moreover, the fact that Emily says the Govt knew and as such proves that the Hijackers were deliberately allowed unchecked onto the planes is easily countered by saying the Govt couldn't have known and had they done so the Hijackers would of been stopped at the airport.

In short no one who was seriously implicating the Govt as being behind 911 would use such a no win hypothetical argument. Still it's fair to say that's one in the eye for Emily. However , that is all it's fair to say.

Next up came Charlie's turn to be educated and at this point I would have found it easy to lob something heavy at my TV screen. Charlie maintained that there was bombs planted in the trade centre and it was these bombs that brought down the twin towers, not the impact of the planes.

Andrew Maxwell then told us that some people believe a powdered substance called Thermite was used and to prove once and for all that this couldn't possibly be true a steel girder was laid on its side and a large pile of Thermite was placed on the end.

Dramatically ordering the trippers to get well back, the thermite was then ignited and promptly exploded in an impressive firework type display. Once the flames had gone out, the Steel girder was examined and the only visible damage was a small hole.

So that was that theory up in smoke if you'll pardon the pun. But so as not to leave anyone in any doubt that explosives couldn't have been used, we were then given a lecture from a demolition expert. He told us that in order to bring the towers down by controlled demolition it would take months of planning and putting explosives in place.

The planting of these explosives would require large teams of experts working for weeks in the central core of the building. For them to do so, unnoticed and unchallenged by the tight security in place in the trade centre would be impossible.

Finally, presumably to complete Charlie's humiliation, we were shown how the towers came down in a scientific display using towers made out of... Errr... Lego. By breaking a random piece off the top of the lego tower, Charlie then demonstrated to the 'construction scientist' how he had watched the section of tower above the impact site first tilt, then fall back into line as the tower came down in its own footprint.

Talking to Charlie like he was talking to an imbecile - although he was - our intrepid expert then patiently explained how the outer steel supports had been severed when the plane struck the tower and how the fire proofing had been dislodged from the steel girders in the buildings central core.

It was then explained that with no fireproofing to protect the steel core the immense heat from the exploding jet fuel had caused the girders to bend in the direction of the severed outer steel.

Then, as the top of the building fell, the weight of this top section collapsed the floors of the section immediately below the impact zone, bringing the top section back into line and starting a concertina effect.

This then - according to the experts - is how the towers came down in their own footprints. Course, this impressive and wholly believable explanation would have be fine had it not been for a few basic facts and the rewriting of the laws governing physics.

So let's first deal with the scientific lego demonstration. Firstly, the outer steel supports on the towers had no strength in them. They were simply there to hold the floors in place. The whole strength in the tower was located in its central core.

And had the steel in the central core heated up to such a degree that the steel did indeed bend, then the top section would simply of fallen off - Just as Charlie said it appeared to be about to do, seconds before the tower came down at free fall speed.

However not only was all the jet fuel burned up in a giant fireball on impact, jet fuel doesn't burn anywhere near hot enough to melt steel. Moreover, testimony from firemen has confirmed that the fires left burning were not very hot.

This fact is proven by the colour of the smoke and flames. Indeed, if you go into a steelworks you will see that the men working with molten steel are all wearing heat protection suits. Yet video footage of the trade centre, clearly shows a woman standing in the opening left by the plane, waving a shirt for help.

Therefore it is impossible for there to have been anywhere near the heat needed to have any effect on the steel whatsoever.

The next problem is the speed that the towers came down. At free fall speed the towers would come down in 10 seconds. As it was they came down in under 12 seconds. It is therefore impossible and against the laws of physics for the towers to have come down at that speed if it wasn't a controlled demolition, even if you believe that the wreckage gathered momentum the nearer it got to the ground.

It is a scientific fact that the only way the towers could have fallen at the speed they did is if the central core was being destroyed and removed as it fell. The only way this could have been done is by explosion but as we have seen, thermite wasn't up to the job.

However by adding Sulphur to Thermite you get what's called **Thermate**. Thermate, once ignited cuts through Steel like a hot knife through Butter. In fact it is used by demolition firms to cut through steel girders in controlled demolitions throughout the world.

Using Thermate on the steel in the towers central core would have brought both the buildings down in the way and at the speed that they did in fact come down. There is no other explanation possible that can be applied to the collapse that doesn't break the laws of physics.
So how did the Thermate and incendiary devices get put into place? Well, for weeks prior to September 11th a whole team of 'Lift Engineers' had been carrying out 'Maintenance' and the towers central core is easily accessible via the lift shafts.

But surely security would of picked up on this? Well yes, Obviously the security firm would have known.

However, the firm employed by the WTC to handle security was called **Securacom**. This is a massive firm who also handled the security at United Airlines and Dulles International Airport. And the man who owns this company is a Mr Marvin P Bush, brother of President George W Bush.

Now, not only is it inconceivable that Charlie Veitch would be unaware of these facts, it is impossible that the BBC would not also be privy to this information. This may be why the BBC neglected to mention WTC building number 7.

You see, had the twin towers never existed, this skyscraper would have been one of the tallest in New York. Yet this building also collapsed in the same way that the towers did, despite not being struck by a plane and despite having no major fires.

However, to mention WTC7 may have led to awkward questions such as to how the BBC news reported live from New York on September 11th 2001, that the building had just collapsed half an hour before it actually did.

Still it is fair to say that, that is one in the eye for Charlie. But thats all its fair to say. Shame on you Charlie. You've sold out.

Rodney, our fourth tripper, we were told studied Biochemistry. We were not told however if he got his degree or not. And I rather suspect that he didn't. After all, If he did then we would of been introduced to Rodney as having a degree in Biochemistry.

Nevertheless, Rodney had a problem with accepting that the size of the hole in the Pentagon could have been made by an aeroplane as large as a 757.

And as I have already said, it has been proved impossible for a 757 to hit the pentagon where it did. But for argument's sake let's say that it was possible. The Pentagon is the most heavily protected building in the world. Moreover, the airspace around the Pentagon has an exclusion zone. So, should an aircraft or missile enter this airspace an alarm would be triggered and surface to air, heat seeking missiles would be automatically launched.

Strangely, this missile system was conveniently deactivated on 911. Similarly there are more security cameras in the vicinity of the pentagon than anywhere else in the world yet to date, two grainy clips of film have been released by the US Govt... And neither shows the existence of a 757 hitting the building.

In fact a quick flick through photographs on the internet will show you the kind of wreckage left by a plane crash. However we are told in the programme by a Mr Alan Pilsner, who works at the Pentagon, that this particular plane disintegrated.

Mr Pilsner whose office is decorated with letters of heartfelt thanks from Donald Rumsfeld and George Bush Goes on to say that he saw the body parts of stewardesses that day. Therefore we can only conclude from this fact, that he either knew the dead stewardesses or that their body parts were still dressed in their uniforms.

And as such, all that I can say is these stewardesses must have been a pretty hardy bunch for their bodies to be left intact enough as to be visibly identifiable from their uniforms. Especially when you consider that they came from a metal aeroplane that disintegrated into thin air.

Furthermore the whole plane must have completely disintegrated before the wings hit the building being as the building itself has no structural damage whatsoever on either side of the 65 ft opening made on impact. Not even broken windows.

Now thats pretty hard to explain coming from a plane with a wingspan 2 inches short of 125 ft. So despite the plane disintegrating before the wings touched the building, Pilsner would have us believe that the tail end of the aircraft carried on travelling through a further nine reinforced walls and untold steel columns before finally coming to rest in the pentagons central gardens.

On the actual day, Donald Rumsfeld was videoed bravely helping carry away what little debris there was left from 'the plane'. Course not only should Rumsfeld have faced criminal charges for interfering with a crime scene, he should not have been there at all. After all it is standard practice for bodyguards to get senior Government heads to a place of safety in an emergency.

Furthermore these tiny pieces of debris - small enough to be carried away by hand - were hardly posing a danger to anyone or anything. They would however have been of incredible help to aircraft crash investigators had they been left where they were. Still it's safe to say that that's one in the eye for Rodney. But that is all its safe to say.

After the debunking of Rodney's conspiracy theory, we were then treated to scenes of our intrepid roadtrippers falling out with each other. This falling out included much shouting, much crying and much walking out of the room, thus giving the impression that anyone who disbelieves anything other than the official version of events must be immature, hysterical, and have a tendency to overreact.. God forbid the BBC should ever make a credible programme using a serious presenter and people with real knowledge of the so called conspiracy theories.

Nevertheless, these tantrum scenes led nicely into Shazin's conspiracy theory. Shazin wanted to know how the people on United flight 93, the plane that allegedly crashed into a field in Pennsylvania, were able to make phone calls to their loved ones.
Now for those not in the know, this was an excellent question. Especially after the Govt released details and recordings of those phone calls, allegedly made by the passengers from their cell phones.

However, it was rather inconveniently pointed out that in 2001 it was impossible to make a call from a cell phone at the hight united 93 was flying at. This fact naturally caused a problem for the 911 commission whilst compiling their evidence for the aforementioned independent report and left them no choice other than to professionally ignore the tapes.

And that way they wouldn't need to be included in the final draft. Course leaving out the phone call evidence could have led to questions being asked about the validity of the report but luckily enough there was a transcript of a phone call available, allegedly made by a stewardess on the plane's phone to air traffic control.

This call must be genuine since it is included in the final draft of the report, mustn't it? However, for a less tongue in cheek, more detailed and scientific account of the phone calls, I refer you once again to the book, '**The New Pearl Harbour**' by David Ray Griffin.

Now obviously this problem with the phone calls could have left the Beeb with egg on their faces. So, there was only one thing for it. The BBC would need a diversion to draw attention away from the fact that it was impossible for the phone calls to be genuine... Enter Greg Fife.

Aircraft crash investigator, Greg was drafted in to explain why the debris from United flight 93 were so small and scattered over a distance of a mile. He also felt the need to explain why the crater left from the impact was so small and shallow. Now in order to do this Greg had to hope and pray that no one amongst the road trippers had ever seen the 100's of photographs available on the internet showing aeroplane crash sights.

After all, if they had then it could have led to even more awkward questions being asked, like why, in all these photos is it so easy to identify the remains of an aeroplane? Greg was apparently also banking on our roadtrippers never having seen the tape in which Donald Rumsfeld slips up and says Flight 93 was shot down.

For had they done so, they may well have had a look at the 100's of photographs available on the internet which show images of the debris left from shot down aircrafts. In these pictures it is very hard to tell what has been shot down because all that's left of the plane is small pieces of debris scattered over.. .Errr, miles.

Still Greg wouldn't lie would he? So to help us mere mortals understand better what happened to flight 93, Greg provided the trippers with a little plastic model of a 757. He then scientifically demonstrated the angle at which flight 93 hit the ground by tilting the toy planes nose downwards. He then built on this demonstration by explaining that it was because of this angle of impact that the crater visible at the crash site is so short and shallow.

Greg then ventured further still by saying that what actually happened on impact was the 757 buried itself roughly 40ft into the ground. This was presumably followed by the 40ft crater containing the plane backfilling itself... Although he neglected to mention that it so obviously did!

Nevertheless, Greg is able to tell us this information because crash investigators were able to locate the black box .An airplane's black box is unique to each and every plane that it is attached to and is identifiable by numbers which are impossible to be removed or altered.

Interestingly enough, the 911 commission requested to examine flight 93's black box as evidence - a request that was subsequently refused. However, i digress.

Now, presumably flight 93 crash investigators had to dig down 40 ft to locate the black box and this would be how Greg knows the depth that the plane disappeared into the ground. Course this depth of 40 ft throws up its own problems in so much as a 757 is over 155 ft long.

Therefore, by my reckoning this leaves 115 ft of aeroplane unaccounted for. Fortunately this is not a problem for Greg. The missing 115 ft of plane is obviously the tiny pieces visibly scattered over a mile. But how would this make sense? I mean surely the remaining 115 ft of wreckage would of piled up on top of the now buried 40 ft?

No says Greg, not at all. However for him to accurately demonstrate what happens in a crash such as this, a scientific experiment would be needed. So, after buying half a dozen eggs, the scientific experiment was ready to begin. Each road tripper was then handed an egg and ordered to throw it in the air and let it smash on the ground. "Now" says Greg triumphantly pointing to the smashed eggs, "Look how far the eggs have splattered on impact".

But unfortunately our Roadtrippers are not convinced. This leads Greg no option but to go more hi-tech and for this he fills 5 balloons with water and orders our 5 roadtrippers to throw the balloons into the air and let them hit the ground.

This then, as far as I can tell, leads to conclusive proof that if a 757 was made of thin rubber and filled with water there would be a lot of wet ground in the event of a crash. And by now even the BBC was beginning to realise how silly they were looking, so having had the roadtrippers change their wet socks the programme returned to the question of the phone calls.

However there was still the real danger that unanswerable questions could be asked, especially by Shazin who was demanding an answer to the unanswerable. Enter Alice Hoglan, grieving Mother of Mark Bingham, one of the heroes who died on flight 93… Apparently.

Not that it would matter too much if she was who she says she was or indeed if Mark Bingham ever existed. After all, no one was ever going to question the woman too hard due to the fact that she promptly burst into tears on introduction. This had the effect of reducing our 5 heroes into floods of tears also.
Nevertheless, after much sympathising and group hugging Alice told us tearfully how her son had called her up on his cell phone from the hijacked plane. In fact she is 100% positive that it was her son because shes heard the tapes a few times and you can quite clearly hear Mark Bingham say, "*Mum its Mark Bingham*".

Now the more cynical amongst us could be forgiven for thinking that after a period of 10 years, a woman confronted by 5 people trying to besmirch her hero son's memory would have reacted with anger rather than being reduced to an emotional wreck. Furthermore, the more cynical amongst us would also be forgiven for finding it strange that a son, when calling his mother would feel the need to introduce himself at all let - alone by his full name.

After all the "*mum*" kinda gives a hint as to the callers identity. Nothing strange about that says Alice, explaining that Mark was a public relations man and as such was used to introducing himself in such a way.

And so, add a few more tears to this explanation and it has to be true. We then have another awkward moment for the BBC when they are forced to admit that it would be extremely easy for the Govt to forge these tapes. Thankfully Alice is able to save the day by saying that she could hear the sound of *"4,5,6,7 men fighting"* in the background.

Course, no one had the heart to ask Alice if it was in fact 4, 5 ,6 or 7 men she had heard fighting that day. In fact no one was able to ask anything through their tears once Alice said that she could see her son now, jumping over the backs of seats to get at the hijackers.

In fact I am not altogether sure that I didn't hear her say over the sound of my own sobbing, that John Wayne himself was leading the charge. Either way it's safe to say that it's one in the eye for Shazin. But that is all that it's safe to say.

Since this article was first published in the Sovereign Independent Newspaper, Charlotte has spoken out about how the program was purposely edited to make the participants appear stupid. She has said that they were continually bullied and their questions unanswered or ignored.

Charlie Veitch, bless him, has since tried defending his participation in the program. In doing so all he has done is made himself look incredibly stupid and on film comes across as a little boy caught stealing while trying to deny it. You cannot defend the indefensible Charlie. It is my understanding that many more higher profile activists including Luke Rudkowski were approached before Veitch and offered better financial incentive. All of them turned the BBC down flat.

Veitch incredibly thinks he has some credibility left and as such believes he can carry on where he left off prior to the shows screening. The last that I saw, Veitch had been forced to make a video pleading for donations. Good luck with that. Idiot.

Chapter 8
Remembering 7/7 on 9/11

I wrote this article for the Sovereign Independent Newspaper on September 11, 2011 - the anniversary of 9/11 - to remind people of Britain's own government orchestrated false flag 7/7.

According to the Writer & Journalist Kevin Boyle, When Tony Farell, the Principal, Intelligence Analyst for the South Yorkshire Police force submitted his 2010 annual review report to his superiors, he was already aware that in doing so he was calling time on his career.

The reason that he was aware of this had nothing to do with shoddy workmanship. On the contrary, after firing Mr Farell, his employers were forced to admit that his work record during the 12 year period he had worked for them was impeccable.

So, just what was contained within the pages of this report that could lead to such dire consequences for Mr Farell?
The simple answer is that the report was far too accurate and truthful for his bosses liking. In summing up his report, Mr Farell had concluded that any major threat of a terrorist attack would come from within the state apparatus, not from Islamic Fundamentalists.

In reaching this conclusion Mr Farell's report had asserted that both 7/7 and 9/11 were 'inside jobs'.
Course, despite the South Yorkshire Police having to admit that Tony Farell's 12yr stint with them had been faultless, he still lost his case for unfair dismissal held in early 2011. And without the funds to employ legal representation to mount an appeal, that should have been the end of the matter. But Mr Farell is made of sterner stuff and as such he launched an appeal regardless.

The basis of that appeal centred around the fact that the South Yorkshire Police failed to review or investigate any of the analysis in his report. The appeal began last week on September 7th.

In giving evidence, the SYP Director of Finance, the man who sacked Mr Farell was forced to admit that the data in the intelligence report *"could be right"*. However the accuracy of the report was of no concern to the appeal tribunal. Their mandate was to only address evidential matters relating to points of law previously overlooked or misapplied.

You see, while the report's accuracy was of no consequence to the tribunal, to accept the findings as correct would have had dire consequences elsewhere. This is because the UK police policy on terrorism is the responsibility of the Metropolitan Police. The Metropolitan Police in turn receive their instructions on Anti Terrorism from the Security Services and it is the latter that Tony Farell, along with many others is accusing of carrying out the terror attacks on 7/7. And therein lies the problem. You see, the only way South Yorkshire Police could of retained the services of Mr Farell would have been to accept the findings of the report. Yet the ramifications in doing so would almost certainly have torn the Establishment apart, and just like 9/11 the powers that be were never going to just stand back and let that happen.

The outcome of Tony Farell's appeal has yet to be decided. Mind you, I suspect that he has more chance of winning the lottery than his appeal. Moreover, defeat will no doubt lead to the evidence in Tony Farell's report being filed alongside that of 9/11 in the annals of conspiracy theories.

And no doubt this confinement will delight those who are either too blind or too stupid to see, along with those amongst us who simply choose not too. However, for the more open minded, rational thinking people, of who we are plenty and rapidly rising in numbers, the emerging evidence that 7/7 was an inside job is now too great to ignore.

Indeed, it is sad to say that 9/11 is always going to overshadow 7/7. Nevertheless, regardless of what a person believes, everybody knows at least some of the facts about 9/11 don't tie in with the Government's version of events.

Yet when it comes to the events of 7/7 the vast majority of people don't even know the Government's version of events, never mind that of the conflicting evidence. Therefore, it is up to people like us to make sure people never forget our own 9/11.

Unfortunately there is far too much that the Government rather us not know about 7/7 to list here. However some of the evidence is far too alarming not too. This includes the following:

1) In the Edgware Road tube train carriage there were 3 holes. All 3 holes were ringed with jagged metal pointing up into the carriage. Of these 3 holes, there was one large one near the first set of single doors and 1 large hole and 1 small directly in front of the first set of double doors. The carriage was sufficiently busy enough for eyewitnesses to confirm that at least one person disappeared down each of these holes. Two survived, the other died. How is this possible, when according to the Government a suicide bomber, acting alone, with homemade liquid explosives in a rucksack on his back was responsible for the carnage?

2) The body count on both the Edgware Rd & Aldgate trains was conducted by Dr Morgan Costello. Dr Costello counted 6 bodies on the Aldgate train and 7 on the Edgware Rd train. These two figures tally with the number of victims killed but does not allow for the 2 suicide bombers. The Government later partly addressed this discrepancy by saying that the suicide bomber on the Aldgate train had been splattered in 52 separate pieces across the carriage. However this is inconsistent with the victims bodies and that of the injuries of the survivors standing next to him. The majority of these serious injuries were to feet and lower limbs.

(3) There were 4 separate training exercises being carried out by the emergency services on 7/7 mimicking the events of what actually occurred. This is a telling sign of a false flag operation with the exact same thing happening in America on 9/11.

(4) Despite us being told that the suicide bombers used home made liquid explosives, Superintendent Christophe Chaboud, a French Policeman assigned to help Scotland Yard with the investigation told the Times Newspaper that initial analysis on the bombs showed them to be that of a sophisticated type used by the military. From 2005 up to date the official story on the type of explosive used has gone from being 'C4' to 'TAPT' before ending up as a mixture of black pepper and boiled-down hydrogen peroxide bought from a local warehouse.

(5) For a much more detailed account of this evidence along with a lot more Google: No one to vote for Kev Boyle.

Today is September 11th 2011. The day quite rightly belongs to the memory of the innocent people murdered by their own government exactly 10 years ago. But while we remember the victims of 9/11, let us also spare a moment or two for those murdered in London on 7/7. May each and everyone of their soles forever Rest in Peace.

Course, if you do not believe that our governments stage their own terror attacks, then you really do need a check up from the neck up.

Nevertheless, there is plenty of documented evidence to be found on the internet to prove the fact. For instance, on February 17, 2012 Tony Cartalucci wrote the following for Prison Planet.com:

The Federal Bureau of Investigation (FBI) has once again proven that the only thing Americans need fear, is their own government, with the latest "terror attack" foiled being one entirely of their own design.

USA Today reports that a suspect had been arrested by the FBI who was "en route to the U.S. Capitol allegedly to detonate a suicide bomb." While initial reports portrayed the incident as a narrowly averted terrorist attack, CBS would report that a "high ranking source told CBS News the man was "never a real threat.""" The explosives the would-be bomber carried were provided to him by the FBI during what they described as a "lengthy and extensive operation." The only contact the suspect had with "Al Qaeda" was with FBI officials posing as associates of the elusive, omnipresent, bearded terror conglomerate. The FBI, much like their MI5 counterparts in England, have a propensity for recruiting likely candidates from mosques they covertly run.

This is but the latest in a string of national terror plots carried out from start to finish by the FBI, who has made a business of approaching likely candidates and grooming them to carry out terror attacks. In September 2011, another FBI terror operation targeting the Capitol was "foiled," involving a patsy who believed he was to take part in an assault that would involve multiple gunmen and even a drone bomber provided to him by the FBI.

And perhaps the most dubious of all, was the December 2010 Portland "Christmas Tree Bomber," who was also approached by the FBI, provided demolition training, including a demonstration with live explosives performed in a Lincoln County park, and a van within which the patsy believed his handlers had provided him a bomb. The van with the inert device was parked next to a crowded Christmas tree lighting ceremony where the patsy attempted to detonate it remotely before being arrested by FBI agents.

It would later turn out that Portland had heroically withdrew from the FBI's Joint Terrorism Task Force, (JTTF), with the operation then being carried out behind Portland Mayor Sam Adam's back only for its conclusion to humiliatingly catch the mayor off guard. The city of Portland would eventually rejoin the JTTF after the fallout from the FBI's own terror plot.

The FBI is carrying out what is essentially a campaign of entrapment fueling what alternative news outlet Media Monarchy appropriately calls "terronoia." And while it is true that these incidents are being used to foment a climate of fear to justify the ongoing "War on Terror," there is a more sinister implication readers must be aware of.

In 1993 the FBI was carrying out an identical "sting operation" in New York City. The target was the World Trade Center, the weapon of choice would be a bomb-laden van, that like the above mentioned attacks, was supposed to contain an inert device. Helping the FBI was an Egyptian informant, Emad Salem, who over the course of the investigation grew suspicious of the federal agents and began recording his phone conversations with them.

From these recordings released by the New York Times, it turns out that the FBI switched out the inert device for real explosives at the last moment resulting in an attack that killed 6 and injured over a thousand. Despite this evidence, the 1993 bombing is still to this day attributed to "terrorists" with the FBI's involvement muted if ever mentioned.

The implications are of course, with the FBI's current nationwide stable of patsies being trained, directed, and provided material support to carry out attacks the FBI then "foils," is at any given moment, any one of these operations can be switched "live" just as in 1993. The resulting carnage can then be used to manipulate public opinion just as it was in 1993, 2001, on 7/7 in London, and in Madrid, Spain in 2004.

The risk rises exponentially now with Israel being confirmed to be training, arming, and directing US State Department-listed terrorist organization, the People's Mujahedin of Iran, also known as Mujahedeen e-Khalq (MEK). The US has also played an extensive role in supporting MEK who is currently carrying out a campaign of terror inside of Iran.
This is part of a plot by the US indicated in its own policy papers, openly conspiring to provoke a war with Iran. This is best encapsulated in this often cited quote from US policy think-tank, Brookings Institution:

"...it would be far more preferable if the United States could cite an Iranian provocation as justification for the airstrikes before launching them. Clearly, the more outrageous, the more deadly, and the more

unprovoked the Iranian action, the better off the United States would be. Of course, it would be very difficult for the United States to goad Iran into such a provocation without the rest of the world recognizing this game, which would then undermine it. (One method that would have some possibility of success would be to ratchet up covert regime change efforts in the hope that Tehran would retaliate overtly, or even semi-overtly, which could then be portrayed as an unprovoked act of Iranian aggression.) "
-Brookings Institution's 2009 "Which Path to Persia?" report, pages 84-85.
The same report would go on to say:

"In a similar vein, any military operation against Iran will likely be very unpopular around the world and require the proper international context—both to ensure the logistical support the operation would require and to minimize the blowback from it. The best way to minimize international opprobrium and maximize support (however, grudging or covert) is to strike only when there is a widespread conviction that the Iranians were given but then rejected a superb offer—one so good that only a regime determined to acquire nuclear weapons and acquire them for the wrong reasons would turn it down. Under those circumstances, the United States (or Israel) could portray its operations as taken in sorrow, not anger, and at least some in the international community would conclude that the Iranians "brought it on themselves" by refusing a very good deal."
-Brookings Institution's 2009 "Which Path to Persia?" report, page 52.

Clearly those in the West intent on striking Iran realize both the difficulty of obtaining a plausible justification, and the lack of support they have globally to carry out an attack even if they manage to find a suitable pretext. Brookings would continue throughout their report enumerating methods of provoking Iran, including conspiring to fund opposition groups to overthrow the Iranian government, crippling Iran's economy, and funding US State Department-listed terrorist organizations (MEK) to carry deadly attacks within Iran itself. Despite these overt acts of war, and even considering an option to unilaterally conduct limited airstrikes against Iranian targets, Brookings noted there was still the strong possibility Iran would not allow itself to be sufficiently provoked:

"It would not be inevitable that Iran would lash out violently in response to an American air campaign, but no American president should blithely assume that it would not."
The report continues:
"However, because many Iranian leaders would likely be looking to emerge from the fighting in as advantageous a strategic position as possible, and because they would likely calculate that playing the victim would be their best route to that goal, they might well refrain from such retaliatory missile attacks."
-Brookings Institution's 2009 "Which Path to Persia?" report, page 95.

With this in mind, and with the 1993 World Trade Center attack as a historical precedent, it is almost a certainty that the West and Mossad are carrying out the current global wave of bombings now being blamed on Iran. This includes two failed bombings in India and Georgia, and a more recent incident in Bangkok, Thailand.
Law enforcement officers across America may be witnessing the FBI conducting through their JTTF what they believe to be a "sting operation" that may end up being the next major terrorist attack on US soil – and the pretext for certain war with Iran.

The fears of Portland Mayor Sam Adams were well founded, and it took an act of terror to strong-arm him and the people of Portland into capitulating to the federal JTTF program. Local law enforcement, for the safety of themselves and the people they are charged to serve and protect, would be wise to keep an eye on the FBI – apparently the most likely source from which terror plots both "foiled" and "successful" are hatched...

Course, these attempts by the Security Services to create fear amongst the population by and large would be pathetic and laughable, would it not be for the fact that the population , by and large, believe these plots to be real.

Indeed, the fact that these false flag plots are so transparent is testament to just how gullible we have become as a whole. Course, for the Government these plots put them in a win, win situation as not only does it keep the public in fear but they also make the Security Services appear as if they are on top of their game...This is why the following old adage should always be remembered : *Anyone who would give up their freedom in exchange for security, is deserved of neither.*

Just sayin'.

Chapter 9
Welcome to Hateland, have a nice day

This is another article that I wrote for the Sovereign Independent and marked the beginning of the covert press agenda to demonise ALL Muslims.

You really have to hand it to the Establishment. They know exactly what buttons to press. In fact the propaganda department has been in full swing this weekend with maximum utilisation of the mainstream media being effectively employed to promote racial hatred.

You see, it all started in the UK on Friday with the 6 o'clock news. The leading, major story of the day was that American Security Forces had received intelligence reports confirming the threat of terrorist attacks planned for over the weekend.We were informed that there was a "credible" but as yet "unconfirmed" threat of a terrorist attack taking place in either New York or Washington.

However, we were not told who made the threat but being the weekend of Sept 11th the insinuation must be Al Qaeda. Our intrepid news reporter, 'live' in New York went on to say that the message from city officials was that: "There's no need to panic but the public should remain vigilant...".

Now if your a bit gullible, as the vast majority of people in 1st world countries appear to be, it is hard not to panic with a headline like that... Harder still when the warning is repeated either on the TV or Radio on the hour every hour.

Still i'm sure the Sheeple must of felt a lot more reassured once they saw the huge army of combat police on parade. After all, no self respecting, crazed Muslim, suicide pilot was ever going to fly a 757 into Ground Zero once he saw the sun glinting off their Rayban sunglasses or the barrel of their sub machine guns.

However, those of us less gullible people saw through the headline straight away but for those of you who don't understand corporate gobbledygook ,the news loosely translated like this:

The Gov't owned media have been ordered to put the fear of god into people by repeating (Confirming) a rumour (intelligence report) started by a govt office bods (security services) which are believable (credible), yet not necessarily honest (unconfirmed). The rumour suggests that you may or may not be subjected to violence (Threat) probably by people (Terrorists) who don't exist (Al Qaeda), so we won't mention them. We haven't a clue where you're probably not going to get hurt by anybody (New York or Washington) but some wannabe important people (city officials) have advised the gullible sheeple (public) to be petrified and keep an eye on the fella next to them, because he hates you and wants to kill you (Don't panic but remain vigilant).

No surprise then that 9/11 II ,the sequel never materialised. Course, that fact hasn't stopped today's papers cranking up the racial tension a notch. Indeed, much is being made of yesterday's demonstration by so called Islamic extremists outside the American Embassy.
And indeed, it's worked a treat as well judging by the comments on Facebook etc. In fact I don't think that I have ever seen the level of racial hatred that this demonstration has evoked… Which is a great pity really because unlike previous years, I hadn't seen a single status about 9/11 that condemned or blamed Islamic extremists.

Now there are 2 possible scenarios to this demonstration. And which ever scenario is correct, there can be no doubt that the media has reported the demonstration to great affect.

In doing so, along with the scare monger broadcasts predicting terrorist atrocities that were never going to happen, the promotion of racial harmony has been put back years.

You see, if the pictures in the papers were to be believed then your average God fearing Christian would have every right to hate and fear the Muslims.

Forced by sheer numbers against the safety barriers! Faces hidden with only their eyes visible! waving placards that predict world domination for Muslims! Burning the Star Spangled Banner! Isn't there a ban on demonstrations? In fact even I was scared for a moment...Alright, I made the last one up, but it's easy to see how people are manipulated into perceiving that we are under threat from the Arab world.

And the sad truth is we really aren't but the government could never have us know that. Indeed, if we knew that the Arab world posed no threat to us then there could be no ongoing war on terror.

And if that were the case then how on earth could we steal their oil?. Moreover, how would the CIA underpin the American economy if they couldn't control the all time high distribution of Afghanistan's Heroin? What would happen to the newly built gas and oil pipelines that the Taliban refused to let the USA run through their country? What about the Trillions of Dollars the World bankers would lose in interest on the loans used to finance the war? Where would racial harmony leave the plans for the NWO ?

Then there is 9/11. How would the anti terrorist bill ever have been passed, not to mention the many other infringements on our civil liberties if there were no Arab Terrorists to protect us from.

In fact Larry Silverstein would have been bankrupted over the cost of removing Asbestos from the World Trade Centre instead of becoming a billionaire through insurance claims!

Indeed, how would the FBI bosses have managed to destroy the evidence relating to the missing Trillions of Dollars stolen by the Bush Administration had building 7 of the WTC not collapsed under the sheer weight of the jet fuel spilled from the hijacked United Airways aeroplanes?

How would United Airways along with many others have made a killing on the stock market had it not been for the terrorists taking their planes for a joyride, for that matter?

Then there is the Pentagon. How would the accountants there have accounted for the billions of dollars in misplaced funds had the Terrorists not overpowered the pilot of the Boeing 757 cruise missile, before getting all confused as to which side of the building contained the Senior government heads such as Vice President Dick Cheney and Defence Secretary Donald Rumsfeld and steered it into the Accounts department instead?

On the other hand, racial hatred not only provides the opportunity for Governments and corrupt corporate fat cats to make easy money, remove our civil rights and pursue their own agenda, it also keeps people divided. Not only Black against White, or East against West, but those who support racism and those who don't.

Indeed, it is these divisions that allow the few to rule the many. And this brings me nicely back to the two scenarios for the demonstration. You see, the general consensus in this morning's papers put the number of demonstrators at 100. And a quick look at the news videos and photographs makes the number of demonstrators appear to be in far greater numbers.

Now if these were truly Islamic extremists, then I would have no time whatsoever for them. Mind you, as demonstrations go a 100 people is hardly a success by any standards. After all, the British Muslim population is expected to top 3 million this year.

A 2010 survey put the number of Muslims in Britain at 2,869,000. Therefore, this being the case 100 Muslim extremists is hardly representative of the British Muslim population. And to put it into perspective the demonstrators represent less than 0.003% of British Muslims.

Moreover, a 2009 survey on the attitudes of British Muslims found them to identify more strongly with the UK and hold the country's institutions in higher regard than the rest of the British population.

Now according to the newspapers, the police kept 'a small' number of Muslims who were opposed to the demonstration away from the main protesters. One of those Anti demonstration protesters, Abdul Sallam 41 travelled all the way from Glasgow to make his feelings known about the demonstrators.

He said " *i'm a Muslim. What they are doing is bringing shame on all Muslims. This is not part of the teachings of Islam. Islam is about peace, but what they want to do is hate other people. I am proud to be British. i love my country. All these people are doing is breaking Britain apart*".

So, notwithstanding the disproportionate representation of Muslim views, the demonstrators were not protesting against Britain. Their anger was solely aimed at America. The picture of a flag (for that's what it was) was not the Union Jack, it was the Star Spangled Banner and the demonstration was largely peaceful with only 4 "extremists" being arrested.

But looking at the situation fairly, do they not have a right to be angry? I mean between 2003-2010 nearly 108,000 Innocent men women and children have been killed in Iraq. Moreover, in a survey taken by 2000 Iraqi adults, 22% had lost one or more family member who lived under their roof.

Furthermore 70% of children in Iraq are exhibiting signs of post traumatic stress and now have the honour of living in the most dangerous place on Earth. Yet their country was invaded under the pretence of being in possession of WMD's… Which was later proved to be false... and also of harbouring Osama Bin Laden… Which was also false.

In short Iraq was illegally invaded. Can you imagine if it had been the other way round and it had been Britain illegally invaded? Living under the same conditions they are now, with three quarters of our children severely traumatised? Yet still no hatred was directed at the British from the demonstrators. And let's not beat around the bush here, Britain is as deeply involved in the invasion, pro rata, as the USA is.

Then the so called English Defence League(EDL) turned up although quite what this repackaged National Front Party is defending England from I haven't a clue. They claim to be a non racist group but their mandate and actions point to the opposite.

The Newspapers put the number of EDL members present yesterday at around 60. This begs the question why were the EDL there in the first place?

Were they there filling in for the KKK? And unlike the so called Islamic Extremists(IE's) the EDL were not kept back from the American Embassy. However unlike the IE's the EDL refused to move when told by the police. Unlike the IE's ,the EDL did scuffle with police and unlike the IE's, The EDL had come to fight ,not protest.

This led the police to arrest 20 EDL members which has led to the usual racists comments such as "*They cam over ere an burn r bleedin flag an ware da mugs that get nicked init?*".

No they dont. That is racist propaganda spread by the likes of the Government, The EDL and the uneducated. From what I could see, the 60 strong EDL were much more intimidating, antagonistic and aggressive than the 100 strong IE's were. And why should that be? The IE's were protesting against the Americans. Would the EDL have been there had it been White Brits protesting against the Americans leading us into an illegal war? A war we cant and wont ever win? A war that in Afghanistan alone has cost the lives of 308 British soldiers and injuries, many life changing to a further 10,608 more… I think not.

So for crying out loud let's aim our anger at the real enemy. As i've said I don't condone or support any extremist group and that includes the EDL.

But what if the IE's were not who they say they were? What if they were CIA plants or worse, British Government plants. Indeed, you have to ask yourself who stood to gain from the demonstration? The so called IE's had nothing to gain except upsetting and alienating the British Population. Isn't that a case of cutting off your nose to spite your face?

In fact such actions can only lead to themselves, their families, their friends and their fellow Muslims being put at risk from race attacks. It can result in their Mosques, factories and shops being vandalised and burnt down. Surely if you are a small minority out to start a race war against the vast majority it would make sense to have a large expanse of water between you before doing so?

The Government and the CIA on the other hand have everything to gain by the demonstration. With this in mind is it so far fetched to accept that this demonstration could very well be a carefully orchestrated plan which has achieved the result it set out to achieve?

With regard to the so called 30 day blanket ban on demonstrations, it's quite difficult to find any information on this subject. Having said that I must confess to not looking all that hard. After all the ban doesn't really have a bearing on this article except to question why yesterday's demonstration was allowed to go ahead.

From what little I could find out it seems that the 30 day order isn't so much a blanket ban, more a select borough ban. This doesn't appear to include the Borough of Westminster although there is a permanent ban on demonstrations and protests around Whitehall.

Mind you, its Interesting that although the media was keen to point out that last weeks EDL protest was a static one (The inference being the banning order only applies to marches), no police action was taken until one of the EDL leaders loudly informed the boys in Blue via megaphone that he was breaching his bail conditions by being there. Likewise,did the so called IE's arrive outside the American Embassy in small groups (it was a small group collectively) with their placards in their pockets? Or could it be that the police know that the ban is unlawful?

Course, I am sure there will be a small number of bigots who read this and imagine me to be a limp wristed, politically correct, left wing, do gooder. Yet if labels need be applied to someone having the belief that all human beings are equal, regardless of race, colour or creed, that the world belongs to us all and not just the few, that no one should ever have to go without food, water,clothing or shelter and that no one should have to live in fear of his fellow man, then I care not what you label me.

Chapter 10
Invasion of the Baby snatchers

When Tony Blair became the British Prime Minister he immediately began to wage war on what he deemed as "unfit parents'. This has led to many perfectly good parents having their children removed from their care.

Disturbingly, many of these children are ever heard of again. The following is the first of many articles that I have written on the subject...

It wasn't so many years ago that in cases where children were taken from their parents by the social services the general consensus amongst the public was that there had to be a good reason.. But not so any more.

Indeed, many parents in the UK are now so afraid of the social services that they think twice about taking their children to casualty should the need arise.

In fact it is certainly is not unfair to say that the fear, mistrust and suspicion afforded to the social services by some, is akin to that afforded to Adolf Hitler's SS. Quite appropriate then that both share the same initials.

Then again, the Nazi SS were extremely efficient and very well organised... The same cannot be said for Britain's SS.

I mean, we are led to believe that the SS are here to protect our children from cruelty and neglect.

Moreover, any decision made by the SS are supposed to be in the best interest of the child.
Which would be commendable if it was true.
You see, what we are seeing now is an organised program of child stealing in order to meet the adoption targets set up under the Blair Government... That and a production line of young children for the filthy rich to rape.

Indeed, there are huge financial incentives offered by the Government to ensure that their targets are met... Although that fact is often denied.

On the flip side, underperforming leads to job losses and reduced budgets. Failure to meet their quotas is therefore not an option.
This is why Social Workers seek out easy targets mostly made up of :
Young single mothers lacking in family support, poorly educated mothers on benefit and children with injuries which are often no more than minor bruises and such like
.

Rarely are these children snatched from middle class families which indeed is a major contributing factor in leading to that misguided belief amongst the more affluent members of society that *'there is no smoke without fire'.*
This view inevitably leads to the SS being defended, even justified in being over cautious, especially when cases such as Baby P explode in the media.

However in cases such as Baby P and Victoria Climbie, the lack of intervention from social workers is actually to blame.
This lack of intervention stems from the social workers often being intimidated and subject to abuse by the parents of the children they are investigating.

Indeed, quite often the social worker is even denied entry into the home to check on the child's well being.

You see, Social workers, despite what people are led to believe, have very little authority.
Because of this, cases such as Baby P are neglected in favour of easier targets.
And it is this lack of knowledge on what social workers can and cannot do that leads to a lot of parents losing their children.

Moreover, aware of the public's ignorance a social worker will resort to bullying, duping and scaring parents into signing over their children.
This was made easier for the heartless SS to get away with by the 1989 Children's Act which in effect meant a veil of secrecy was thrown around court proceedings involving children.

And in turn, this is another reason that so few people from the middle classes and upwards know what is really going on.
Course, as I have just said, this secrecy and wall of silence imposed around child welfare was supposed to have been put in place to protect the child.

However, far from doing so it has allowed the SS to act in a corrupt and totally unprofessional manner. So much so in fact that it isn't unfair to say that the child's welfare and wishes are secondary to performance targets.

Reporting restrictions on court proceedings mean children are removed from loving and perfectly capable parents on the flimsiest of evidence.
And because of these 'secret courts' parents have no recourse from anywhere because just discussing their case with anyone other than their legal advisers can result in a prison sentence.

And of course, more often than not it will be a parents legal team's incompetence that will lead to them losing their child/children. Invariably the vast majority of child order cases see the parents being represented by legal aid solicitors.

Now, far be it for me to suggest that the outcome of a case is decided beforehand or that the SS and Law Society are acting in complicity. However recent Parliamentary figures show that child care orders average around 8000 a year. Of these only between 0.1 and 0.2 percent are refused.

Moreover, Ian Joseph - a Monaco based businessman - was so alarmed about what goes on in our law courts that he set up a website specifically to help parents who have had their children snatched by the state.

Indeed, it is also true to say that I have pointed many a panicked parent in Ian's direction.
Course, the first thing he tells parents who are receiving legal aid is that if they want their children back then they have to get rid of their solicitor and represent themselves... Sadly a far too daunting a task for many.

Liberal Democrat MP, John Hemming is also an outspoken critic and long time opponent of the way family court proceedings are conducted. Although it has to be said that Hemming is an MP and a self confessed *"love rat"*.

Unfortunately, such is the scale of the problem both are limited on what they can do.
John Hemming, knowing the likely outcome of court proceedings will often tell parents to flee the UK for either Southern Ireland or Sweden... How scary is that!

Furthermore, the fact many couples follow his advice only goes to show that the accusations against them are false in the vast majority of cases.

But does this major, life changing step mean you get to keep your unborn child?

Well, I do in fact personally know one such couple very well who John Hemming helped relocate to County Wexford in Southern Ireland.

Course, they cannot be identified by their real names so i will call them Steve and Emma.

This is their story...

Emma, now aged 30 was living alone with her daughter (Child A) in Essex when she Met Steve now aged 37.

The couple were both delighted when Emma found out that she was pregnant with Steve's baby (Child B).

However Emma was ill throughout the pregnancy with Pre-Eclampsia and with Steve out at work, the couple had no choice except to get a babysitter to look after Child A.

It was at this time that Child A was found to have a vaginal injury. Worse still, and to their horror, Steve was accused by the SS of being responsible despite there being no evidence whatsoever to support this claim.

Child A, a month short of being 2 years old was then forcibly taken into care.

Worse was to follow when Emma gave birth to Child B on Christmas eve that same year.

In fact just 5 hours after giving birth Child B was taken from Emma and handed over to foster parents.

And that being despite no charges being brought against Steve for the injury to Child A.

Worse was to come however because the couple were unable to stop the children from being adopted.

So, when Emma fell pregnant with Child C she was told by the SS that the baby would be taken into care immediately after Emma had given birth.
At this point out of sheer desperation the couple contacted John Hemming, who advised them to go to the Republic of Ireland.
He told them that even if the Irish SS got involved, the couple would at least receive a much fairer hearing over there.

Arriving in County Wexford on the 1st of June 2009, Emma gave birth just 3 days later.
However, with no Medical records available the hospital staff had no choice but to contact England.

And of course in doing so, the hospital was made aware of Emma's previous history.
Therefore with limited information to hand, the Irish social services - at the request of the English Social Services - had no choice except to take Child C into care pending reports.
Indeed, in contacting the English SS the Irish SS were told that under no circumstances should Child C be returned to the couple.

Now remember, this was despite there being no evidence or criminal proceedings to suggest that either Steve or Emma were a danger to the Baby.
Thus began the long drawn out legal procedure of preparing reports for a court hearing.

Despite this the couple were allowed to see Child C twice weekly at a contact house.
During this period, everything seemed to be engineered towards gearing up for Child C being returned to Steve and Emma's custody.

In fact it is fair to say that things were looking so good that the couple were not worried when Emma fell pregnant again.

However, concerned over the slow pace that things were moving, the couple's Solicitor - at their behest - tried to speed proceedings up by asking for a review of the evidence regarding the injury to Child A.

This review brought to light the facts that Child A had only been subject to one injury(inconsistent with parental abuse) and neither had she been 'Groomed' as had been previously suggested by social workers.

More importantly, the review revealed that the babysitter Emma had been forced to use whilst she was ill - a registered childminder who had been working with disabled children - was under investigation for child abuse.

Emma was also becoming increasingly concerned about the level of care offered to Child C by her Foster carer.

She therefore voiced these concerns to social workers, which included the complaints that Child C often had head lice, sore looking rashes and the fact that Child C called her Foster carer Mummy.

However, when Emma gave birth to her 4th child (Child D) the couple were devastated to learn that he was to be removed from their care. Again I will remind you that there was no evidence of neglect to Child A who was removed from Steve and Emma because of concerns over Steve.

Furthermore, this was despite there being no evidence to back these concerns up and him never being charged with any offence.

Child A was only 2 at the time and the couple never had any of the 3 subsequent children in their care for there to be any concerns about their parenting skills.

Nevertheless, Child D was placed in foster care with his sister and Steve and Emma now got to see him twice weekly along with Child C.

Moreover they had been categorically told that the SS plan was for reunification.
However at a court hearing in April of this year, the couple were horrified to learn that despite what they were told about reunification, the SS intend to keep both children in permanent foster care.

Alarmingly, not only does this course of action contradict what they were told by social workers, the fact of the matter is that no one had even bothered to discuss this course of action with them and neither has it been discussed with them to date.
Sadly, Steve and Emma are now left in limbo.

Yet despite the agony of having their 4 children taken off of them they have somehow managed to stay together as a couple, whereas most relationships would have collapsed under the strain years ago.

Childs A and B were removed on the flimsiest of evidence and quickly adopted out effectively making it impossible to get them back. The fact that they gave up their home, family and friends in order to flee to Ireland for the sole purpose of keeping their unborn baby apparently counts for nothing.

Moreover, the couple are acutely aware that should their Irish children be returned to them, then they will be forever under the scrutiny of the social services.
Therefore, that fact alone would be enough to ensure that Steve and Emma were nothing short of perfect parents.

Unfortunately, without the financial backing it is hard now to see where the couple go from here.

So, is there anything that couples in a similar position to Steve and Emma can do?

And to answer that you have to understand that Steve and Emma put their faith in the British legal system.

And when that let them down they followed the well intentioned advice of John Hemming to flee the country.

They then put their faith in the Republic of Ireland's legal system and that too has let them down.

Therefore, in theory the answer is no.

In reality however there is but you have to take command of the situation from the start.

You see, you cannot afford to show any weakness in your resolve to hang onto your child.

Indeed, to do so will result in you being bullied into submission.

So firstly, never trust a social worker.

And I am not saying that they are all bad, but by far the vast majority are.

Do not be fooled by their friendly approach as this is more often than not a trick.

And above all, always keep in mind that they have no authority to do anything without a court order.

You also need to make sure that you film or record everything.

Course, nine times out of ten they will tell you that you are not allowed to film them but stand your ground and remember that you are allowed to film who and what the hell you like in your own home.

Be polite, but not friendly or openly hostile.

Offer no other information other than what they ask for and do not be rushed into making a rash reply.

If they try to get you to sign consent forms to take your child tell them to *"do one"* until they have a court order.

Always check that you are dealing with a fully qualified Social worker who is registered with your social service department... You would be surprised how many aren't!

Also remember that you can tell them to leave at any time.

Course, if they do feel that they have a strong case against you then the chances are they will return with a court order.

And that being the case then I am afraid that there is nothing you can do to prevent your child being taken.

However, as the statistics have shown you are wasting your time employing a solicitor.

You must - as Ian Joseph will tell you - represent yourself in court.

After all, the fact is that no one will fight harder or argue more passionately for the return of your child than you will.

Course, if your child is unborn and you've been told that your baby will be removed from you at birth, then there's little you can do at that time to prevent it.

However you will inevitably be told sooner rather than later that you have to register your baby for a birth certificate and this is where you really need to make a stand.

And that being the case, flatly refuse to register your child's birth.

After all, at that stage you have nothing to lose and everything to gain.

Course this refusal will lead to you being bullied and threatened with all kinds of things - including prison.

But again, stand your ground.

No charges will be brought against you if you don't consent.

You do however need to be clued up on the workings of Admiralty law before you take this course of action.

Nevertheless, without a birth certificate the SS have no choice but to return your baby.

This was evidenced following a FOI request submitted to Torbay Council under the freedom of information act.

The request was in the form of a question asking if a child is not registered at birth, do they have the authority to remove the child?

Torbay Council's answer?
No they don't.
Source:
https://www.whatdotheyknow.com/request/right_to_any_child_with_no_birth

However, you should be aware that having no birth certificate could present problems for your child later in life although There is an interesting article to be found at the link below about a couple who refused to register their child and have had no problems to date.
http://self-realisation.com/equity/case-studies/denial-of-consent-to-register-children/

Moreover, you can cross that bridge when you come to it as for now, the important thing is keeping your child where he or she belongs and that is with you.
What's more, if the Social Services really had the child's best interest at heart, they too would be working to keep children with their parents.

I cannot in fact stress enough that removing a child from his or her parent's should only be done when ALL other avenues have been explored.
Sadly this is not the case so think on, sometimes - just sometimes, there is smoke without fire.

Two years after writing this article Child C and Child D were finally returned to Steve & Emma. They are all still living happily in the Republic of Ireland.

** On the 9th of February 2012 it was announced that the number of children referred into care in England has hit a record high. According to the BBC:

"Last month, local authorities made 903 court applications to take children into care - the highest since courts service Cafcass was set up in 2001.
"Numbers have been rising since late 2008 and the infamous Baby P case involving the death of a toddler while on the at-risk register in London.
"Cafcass boss Anthony Douglas said: "All agencies need to factor in these much larger increases into their planning."
It is the first time England's referral figures have passed the 900-mark in a month, and compares with 803 the month before and 698 in the previous January.

*** My claims in the above article were reinforced on the 18th of Feb 2012 by Christopher Booker writing for the Daily Telegraph:

Such is the reign of terror now being imposed on innocent English families by social workers that scores of parents have been fleeing with their children to Ireland to escape their clutches. I have followed a dozen such stories over the past two years, and in all of them two things stand out. One is that the English social workers seem prepared to stop at nothing to get the children back. The other is the extraordinary contrast between them and the Irish social workers, who again and again have satisfied themselves that the children are at no risk from their loving parents and are astonished by the ruthless behaviour of their English counterparts.

Several of these stories I have reported more than once and they do not have happy endings. A mother and baby were

pursued to Ireland by six social workers and police, who sat in Dublin for 10 days of court hearings, until a judge ruled in their favour (with the social workers seen giving "high fives" on emerging from the court). When the mother again escaped to a remote cottage, she was violently knocked down by a policeman, so that her baby could be taken back to England.

Vicky Haigh, a former racehorse trainer, managed to escape to Ireland before her daughter was born. But then she was brought to England to be quite bizarrely punished, in a case relating to her beloved older daughter, with a three-year prison sentence – leaving her baby to be looked after in Ireland.

A 14-year-old boy lived happily with his mother in Ireland for six months until, after an equally bizarre judgment based on evidence neither he nor his mother were allowed to see, he was deported miserably back to care in England.

Last week, another such story came my way. It concerns a respectable family which was hit with disaster last summer, after the semi-autistic 8-year-old son –who tends to make things up – had lashed out at his 13-year-old sister, leaving bruises. When these were investigated, the boy told the police that his father had done it. The girl denied this – and the boy admitted in video evidence what had really happened – but the police stuck with his earlier story and arrested the father. Although he was never charged, the interventions of social workers became so menacing that, last October, the family escaped to Ireland, where the father has his roots.

There they have happily settled, and the 13-year-old daughter has become a star pupil of the local school. But the social workers eventually tracked them down – after the children's grandmother, back in England, had been arrested by 10 police officers, handcuffed, held for three hours in a cell, and told she would be charged with perverting the course of justice unless she revealed their whereabouts. The English social workers pressed their Irish counterparts to co-operate in getting the children back to England (there are no court orders), but were told there was no reason for this because the children were in no danger.

The social workers then tried to lean on the school principal, saying that the children were "at risk of emotional harm". The sensible headmistress gave them very short shrift, saying that the English social workers had behaved deplorably in trying to destroy a perfectly normal family, and that England's loss was Ireland's gain, since the girl was a brilliant pupil, who was learning five languages. Thanks to their origins, the family will soon be safely confirmed as Irish citizens.

What is striking about these stories is how often the parents emphasise the contrast between the two countries' social workers. "In England," says this father, "we were treated like dangerous criminals. In Ireland the social workers could not be more different, warm, friendly, treating us like human beings." And of course it is in England that the number of children taken into care has soared to a record level, just having topped 900 a month. There is a phenomenon of group psychology here that deserves much wider attention than it is being given.

Chapter 11
Disgraced Peer apologises - Exactly for what is anyone's guess

ALL of our MP's & Lords are self-serving crooks. However, when they are caught it clearly becomes obvious that there is one rule for us and another for them.

What follows is a report that I wrote for the Sovereign Independent Newspaper about the criminal Lord Hanningfield.

It has been revealed that the Disgraced Tory Peer, Lord Hanningfield was released from a low security Kent prison after serving only TWO months of the NINE month jail term that he received for SIX counts of fiddling his House of Lords expenses.

On his release in September 2011, Hanningfield was immediately re-arrested by Essex Police relating to allegations that he misused his Corporate credit card while he was leader of Essex County Council.

Speaking on the 30th of October 2011 in the Sunday Express, Hanningfield, appeared to issue an apology for fiddling £13,379 in government expenses. But did he?

The expenses relate to overnight stays in London that Hanningfield claimed for, when in fact he was actually driven back to his luxurious Essex home in a Government provided chauffeur driven limousine.

The arrogance of this man is breathtaking. After his arrest in early 2010, Hanningfield tried to avoid going to court by claiming Parliamentary privilege. When that failed, Hanningfield used every opportunity available to chant his mantra "*I have done nothing wrong*", even after he was found guilty and sentenced in July 2011, which he immediately unsuccessfully appealed against.

Even Hanningfields apology smacks of insincerity and in issuing it he still refuses to accept that he had committed a crime.
The carefully worded apology states "*After much consideration, during and after my conviction, i have come to realise that i owe my friends, family and the public a heartfelt apology for the difficulties and problems my actions have caused*".

You will note that nowhere in that apology does Hanningfield say that he is sorry for the actual crime he committed.

He then goes on to say "*I have come to accept the situation in which i found myself was, unfortunately, one caused by my own negligence and for that i am truly sorry*".
Yet once again you will note that Hanningfield does not apologise for the crime. In fact it's hard to judge if he's apologising for his 'negligence' or if he's just feeling "truly sorry" for himself having had to spend time in prison.

Course, if someone goes to a business meeting and then straight afterwards get driven home at someone else's expense, it doesn't take a genius to work out that they are not entitled to claim for the cost of an overnight stay in a hotel. That isn't negligence. That is fraud... Something that Hanningfield was guilty of at least 6 times.

Hanningfield then ends his apology by boasting that he didn't claim legal aid to defend himself against the action.

Is he for real?

But not before he says "*I must, though, stress that there was no intention on my part to break the law, but i recognise i did so – and for that in itself there are no excuses*".

Sooo, no apology for the crime there then either.

Hanningfield also claims that he is not guilty of the new charges brought against him, for which he is on police bail until January 2012. I myself suspect that in this case there really is, no smoke without fire.

Two years later, Hanningfield received substantial damages from Essex Police for wrongful arrest.

** *On the 9th of April 2012, Press TV reported the following in regard to Lord Hanningfield:*

The British House of Lords offers two criminal peers, imprisoned for fraud, the same opportunity to rob the public money as they enjoyed before, by welcoming them back on their seats after Easter.

The Tory peers Lord Hanningfield and Lord Taylor of Warwick were convicted to 12 months and 9 months in prison, respectively, for submitting false expenses to the Lords.

Hanningfield was found guilty of presenting false claims of £13,379 of taxpayer money and Taylor followed suit with £11,000.

However, as the upper chamber's regulations do not include any requirement for peers to resign or be expelled, the two will be reinstated in the same potentially-ripe position for embezzlement even without a probation period after their prison terms.
The prospects of two fraudster peers returning to the ultimate decision-making body of Britain raises serious questions about special privileges enjoyed by the Lords including the hereditary right to claim an upper chamber seat.

According to the Rehabilitation of Offenders Act 1974, an ordinary criminal convicted of burglary or mugging has to endure a rehabilitation (probation) period of at least one year to receive a qualification to work from the Criminal Records Bureau (CBR).
The CBR's certificate will only accredit such a criminal for jobs that do not leave him in a position to repeat his crime.

Chapter 12
Putting a stop to the car insurance racket

Another Sovereign Independent article that I wrote in relation to the car insurance scam.

There can be no denying that car insurance is a corporate money making protection racket that has the motorist held by the proverbial 'short and curlys'. New laws recently introduced by the government mean that you cannot even keep an uninsured car in your garage unless you declare it as SORN.

And while this new rule will cause further misery to thousands of law abiding motorists and car collectors, it is likely to have no effect whatsoever on those the government say the new law is aimed at, namely uninsured drivers.

After all, let's face it, anyone driving on the road uninsured isn't going to worry about parking their motor up without declaring it SORN. The new law will however entitle the police to seize and destroy many more cars and drag the innocent keepers into court, where they can expect to be fined anything up to £1000.

However, to my mind, instead of heaping further misery upon the easy target motorist, while at the same time adding to the millions of pounds in profits made by the big insurance companies, the government would be better off putting a cap on the high cost of insuring a car.
In fact, by making insurance more affordable, normal law abiding citizens would be less likely to be pushed into risking driving an uninsured motor. But we all know that will never happen.

Indeed, I don't think that any sane person would disagree that having car protection for yourself and others is a bad thing. However the fact that car insurance is obligatory means that the insurance companies have been given carte blanche to rip us off. I know this from personal experience which is as follows.

I had been insured with Kwik Fit, over a 7 year period. Back then, as I do now I pay my yearly policy in monthly instalments via direct debit. Throughout this time I never had a claim yet despite this fact my policy rose on average by £10-15 per year.

Then after the 7th year Kwik fit sent me a renewal notice, which I noticed had jumped up in price by nearly £150. Anyone who pays a yearly contract such as an insurance policy by direct debit will know that after the initial 12 month contract is up, unless you inform the company involved to the contrary the contract will re-commence for another year.

Now I suppose that I could have tackled Kwik fit about this price hike, but to my mind 7 years of loyalty deserves more so I simply cancelled my direct debit and moved to Tesco insurance who were willing to insure my car for more or less the same price as Kwik fit were before they tried ripping me off.

Now, after my year was up with Tesco insurance, they sent me a renewal notice which was for around £100 more than the previous year. So. once again I just cancelled the Direct Debit and moved to Swinton insurance who were cheaper by far than Tescos were in that first year.

However after a month with Swintons I bought a new, more powerful car. Before doing so I looked at insurance prices on 'Go Compare' and as luck would have it, Swintons were also the cheapest according to this website and would be prepared to insure my new car for roughly £60 more than what I was paying them now.

So, on the day that I bought the new car I cancelled my insurance for my old one with my local Swinton branch who then Quoted me £100 extra to insure my new car. When I told them that they were quoting me £40 more than they were quoting me on the Go Compare website, I was told by the Swinton agent that I would have to go through the Go Compare website to make this price.

I was also told categorically that since I would still be insured on the new car by them, i would not be subject to cancellation fees for terminating my insurance policy early.

Nevertheless, despite this fact, I received a letter from Swinton informing me that unless i pay them a £33 cancellation fee within 7 days then they intended to help themselves to this money by deducting it from my bank debit card... Very nice of them!

Tescos Insurance have in the meantime also gone into Corporate greed overdrive and are threatening me with court action unless i pay them £438 for an insurance policy that I never used and didn't give my permission for them to set up.

Indeed, it is this kind of bullying that a huge number of people give in to and pay up rather than risk being hounded by debt collection agencies or worse still facing an appearance in court, thus making untold amounts of money for these companies.

I myself am a bit wiser to these bully boy tactics and as such, in the case of Swintons I just cancelled my debit card and ordered a new one. Nevertheless in doing so it has caused me unnecessary aggravation in so much as I have to wait 7-10 days for a new card. In regards to Tesco's demand, I have appropriately filed their letters in the bin.

However, to ensure that the insurance rip-off continues, the following was reported by the Daily Mirror newspaper in February 2012:
Cameras at petrol stations will automatically stop uninsured or untaxed vehicles from being filled with fuel, under new government plans.
Downing Street officials hope the hi-tech system will crack down on the 1.4million motorists who drive without insurance.

Automatic number plate recognition (ANPR) cameras are already fitted in thousands of petrol station forecourts.
Drivers can only fill their cars with fuel once the camera has captured and logged the vehicle's number plate.

Currently the system is designed to deter motorists from driving off without paying for petrol.
But under the new plans, the cameras will automatically cross-reference with the DVLA's huge database.
When a car is flagged as being uninsured or untaxed, the system will prevent the fuel pump being used on that vehicle.
The proposals will have a huge impact - forcing drivers to insure and tax their car if they want to drive.
One in 25 drivers in the UK do not have insurance - one of the worst records in western Europe.

According to recent figures, around 160 people are killed and 23,000 injured by uninsured and untraced drivers every year.
Downing Street officials are due to meet representatives from the major fuel companies in the next few weeks to discuss the idea.
But some petrol retailers said the proposals were a "step too far" - claiming they put cashiers at risk.

Brian Madderson, from RMI Petrol, which represents independent petrol stations, said: "Staff are already getting stick from motorists for high fuel prices.
"This proposal will increase the potential for conflict. Our cashiers are not law enforcers."...

Course, while it is unlikely that the British government will ever put a stop to the car insurance rip off, Roger Hayes of the British Constitution Group could unwittingly force insurance firms to slash their prices in order to survive.

You see, Roger is committed to setting up what he calls 'The Lawful Bank' and is now engaged in trying to ascertain the number of people who would be willing to use this bank. Once he has sufficient numbers the bank will be set up.

The Lawful Bank will operate using the fractional reserve banking system which is employed by all the high street banks. However, unlike the high street banks, it is the customer who will reap the benefits of this banking system. One of those benefits, according to Roger is car insurance which he estimates will cost a customer around £100 per year.

*Unfortunately Roger's plan never came to fruition, sadly because of lack of support. Meanwhile, the car insurance rip off scam still continues to this day

Chapter 13
The Cancer Con

Cancer is easily curable and I know that fact from personal experience. Course the Establishment do not want you to know that it is. So, what follows is the first of many articles that I have written on the subject and again, this one was written for the Sovereign Independent Newspaper...

Sometime last year I read a statistic about Cancer that left me totally gobsmacked. The statistic dealt with the drastic increase in numbers of those likely to be affected by Cancer throughout the 20th century. The figures given were that in the year 1900, around 1 in 100 people were affected by Cancer. By the 1950's that figured had increased to 1 in 10 before rapidly rising again to a staggering 1 in 3 by the year 2000.

Now obviously a lot of the increase between 1900 and 1950, can in theory, be explained away by the average life expectancy being a lot lower during that period and no doubt the two world wars also had a bearing on the figures.

However, even reducing that number by a generous 75 % will still give you a figure rising from 1 in 25 to 1 in 10 during that period. A staggering increase by any standards.

By the 1950's life expectancy had increased sharply and with the absence of any world wars the rise from 1 in 10 to 1 in 3 by the year 2000 isn't so easily explained away. To further fan the flames, statistics released in 2011 suggest that 48% of people will now be affected by cancer at some point in their life.

That means that in just over a decade, the already alarming 1 in 3 has risen to nearly 1 in 2 and if you apply that figure to the average family of 2 adults and 2 children, it is hardly surprising that people rush to the Doctors at the drop of a hat.

Between 1950 and the Millennium the incidence of all types of Cancer rose a staggering 85%. Moreover this statistic is based on the age adjusted rate. In other words, the increase has nothing to do with people living longer.

Further proof of this is evidenced by the fact that over the 2 decades leading up to the year 2000, the fastest growing rate of Cancer for any age group was that found in children.

Furthermore ,there has been a major shift in the type of Cancer people are developing. For instance, Breast Cancer now affects 1 in 3 women and accounts for the highest number of deaths in female cancer patients.

However ,during the first half of the last century cases of Breast Cancer were virtually non existent. Once again, this can't be explained away by the fact that life expectancy was so much lower between 1900-1950, since breast cancer is common amongst relatively young women.
Similarly, Testicular Cancer, although still fairly uncommon has seen the biggest increase in numbers of all the other cancer types more commonly found in men. Once again, Testicular cancer is almost exclusively found in younger men, especially within the 15 - 35 year old age group.

Further contradictions can be found contained within the numbers when you consider the improvement in working conditions. You see, the laws on Health and Safety in the workplace became much more stringent and rigorously enforced during the second half of the 20th century.

Gone were the days of working in factories and mills where the air was thick with cancer giving particles. The latter half of the century also saw the banning of asbestos which at one time inevitably lead to those who worked with it developing Asbestosis, a form of Lung Cancer.

Interestingly enough, cancers whose development are specifically linked to Cigarette smoking such as lung cancer, only account for a Quarter of all Cancer related deaths. This is despite the fact that people smoked in far greater numbers up until the mid 1960's. In fact it is only after this time that the number of people who smoked slowly started to fall.

So, no matter how you massage the figures there is still an enormous leap in the number of people getting cancer. Worse still the trend is showing no sign of slowing down. That is to say the trend is showing no sign of slowing down for the vast majority of us.

However, for the social elite cancer is an entirely different story. You see, while the statistics point to 1 in 3 of us developing cancer, when is the last time that you heard of a member of the Royal family getting Cancer?

I mean, the Queen mother lived well past the 100 mark. The Queen & Prince Phillip are still going strong and there are not many 90 year old's still competing in equestrian events i'll wager.

Charles, Anne, Andrew and Edward haven't had Cancer. Neither have the 8 Grandchildren. So suffice to say then, the Royal family don't even fall into the 1 in 10 category last seen in the 1950's.

However, it isn't just Royalty that are seemingly immune to Cancer. Indeed it's very rare that you ever hear of anyone with power, influence and money being affected. Stranger still, even when the super rich are unlucky enough to be blighted by the curse of the common man, the rule of thumb doesn't appear to apply either.

Take the actor Michael Douglas for instance. After years of smoking he fell victim to Throat Cancer. Course, on the surface of it that isn't unusual for a 66 yr old smoker. Worse still Douglas must have been ignoring his sore throat and niggly cough because by the time he was

diagnosed, the supremely wealthy actor's cancer was classed as Stage 4.
And there isn't a stage 5. Therefore anyone with stage 4 cancer is realistically staring death in the face.

In fact it means that your cancer has spread from its source into the lymph nodes and other parts of the body. So with that in mind it seems almost unbelievable that last month, a healthy looking Douglas and his wife Catherine Zeta Jones were photographed by the Paparazzi having a leisurely smoke.

You see, Douglas has been told that the Cancer has gone, a fact that even the Rothschild owned media were unable to contrive a reason for. And as such The Guardian Newspaper hailed it a "*Modern Miracle*" .Hmmm. well they would wouldn't they?

Nevertheless, in the absence of "Modern Miracles" happening to the general population, the millions of people afflicted with cancer every year are forced to put their lives in the hands of what is laughingly termed as 'Modern medicine'.

This usually comes in the form of Chemotherapy. Chemotherapy or 'chemo' involves the patient having large doses of powerful drugs administered to them, usually intravenously.

These drugs supposedly kill the cancer cells. Unfortunately more often than not they kill the patient as well - not that any Doctor will volunteer that information to the patient.

However, a Doctor will tell you that Chemo will destroy your immune system and no doubt he will also mention that the other side effects are hell and the chances are that you will lose all of your hair, vomit almost continuously, suffer severe fatigue, swell up like a balloon and be left sterile.

But it is more than his job is worth to admit that more people die from chemo or from other causes brought on as a direct result of having chemo, such as heart failure, than actually die of cancer.

Cancer Research UK spend around £332 Million annually in their bid to find a cure and the USA is typically the biggest worldwide investor with the Government backed 'National Cancer Institute' receiving an annual budget of almost $6 Billion.

To give you a further insight into the kind of money spent on research, The American Cancer Society raised a staggering $848 Billion in 2005. It would therefore be nigh on impossible to put a figure on the Trillions and Trillions of Pounds invested globally in Cancer research over the past 50 years or so.

This begs the question, "*What the hell are these researchers doing?*". I mean think about it for a moment. When HIV first began to spread rapidly in the late 1970's, early 1980's, there was no known cure and scientifically very little known about the disease. Yet barely 30 years later, although still incurable, given the right medication, a person with HIV can live an almost normal life.
And that includes having children and also having nigh on the same life expectancy as a non sufferer. Unless you are a HIV sufferer in Africa of course... But that's a different story.

However, Cancer and HIV are totally different things and as such the two can only be loosely compared. Nevertheless, given the time and money spent on cancer research surely we should be able to expect better than Chemotherapy by now?

The NHS spends around £4.5 Billion a year on Chemo to treat cancer sufferers yet it is estimated that 75% of those who die, do so because of the Chemo rather than the cancer itself.

Furthermore, it has been recognized throughout the medical world for well over a decade that Chemo cannot completely eliminate tumours of the Lungs, Colon or the Breast. In fact statistics show that only 2.4 % of Cancers respond successfully to Chemotherapy.

Despite this fact Chemotherapy is still used to treat all three of the aforementioned cancers, with the NHS spending £100 Million annually on the Breast cancer drug, 'Herceptin' alone. It would however be unfair to hold the NHS Doctors responsible for treating patients with drugs that do a person more harm than good.

After all, the vast majority of Doctors and Nurses within the NHS are dedicated, overworked and underpaid professionals who do the best that they can with the medicines that they are given. At the same time they find themselves having to work in poorly equipped,below par, unhygienic Hospitals and within the confines of a woefully inadequate budget.

And while the £4.5 Billion handed over to the NHS by the British Government for treating cancer may sound like a huge sum, it actually works out at a measly £76 per head. Nevertheless, whilst there can be no doubting the dedication shown by the medical teams working for the NHS, the saying; "*You pay Peanuts, You get Monkeys"* is also hugely applicable.

In stark contrast, the exact opposite is true over in the USA, where the highly paid Doctors work in clean, modern, well equipped hospitals. They are however, more likely to be dedicated to the Dollar bill than the dying patient. Course, this is only because treatment is paid for by medical insurance over there, which doesn't explain why American cancer patients are also treated by Chemotherapy.

However, Better Surgeons, better working conditions and better equipment would explain why only 40% of Cancer patients die in the USA in comparison to 60% of patients in the UK.

Indeed, it is not really surprising then to learn that the UK also has by far the worst survival rate of all our European counterparts.
So by doing a quick recap of the statistics and the available information we can say with a high degree of certainty the following things:

(1)that over the past 110 years cancer has gone from affecting an acceptable 1 in every 100 people to a totally unacceptable and apparently inexplicable 1 in every 2 or 3 people.

(2)The above doesn't apply to the Social Elite who appear to be more akin with the 1 in 100 statistic.

(3) Despite at least 50 years of allegedly serious research into cancer, funded by an indeterminately huge amount of money, the advances in treatments, despite what we are led to believe is negligible. Furthermore, the general consensus is that we are losing the so called war on cancer.

(4)Despite 48% of people now likely to be affected by cancer, and the UK's shameful survival rate amongst patients in comparison to our European and US counterparts, the government remain apathetic towards the epidemic as well as to the reasons for the unequalled leap in numbers. Similarly the British governments level of concern is all too apparent by their unwillingness to invest in better qualified Doctors, treatment and equipment.

Now obviously I am in no doubt that some of you reading this article will nevertheless, pour scorn on the above by claiming that statistics can vary greatly depending on which side of the fence the statistician stands.

And I would also be the first to admit that statistics can be massaged and/or tailored to suit a users need. However in writing this article i have also drawn on personal experience to back up the statistics.

You see, my immediate family is quite small. My Mother was an only child and my Father had only the one Brother. This obviously means that I only have one blood uncle and one Aunt through marriage. I am the 2nd eldest of 4 boys produced by my parents.

And in keeping in line with the Statistics, I can reveal that my paternal Grandfather suffered various bouts of cancer before finally dying from the disease. My maternal Grandmother officially died of a Heart attack but the autopsy revealed that she also had cancer.

My Father who is now in his 70's is currently battling Cancer. Ten years ago, while in my thirties (relatively young, again in line with the statistics) I was found to have a tumour containing 2 types of cancer, one aggressive, the other with a tendency to stay localised.

Both types however were malignant but luckily I sensed that something wasn't right very early on and as a result the tumour was removed without the cancer spreading thus saving me the need to undergo Chemotherapy.

Now, while that is counted as a blessing I still had to endure 2 further unnecessary and avoidable operations as a direct result of the hospitals poor communication between departments and through a lack of experience and skill on the surgeons behalf.

In fact at one point they were contemplating sending me to a London hospital to fix the damage caused by their surgeons incompetence. I also had to attend the hospital twice monthly for the first 2 years following the original operation. But notwithstanding the negligence which led to the 2 avoidable operations, I was also able to witness first hand through my twice monthly follow up appointments the hospitals inability to keep tabs on the most basic of information, the poorly trained extremely stressed medical staff and the inevitable 2 hour wait past appointment times, mainly due to chronic staff shortages.

Neither could I fail to notice that the higher up the rankings the medical staff were, the less compassionate and understanding they appeared to be, while at the same time there was a marked rise in their arrogance and aloofness.

In addition to My Grandfather, My Father and Myself, either dying, battling or being in remission from Cancer, two of my Mother's Aunt's and her Uncle have also died from Cancer - the younger of the two Aunts only being in her mid 40's when she died.

I also lost a very close friend who died from Testicular cancer at the age of 23 in the early 1980's. Indeed, the intensive Chemotherapy that he underwent and which left me unable to recognize him failed to stop the cancer spreading to his Brain.

My younger Brothers, Father in Law also died from cancer a couple of years ago which at the time was within a few short months of him being diagnosed. My older brothers girlfriend died of cancer while in her early 20's.

Moreover, my youngest brothers life long friend died at the age of 20 during the course of a relatively minor operation following an accident on a push bike. He was found to be riddled with cancer during the operation as was the Mother of another close friend of mine who also died during a routine exploratory operation.

My parents friend and neighbour who lived directly opposite them died of cancer while in his 50's and there are countless other people who I have known throughout my life who have either had or died of cancer. Hell! we have even had to have 2 family pet Dogs put down because of Cancer.

However, the one case that backs up and highlights what i've been saying more than any other is that of my one time girlfriend, who went on to become a very close personal friend as well as my boss at work.

You see, sometime in late November,or early December 2006 - I forget which - she was referred to hospital after finding a lump in her Breast which she was subsequently told was just a Cyst.

By late January 2007 the lump had grown a lot bigger and she was experiencing a nagging ache to the side of the breast which extended to her underarm. She was again referred to the hospital in February. This time the hospital did an immediate biopsy of the lump, quickly followed by the removal of a malignant tumour from her breast along with some lymph nodes from her armpit.

She was then told that she was to undergo 6 months of intensive Chemotherapy to be followed by - if I remember rightly - 3 months of

Radiotherapy. Radiotherapy is another outdated form of Cancer Treatment. In fact I've never understood the wisdom behind treating cancer with something that causes cancer. But i digress...

Following the 6 months of Chemotherapy my friend was looking forward to a couple of weeks break in her treatment, prior to her starting the Radiotherapy. And on the Saturday afternoon of the August Bank Holiday weekend, which was little more than a week following her last chemo session, we were sat outside the cafe next door to where we worked - having a chat and a cup of Tea.

It was here that I noticed that all the veins in her arm had collapsed leaving what looked like rows of deep trenches in her skin. These trench like grooves ran from the inside of her elbow joint nearly all the way down to her wrist. The collapse, she told me, was a direct result from where she had been intravenously administered the Chemo.

Nevertheless, after having a Brief chat about her arm, we concluded work for the day and I left her with the parting words that I would see her Tuesday Morning... That was the last time that I ever saw or spoke to her again, because she died of a massive heart attack on the Bank Holiday Monday. She had no history of heart problems whatsoever and had only very recently turned 46 years of age...

At this point I should say that long before I woke up to the fact that we live in an illusion of reality, I had already realised that something wasn't right with regards to cancer. Indeed I had long cottoned onto the fact that those with power and money seemed by and large to be unaffected by the disease.

This led me to the conclusion that the Social Elite knew something that the rest of us didn't. Fast forward a couple of years and I now had no doubts whatsoever that there was a cure for cancer. What's more, there is now an abundance of evidence to back this up.

Two of the more damming pieces of evidence revolves around that of two totally unconnected Doctors, the first of which is evidenced by the transcripts of 3 secretly recorded tape recordings of reminiscences given by Dr Lawrence Dunegan in 1988.

Dr Dunegan had been invited to attend a meeting of student Doctors destined to be future leaders in medicine,in Pittsburgh USA on March 20th 1969. The meeting was hosted by prominent Doctor, Richard Day. Before addressing his assembly Dr Day, who at the time was the Head of the Rockefeller controlled eugenics organisation, '**The Planned Parent Federation Of America** ' ordered that there should be no record taken of his speech.

Dr Dunegan however disregarded the order and surreptitiously took down notes on napkins.It was these notes that formed the basis of the secretly recorded interview that Dr Dunegan gave to Mr Randy Engel in 1988.

Dr Dunegan told Randy that during the course of this 1969 speech, Dr Day said *"We can cure almost every cancer right now. The information is on file in the Rockefeller Institute, if its ever decided it should be released"*...

However, there is a lot more to this story and it is well documented on various internet sites. A particularly well written and detailed account can be found at this link: :
http://www.overlordsofchaos.com/html/new_order_of_barbarians.html

The second piece of damning evidence revolves around the work of an Italian Doctor, Tullio Simoncini, a brilliant and courageous man who refused to buckle under the enormous pressure that he had to face and which he still continues to face to this day.

Dr Simoncini has had to endure being disbarred from practising medicine as well as having to endure the indignity of serving a 3 year prison sentence imposed on him. His Crime? Dr Simoncini had discovered that Cancer is a fungus caused by Candida, a yeast type organism found in small amounts within the human body.

In doing so he was able to devise a cheap remedy of unparalleled success in curing cancer. This was true even in cases where the cancer was so advanced that all other treatments had been stopped.

However, instead of being feted as a genius and touted as the saviour of untold lives, Simoncini, was ordered to stop work on his program and to remain silent on his findings.

Along with this evidence which points to the fact that Cancer is highly curable, also comes the question 'If cancer can be cured, why is it being kept a secret' ?
Course, for those of us who recognise the true evil that is ingrained into the very core of the Social Elite, that question is easy to answer. However for the benefit of those who haven't I will explain in brief why we are deemed not worthy of access to the cure.

You see, it is a two pronged answer, the first of which boils down to money. The Pharmaceutical industry is a multi trillion pound business, with huge fortunes to be made by those at the top. A single new drug typically costs around £500 million to produce.

Course these new drugs are always hailed as a miracle cure but take between 10-12 yrs to produce. Over that period of time, the said miracle drug is by and large forgotten by the general public but needless to say, these so called wonder drugs never live up to their hype - as is evidenced by the rapidly rising cases of all cancers.

Furthermore the industry is inherently corrupt, with billions of pounds in bribes being passed back and forth. The sheer greed that exists amongst those with power ensures that human lives will never take precedence over the vast fortunes to be made from cancer.

The second part of the answer relates to control. The Social Elite have an all consuming desire to exercise total control over the world's resources and its population. Indeed it is their quest for total world dominance that drives their Psychopathic needs.

So, notwithstanding the huge boost given to their already vastly over inflated egos by having the answers to the many secrets we are not privy to, Cancer is a huge weapon in their quest to reduce the world population.

This would explain the quantum leap in the number of cancer cases over the past 110 years. And having spent many years researching the activities of the Illuminati, I am left in no doubt whatsoever that we are deliberately being exposed to cancer by design. This exposure takes place largely within the food we buy. An in depth explanation, with statistics to back this claim can be found here :
http://intuitivefred888.blogspot.com/2011/03/cancer-rates-1900-to-2000-and-beyond.html

Further evidence to support this claim came directly from the Horse's mouth so to speak, when Prince Charles recently appeared on the ITV television program, 'This Morning'. You see, while showing the shows presenter around his organic vegetable garden, the monotonous, uncharismatic heir to the throne couldn't help but boast that he and his family were totally self sufficient in the food department. God forbid the buffoon should ever have to be exposed to eating the genetically modified, chemical infested stuff that we are forced to buy from the illuminati owned supermarkets.

And as well as being exposed to the cancer giving chemicals in our food we a forced to swallow them in the form of fluoride in our drinking water. Fluoride is a poison known to cause cancer. Yet while the government are all too aware of the health risks associated with fluoride they have insanely increased the levels of this poison in our drinking water.

This was done following the government's commissioning of a report from Cambridge University looking into the long term effects fluoride had on the human body. The government then used carefully chosen keywords from this report as proof that fluoride was safe.

However the author of the report has stated on camera that far from giving the Government the green light to increase fluoride levels, his recommendation was that levels should in fact be reduced.

You see, there is absolutely no need to use fluoride in drinking water as our teeth get all the fluoride that they allegedly need from toothpaste. In fact Sweden - a country that banned the use of fluoride in drinking water years ago (As have most Continental European Countries) - Commissioned a major survey into the effect the ban had on the nations teeth.

The report came back clearly indicating that there had been no increase in tooth decay.

However, as if to reinforce my view, naturalnews.com released an article in May 2012 stating the following:

Ingesting artificial fluoride chemicals does not prevent tooth decay, but rather destroys your insides and leads to the development of cancer and other illnesses. These are the disturbing findings of an assessment recently compiled by award-winning chemist, author, and founder of ThePeoplesChemist.com, Shane Ellison.

Frustrating more than 50 years of bad science that has claimed the exact opposite, Ellison's appraisal of fluoride's negative effects on the body shows once again why removing fluoride from public water supplies is crucial to public health. And health freedom advocates must step up to be the educational catalyst for bringing about this change nationwide.

"Once ingested, fluoride compounds attack the structural integrity of our insides," says Ellison. "Collagen, a web-like network connecting our skeletal system to muscles, is torn apart by fluoride. We feel it as joint stiffness, ligament damage, and aching bones. This same mechanism leads to browning of teeth, an outcome known as fluorosis."

Ellison adds that laboratory studies dating back decades have shown that fluoride spurs the mutation of mammalian DNA cells, which can promote the growth of cancer cells. Various population studies, he says, have shown that fluoride ingestion can increase a person's risk of developing bone cancer by as much as 700 percent.

And finally, fluoride has never been shown to actually prevent cavities, which is the excuse most often used to continue lacing public water supplies with this toxic poison. On the contrary, fluoride ingestion actually promotes tooth decay, and even the U.S.Centers for Disease Control and Prevention(CDC) admits that there is no verifiable, scientific proof that fluoride in any way prevents cavities.

So why does artificial water fluoridation continue to persist in many towns and cities across America today? A combination of ignorance and pride both appear to be factors, as the medical establishment largely refuses to accept modern science showing that fluoride is unsafe because it has been claiming for many decades that fluoride is safe.

John Garfield fromThe University Daily Kansanrecently wrote his own assessment of the dangers of fluoride, noting that the best available science links fluoride consumption to thyroid disorders, endocrine disruption, reproductive damage, skin problems, brittle bones, immunodeficiency, premature puberty, and lowered IQ (http://www.kansan.com/news/2012/apr/26/water-fluoridation/).

The evidence is so strong against fluoride these days that nearly 40 U.S. communities stopped fluoridating their water in 2011 (http://www.naturalnews.com), and many more, including Albuquerque, N.M., Bolivar, Mo., and Myerstown, Penn., have ended water fluoridation in 2012.

And as if exposing us to the risk of cancer via our food and drink supply isn't sufficient enough, The Government are further polluting the air we breath with god knows what via chemtrails.

Chemtrails is the name given to the visible vapour trail left behind as a result of an aeroplane discharging Chemicals at high altitude.They first began to appear in our sky around 1997. Chemtrails are not to be confused with Contrails, the name given to an aeroplanes equivalent of a car's exhaust smoke.

Contrails will disappear after 5 minutes or so whereas chemtrails can hang about for hours. Chemtrails are often visible in a criss cross formation as a result of the aeroplane flying back and forth so as to ensure blanket covering of an area.This is achieved in very much the same way as a farmer will use a Biplane' for crop spraying.

Course, while many would have you believe that Chemtrails are no more than a Conspiracy Theory, the sheer volume of photographic evidence available on the internet confirms Chemtrails are far more likely to be Conspiracy Probability.

Something is certainly responsible for the sharp decrease in Male fertility over the past 10 years and as such would it not make sense for a group of people intent on orchestrating a large population reduction program to target the source?

Indeed, if that was the case, would it then not be unreasonable to assume that whatever is being used to reduce fertility in the male population could have the potential to also cause Cancer?

Once again, assuming that fact is also correct, would that not then account for the previously unexplained reason for the sharp increase in the number of men developing Testicular Cancer?

Finally, no one would deny that cancer is a life changing illness. Speaking from my own experience there is a marked change in the way you view life before developing cancer to the way you view life having survived it.

On the whole I would suggest that the shift in perception is for the better. However the route you have to take to achieve the shift is precarious and undesirable to say the least. As far as the UK route is concerned more cancer sufferers fail to make it to the other end than those of us who do.

And the more precarious the route becomes the more desperate the victim becomes in a frantic search to find a life line to hang on to. The Blind panic caused by the desperation to find a life line can often lead to that person putting his faith in the nearest one to hand, only to find that he or she made the wrong choice and that lifeline has no substance to it.

So, as I have already stated, there is absolutely no doubt in my mind whatsoever that cancer is highly curable. Neither do I have any doubts that we are being deliberately exposed to the risk of cancer and that those who succumb are receiving treatment akin to a medical variation of Russian Roulette.

However, I have only reached these conclusions through my own research into the subject along with my own personal experience of cancer and most importantly of all, my inner self telling me it is so.

I would therefore advise anyone - who having read this article - is now planning on skipping their next bout of Chemotherapy in favour of an alternative treatment, not to do so unless they have properly researched the subject and if their inner self tells them that it is the right thing to do.

I say this because there are literally hundreds of website on the internet guaranteeing you your survival if you follow their advice. Sadly the only guarantee the vast majority of these sites should be offering is that you'll end up dead very quickly if you follow their instructions.

*On February 23, 2012 **Jurriaan Maesse** for Infowars.com wrote the following on Fluoride:

A mention on the website of the World Health Organization (WHO) admits that there were suggestions by member or members of the Chemical Aspects Working Group meeting in Tokyo, held in 2002, to omit information on the "adverse health effects" of fluoride to "prevent controversy." Here is the full quote from the WHO's website:

*"At the Chemical Aspects Working Group meeting (Tokyo, 2002), the group was informed that the monograph was being finalized, and there was considerable discussion on various aspects of the draft,**including a suggestion that the monograph should not mix discussion on the beneficial use of fluoride with adverse health effects to prevent controversy**. The monograph was not discussed at the Guidelines for Drinking-water Quality Working Group meeting (Geneva, 2004). The document is in editing and layout (2005). A presentation to the Working Groups of the WHO Oral Health Programme on the importance of fluoridation was made in 2005."*

In the <u>questionnaire</u> *for the working group, posted on the WHO's website, the Working Group's members are assured that their comments "will not be posted to the public website." Well, it seems the WHO not only lies to the world, they lie to their own underlings as well. But no matter: the most important thing here is that the WHO deliberately contemplated omitting crucial information about fluoride's damaging effects from its future publications- which in turn act as guiding principles, commandments almost, for states all around the world.*

As it turns out, the WHO not only omits and deletes. That would make the whole affair some sad sort of cover-up or whitewash. No, the WHO- knowing perfectly well that fluoride is most damaging- actively promotes the use of fluoride and works to distribute it through the world's water-supply. A <u>WHO publication</u> *of the Expert Consensus Meeting Group Report even advises adding fluoride in the water-supply for specific segments of the population.*
The "consensus" reached among the "experts" reads, that higher income groups often already consume enough fluoride for their purposes, which- by the way- has decidedly nothing to do with some dental battle against tooth decay.

"For example", we can read in the report, "in countries such as those in Scandinavia, where public dental awareness is very high and alternative vehicles for fluoride (e.g. fluoridated toothpaste) are widely available and widely used, a decision to not fluoridate the

water, or remove fluoride, or to supply drinking water with suboptimal levels of fluoride would likely be of little consequence.

The report continues with the statement that for segments of the population which do not have wide access to fluoridated toothpaste, the WHO would me more than willing to dump trace amounts of it into the water-supply, free of charge:
"On the other hand in developing and developed countries where public dental health awareness in some population groups (e.g. lower income) might be much lower, water containing either natural or added fluoride at concentrations of 0.5 to1.0 mg/l would be important for dental health."

This idea perfectly coincides with the ruling guidelines of the WHO Oral Health Programme, which include a "particular focus" on "the disadvantaged and under-served population groups.":
"The WHO Oral Health Programme, jointly with the FDI World Dental Federation (FDI) and the International Association for Dental Research (IADR), have embarked on an action plan for the promotion of using fluoride, particularly focusing on the disadvantaged and under-served population groups."

Furthermore, the WHO's Guidelines for drinking water quality states:
"In setting national standards for fluoride or in evaluating the possible health consequences of exposure to fluoride, it is essential to consider the intake of water by the population of interest and the intake of fluoride from other sources (e.g., from food, air and dental preparations)."

Dr.Richard Shames, graduated Harvard and University of Pennsylvania, after in-depth research into the effects of Fluoride on the human biological system, noted:
"(…) the Nazi concentration camps used fluoridated water to suppress the will and vigor of inmates. This appears to have been during the 1930s and was the first known example of fluoridated water supplies for a specific population."

Fluoride, in whatever amount, is nothing less than a chemical weapon. Considering it is applied to entire populations or certain groups within a population, the definition is chemical warfare- a tool most useful to eugenicists who are intent on depopulation the planet.

Chapter 14
Playthings For The Powerful

Another article that I wrote for the Sovereign Independent which looks at the sexualising of our children...

No doubt the fact that California has just passed Bill AB499, allowing children as young as 12 to be vaccinated against STD's without their parents knowledge, will raise a few eyebrows.

However I can't imagine anyone being unduly shocked. After all, Bill AB 499 is just another piece in a long line of Government legislation designed to hasten the premature sexual awakening in our children.

Course, anyone who doubts the existence of such an agenda being implemented by the US and European Governments hasn't been paying attention. You see, like all Government agendas, the key to their success is achieved via deception,stealth and time.

However, such is the success of a previous agenda which involved the dumbing down of an already apathetic public, that the art of deception is hardly needed. That is to say that the Government no longer try to justify the premature sexual awakening of our children by misleading the public into thinking it is to combat the epidemic of teenage pregnancy and to help stop the spread of sexually transmitted disease.

In fact it was by originally highlighting these so called epidemics that the Government were able to introduce into schools the teaching of the onset of puberty to children as young as 6, graduating to teaching full on sex education to children as young as 11.

It was also this deception that led to teenagers under the age of consent being allowed access to the contraceptive pill and condoms without their parents being informed.

Indeed, had pre teen sex education been the key to combating this epidemic of teenage pregnancy a quick look at the statistics confirms that this government policy has failed miserably. On the contrary, teaching sex education at a younger age has resulted in a rise in pregnancy of pre teen children.

There has also been a significant rise in the number of sexual assaults carried out by children, with recorded attacks such as that by two 7 yr old boys on a 5 yr old girl. Indeed, the killing of 5yr old James Bulger by two 12 yr old boys had a degree of sexual perversion attached to it.

What's more, my own 15 yr old daughter knows of girls who were having sex at the age of NINE. Meanwhile, thirty years ago it wasn't uncommon for schools to have one or two cases of 15 yr old girls getting pregnant but now the government has had to set up special schools specifically for the teaching of under age mothers.

So with the teaching of sex education to children not emotionally mature enough to deal with the information a resounding failure, the sensible thing to do would have been to reverse this policy. However, instead of doing so many European countries simply lowered the age of consent.

For instance, the age of consent in France is now 15. In Germany and Portugal - the latter being the European Mecca for Paedophiles - the age is 14. Meantime, Spain has the distinction of having the lowest age of consent amongst the European Community. Over there it is legal to have sex at 13.

And while the UK opted to keep the minimum age of consent to 16 years of age between consenting heterosexual couples, the government did bring down the age of consent for homosexuals to the same age. In lowering the age of consent many men - and women for that matter - who would once of been branded paedophiles were vindicated and children were given the clear message that it is ok to have sex.

Course, the fact that the UK didn't lower the age of consent shouldn't lead you to the conclusion that the British Government has stronger morals than their European counterparts. Once again this is all part of the deception. You see, despite Britain leading the tables on under age pregnancy, the vast majority of the time under age girls are made pregnant by someone over the age of consent.

Yet very rarely does this fact lead to criminal charges being brought against the guilty Father to be. In fact it is only in cases where the potential Father is well into his 20's and above that we see them being dragged into court. And even then the outcome of any such court action is minimal.

Now I have already discussed the reasons behind this inertia in the law courts in an article that I wrote for the Sovereign Independent Newspaper a few weeks ago. And for the benefit of anyone reading this who hasn't read that article, you can find it on the Sovereign Independent website under the title of '**Why the justice system favours paedophiles**'.

And once you are in possession of the full facts and realize that the people in power are out to exploit our children rather than protect them, the reasoning behind AB499 and such like then becomes clear.

In fact the more critically that you look at today's society the clearer it then becomes that the whole system is geared up to the premature sexual awakening of our children. However such is the power of manipulation and level of mind control exerted on the population by the Establishment that people are blind to what is going on.

Indeed, we are led to believe that there is no harm in major retail outlets selling padded bras, sexy lingerie, high heels and make up ranges designed specifically for and aimed at girls between the ages of 9-12.

After all, what little girl doesn't like to dress up?

Alcohol is also being made a hell of a lot more appealing, not to mention tempting to youngsters when it comes in a lovely shade of Blue and is called an *Alcopop*.

The Cambridge Dictionary does in fact describe an *Alcopop* thus: *A sweet, fizzy(=with bubbles) Alcoholic drink.*

Yet isn't it children who drink Pop, a sweet fizzy(=with bubbles) drink?

And are we not encouraged to be open with our children and freely discuss matters of sex? I mean rarely do films other than horror movies qualify for an 18 certificate these days. In fact from films and TV programmes right through to magazines, children are led to believe that if you don't do *'it'* then you belong in the crowd of 'nerds'.

Indeed, a quick look at my daughter's Facebook reveals an endless stream of wall posts along the line of "*All men are W*****s*" and "*Why cant i find a BF who will treat me like a princess*".

Yet had Facebook been around thirty years ago these would have been the rantings of a three times divorced emotional cripple, not the words of 12 and 13 year old schoolgirls.

And that, I am afraid is what parents have been deliberately manipulated into believing is '*normal*', achieved slowly over time by governments past and present. Or to be more accurate, I should say which started slowly, because the 'sexploitation' of today's young is speeding up at an alarming rate.

Course, the eventual goal is to persuade the masses that sex with children is ok. Thankfully, as it stands at the moment the vast majority of normal people find this concept quite rightly abhorrent.

However, on the other hand the social elite and by those I mean Royalty, members of the aristocracy, family dynasty's of immense wealth, the judiciary, Politicians and celebrities all see nothing wrong with child abuse and paedophilia.

Both practices have been widespread within the upper echelons of society for centuries and those amongst the social elite who don't indulge themselves in the practice's, condone it.

This must be so, if for no other reason than the sheer number of paedophiles amongst the world's elite makes it inconceivable that those who don't indulge are not aware of what goes on.

Course, condoning such behaviour can only mean that those non participants accept it as par for the course. In doing so they become every bit as vile and repulsive as those who take part. I mean, think about it for a moment. If I as a 'commoner' was friends with a paedophile, I would be held in the same contempt by the general public as the paedophile himself.
And a person who doesn't apply the same morality to those within high society seriously needs to question his or her mindset.

Sadly, such is the awe afforded to fame, power and wealth and those who possess it, that getting people to view these monsters for what they really are is a never ending, thankless task. In fact all rational thinking certainly disappears that for sure.

Moreover, rather than see that power and money corrupt, people attach an almost god like status to those who possess it and it is this attachment that allows the elite to get away with what they do and on the scale that they do it.

Sure, the majority will accept that politicians are a little corrupt, but the general belief is that they are working to enrich our standard of living.
Sure, the majority will accept that the royal family is out of touch with the common man, but the general belief is that we should be proud of

them, after all our Royal family sets us apart and makes us the envy of the world.

Sure, the majority accept that family dynasties were founded by ruthless businessmen, but the general belief is that you have to be ruthless to get ahead in business. Ruthlessness is therefore to be admired.

Sure, we accept that Celebrities behave badly at times, but the general belief is 'so what, i'd do the same in their position'.

In short nobody believes the social elite capable of the true evil that engulfs them. To speak out against them inevitably leads to you being branded a conspiracy theorist. And to any *'sane'* persons way of thinking, the term *'conspiracy theorist'* has, through attachment and repetition, come to mean *'gullible weirdo'*.

Worse still, being labelled as such apparently entitles any *'level headed, right minded person'* to take it as read that anything that comes out a conspiracy theorists mouth is crazy bulls**t.

Yet what those sane, level headed, rational people fail to grasp however is that to voice a conspiracy theory is by definition to voice an opinion that people have been secretly planning or have carried out an illegal act.
And then, once a piece of evidence, no matter how flimsy is available to back up that opinion, the theory is no longer a theory... It is now a possibility.

Then when you add enough evidence to that possibility so as to overshadow the evidence to any alternative theory and that possibility then becomes a probability.

However getting people to accept that most conspiracy theories are in fact *conspiracy probabilities*, isn't easy. The saying; *'there is none so blind as those who will not see'* springs to mind.

I mean take the British Royal family for instance. On April 29th 2011 Prince William married Kate Middleton. Support for the royal family

was at an all time high that day, yet the very people the nation were cheering for were the ones who are mugging the nation off.
After all, despite being arguably the richest person in the world, the Queen happily sat back and let her subjects pay for her grandson's wedding... And we didn't even get an invite.

Yet not only did we pay for it, we paid for it at a time when we are being forced to live with drastic government cuts. And despite these cuts, the country still pays her Millions of Pounds a year. But that's ok because she's the Queen.

Worse still, while we struggle to put food in our families mouths we pay for her buffoon playboy son to travel by helicopter to get to St Andrews for a game of golf with a Paedophile.

But apparently that is okay because he's a Prince. Yet to my way of thinking it is not ok because this bunch of inbreds view us with scorn. In fact Prince Phillip - a known Nazi sympathiser like the rest of them - stated in print that when he dies he would like to come back as a deadly virus to wipe out the world population. Charming.

Still, that's more ambitious than his eldest son who is content to come back as a Tampon. And again, apparently that's okay because he's the lovable racist who is married to the Queen.

And that would be the Queen who should have been hanged for treason in 1973 when the Treaty of Rome was signed by the paedophile prime minister Edward Heath. But these are all facts, not conspiracy theories. Indeed there are countless conspiracy theories involving the royal family, which given the sheer weight of evidence are more accurately *conspiracy probabilities*.

However to discuss them wouldn't be relevant to this article. The conspiracy theory that is relevant and is in fact a conspiracy probability is the one put forward by David Icke.
David Icke, along with others, has done extensive research into the Royal family and has publicly accused ,in print and in person not only the Queen, but also the Queen Mother, Prince Philip, Prince Charles,

Prince Andrew and Princess Anne of taking part in Satanic rituals that involve children as human sacrifices.

Unfortunately, to go into the mountain of evidence that David Icke puts forward for reaching this conclusion isn't possible to include in this article. It is however freely available in his book **'The biggest secret'**.

And for anyone who doubts his claim, then I would strongly suggest that they do the research. Similarly David Icke has publicly named, as have others, every American President since and including John F Kennedy through to and including George W Bush, as either being Paedophiles or taking part in child abuse.

As I have with the Royal family, I have also researched the evidence which points to these ex Presidents being either Paedophiles and/or Child abusers and im left in no doubt that the claims are true.
It is also suffice to say that all of these Presidents were puppets of the Rothschild's and none - with the exception of George Bush Snr - had the necessary intellect to be the most powerful man on the planet.

So there we have not only the British Royal Family embroiled in paedophilia, child abuse and murder, we also have every US President since JFK involved also. And this is how it has been for centuries.

Indeed, people throughout history, who we have been taught from a young age are to be admired, or who's work we are made to read or those who are turned into heroes on the silver screen are in fact all Illuminati paedophiles.

The list is endless but includes the likes of:
- Leonardo de Vinci, painter of the Mona Lisa,
- William Shakespeare whose work includes Romeo and 13 yr old Juliet,
- John Ruskin, Author and great moral voice of the 19th century,

- Sir Hugh Walpole, School headmaster turned novelist,
- Oscar Wilde, Homosexual playwright, not to mention 1st Baron, Baden Powell of Gilwall, who founded the Boy Scout & Girl Guide movements.

All to a man; paedophiles!

And then there are soldiers, immortalised as heroes in film such as T E Lawrence AKA Lawrence of Arabia and Field Marshall, Viscount Bernard Montgomery. Both Paedophiles.

Other examples would be the horror writer, Edgar Allen Poe, the Composer, Benjamin Britten and the artist T S Lowrie, who was immortalised in the Brian & Michael hit number 1 song, **Matchstalk men & Matchstalk Cats and Dogs**. Again all Paedophiles.

And then there are people whose work was brought to life by Walt Disney - another man with plenty to hide. These include Lewis Carroll who wrote the drug induced, **Alice in Wonderland** and J M Barrie, Benefactor of Great Ormond Street children's hospital, not to mention the Author of Peter Pan… Both Paedophiles!

Others include, Lord Gordon, Lord Boothby and Lord McAlpine. All Paedophiles. Ex Prime Ministers and Political Party leaders, Edward Heath, Pierre Trudeau and Jeremy Thorpe. All Paedophiles. And then there are those who were idolised by kids, past and present. These include to name but a few, movie heart throb, Errol Flynn, Country singer Boxcar Willie, Rock 'n' Roll singer, Jerry Lee Lewis who married his 14 yr old cousin. All Paedophiles.

There is also testimony to suggest that Elvis Presley had a penchant for 12yr old girls. Others that we know about are Glam Rock star, Gary Glitter, Bay City Rollers drummer, Derek Longmuir and the 'Rollers' manager Tam Paton. All convicted Paedophiles.

Celebrated film director Roman Polanski - another Paedophile. Motown legend Michael Jackson and rock legend Peter *'i was only doing research '* Townsend. Both Paedophiles. Ex Radio 1 DJ's, Alan

Freeman, Jonathan King and Sir Jimmy Savile. All Paedophiles. And these are only a few of those who have been exposed. What of the ones who are still hidden?

Indeed, Politics in particular is riddled with Paedophiles. In Britain, where ever possible, scandals are buried. Political parties close rank and help each other as is shown by the Robert Boothby scandal of the 1960's. Therefore to gauge the extent of paedophiles in politics we must look to America.

Here are but a few of those caught in recent years:

JO MONTLEONE JR, City councillor. Found guilty of fondling under age girls.

JEFF NIELSON, Congressional Aid. Arrested for having sex with a 14 yr old boy.

PATRICK McGUIRE, County commissioner. Questioned by police over allegations of molesting girls between the ages of 8-13.

LARRY CORRIGAN, Prosecutor. Arrested for trying to solicit sex from a 13 yr old girl.

JEFF RANDALL, Mayor. Jailed for molesting Two boys aged 10 and 12.

MARK FOLEY, Congressman. Forced to resign for sending sexually explicit Emails to a 16 yr old boy.

RANDALL CASSEDY, Newspaper Executive. Pleaded guilty to soliciting sex from a 13 yr old girl.

LARRY FLOYD, County Constable. Pleaded guilty to soliciting sex from an 8 yr old girl.

MARK PAZUHARICH, Judge. Given 10 yrs probation after pleading no contest to fondling a 10 yr old girl.

BOBBY STUMBO, Republican party leader. Arrested for having sex with a 5 yr old boy.

ARMANDO TEBANO, County chairman. Pleaded guilty to fondling a 14 yr old girl.

JOHN COLLINS, School teacher and former city councillor.Pleaded guilty to molesting girls aged 13-14.

PHILLIP GIONDANO, Mayor. Jailed for abusing girls aged between 8-10.

TOM ADAMS, Mayor. Arrested for distributing child porn on the internet.

JOHN GOSEK, Mayor. Arrested for soliciting sex from two 15 yr old girls.

DAVID SWARTZ. County Commissioner. Jailed for 8 yrs for molesting 2 girls under the age of 11.

EDISON ALDARONDO. Legislator (Law Maker). Jailed for 10 yrs for repeatedly raping his daughter between the age of 9-17.

STROM THURMOND,Senator. Had a child by a 15 yr old.

MIKE HINTZ. Pastor who received a Commendation from George W Bush. Had an affair with an under age girl.
PETER DIBBLE, Legislator (Law Maker). Pleaded no contest in relation to having an inappropriate relationship with a 13 yr old girl.

LARRY E KING JR, Republican fundraiser. Organised child sex party's at the White House during the 1980's.

CRAIG SPENCE, Lobbyist.As above.

DON LUKENS, Congressman. Jailed for having sex with an under age girl.

DON CRANE, Congressman. Had sex with an under age girl.

RON KLINE, Judge. Pleaded guilty to possessing child porn.

ROBERT BOWMAN, Congressman and Anti Gay Lobbyist. Charged with having sex with a 16 yr old boy he picked up in a gay bar.

JOHN HATHAWAY, Republican Senate Candidate. Forced to withdraw his nomination after admitting to having sex with his children's 12yr old babysitter.

PAUL INGRAM, Republican party leader. Pleaded guilty to 6 counts of raping his daughters.

KEITH WESTMORELAND, Legislator. Pleaded guilty to 7 counts of indecent exposure to minors.

JACK GARDNER, County Commissioner. Pleaded guilty to molesting under age children.

KEOLA CHILDS, County Commissioner. As above.

MERRILL BARKER, County Commissioner. Pleaded guilty to sexually assaulting an under age boy.

FRED SMELTZER JR, City Councillor. Jailed for 6 months for raping a 13 yr old girl.

LARRY SCHWARZ, Parole board officer. Dismissed after being found in possession of child porn.

MARK HARRIS, City Councillor. Jailed for having sex with an 11yr old girl.

JON GRUNSETH, Businessman. Withdrew his bid to become Governor of Minnesota after it emerged he had swam naked in his pool with 4 under age girls including his daughter.

NICK ELIZONDO. Director of the young Republican Federation. Jailed for 6 yrs for molesting his 6 yr old daughter.

DONALD RUMSFELD, Secretary for defence. Authorized the rape of children in Iraqi prisons in order to humiliate their parents into providing information about anti American insurgency's
.
And they are just the ones who were caught. Don't ever make the mistake of thinking that our and other European Politicians and people with power are any different from the Americans.
The people who pull the strings of America's Politicians are the same puppet masters as ours and our European counterparts.

In fact following a court case in connection with an international child porn ring, that took place in Britain in July 2011 an undisclosed number of Policemen, Teachers and Social workers were forced to resign. In every area of jobs that carry responsibility and high society, paedophilia is rife.

These paedophiles now want to 'normalise' sex with children. Those of the social elite not involved are guilty by association. Their refusal to blow the whistle on what's going on can only mean they condone it.

I will remind you of what I said earlier: If I had a good friend who was a known paedophile, I would be viewed with as much contempt and suspicion as the paedophile himself. So why does money, power and fame excuse this behaviour?

And as far as my thinking goes, as long as we allow our politicians to carry on de-criminalizing paedophilia and as long as we continue to ignore and forgive the behaviour of celebrities, then we can never claim to have our children's best interests at heart.

On the 10 of February 2012 the Telegraph newspaper announced that girls as young as 13 have been fitted with contraceptive implants at school without their parents knowing.

The procedure was carried out in Southampton, Hants, as part of a government initiative to drive down teenage pregnancies.

As many as nine secondary schools in the city are thought to have been involved.

But it has caused a backlash from parents who weren't aware that their daughters had been fitted with the 4cm device, which sits under the skin.

It is currently unknown exactly how many youngsters have taken part in the scheme.

** *On the 24th of February 2012, Alex Newman of* **The New American wrote***:*

Members of the European Parliament (MEPs) have started to ask questions about why taxpayers in the European Union (EU) are being forced to finance a giant homosexual lobbying group with past links to organizations promoting pedophilia. Gay and lesbian activists responded to the concerns by unleashing a wave of attacks.

Researchers using publicly available data found that the International Lesbian, Gay, Bisexual, Trans and Intersex Association-Europe (ILGA) received more than two-thirds of its funding directly from taxpayers through the European Commission. When tax money provided by the Dutch government was added in, over 70 percent of the group's funds last year came from taxpayers. The rest came from billionaire leftist George Soros and two other major donors.

"It appears to be a puppet organization in the hand of a very small group of donors, of which the Commission is the most important one," noted European human rights lawyer J.C. von Krempach, who shined the spotlight on the issue late last year in a series of articles. "Is this really a 'non-governmental' organization, or part of 'civil society?' Or is it an inofficial EU Agency?"

Despite the close ties to governments, the lobbying group has a highly controversial past, according to critics. In the 1990s, for example, after international pressure and a global scandal erupted, the ILGA was forced to purge several groups from its membership ranks because their primarymission was promoting pedophilia. Among the more controversial members*was the infamous North American Man/Boy Love Association (NAMBLA), a group which seeks to legalize and normalize pedophilia.*

*ILGA also fought a long battle to become an officially recognized "non-governmental organization" with the United Nations. Of course, it was repeatedly rejected for its myriad ties to supporters of pedophilia as member governments balked. Eventually pressure from European governments*forced *the UN to grant accreditation.*

But questions about the lobbying group's eligibility for official NGO status are now making headlines again, and some analysts expect *the organization's status to come up for review in the not-too-distant future. Indeed, ILGA fails to meet the UN's own established criteria, one part of which states that a "major portion" of an NGO's funding cannot come from governments.*

When the EU taxpayer funding scandal first made headlines in December, concerned MEPs and organizations such as the U.S.-based Catholic Family and Human Rights Institute (C-Fam) sounded the alarm. In essence, according to critics of the arrangement, the EU is just using taxpayer money to lobby itself while litigating in European courts and bullying member governments.

"We might call it political ventriloquism," noted von Krempach, saying ILGA promotes an "extremist agenda" that includes silencing Christians and Muslims while demanding worldwide recognition of "same-sex marriage" and adoption rights for homosexuals. "Through this 'advocacy group,' the Commission speaks to itself."

In the European Parliament — not exactly a legislature *in the traditional sense of the word, but a powerful EU body nonetheless — surprised parliamentarians asked some questions about the funding. From Poland to the UK, MEPs were concerned that taxpayers were being coerced into financing a questionable lobbying group.*

"In reality, the EU has no competences as regards the recognition of marriages or family law," noted Polish MEP Konrad Szymanski with the European Conservatives and Reformists Group (ECR) in a statement to the Commission. "On what legal basis is the Commission giving out operational grants to associations whose main activities are outside the scope of the EU's competences?"

In his written request for answers, submitted late last year, Szymanski also asked why the EU was funding groups working to change the laws of member states — "this being especially questionable in the case of countries such as Poland, which is under this kind of lobbying pressure regarding its family law and which has declared its legislative independence in that sphere."

Szymanski also sought to find out whether the Commission recognized that it was actually breaching EU principles enshrined in European treaties by funding the group. The Commission responded earlier this month by claiming that it does indeed possess the authority to fund homosexual lobbying because it has the power "to take measures combating discrimination on ground of sexual orientation."

More recently, MEP Godfrey Bloom of the UK Independence Party (UKIP) also asked the European Commission to explain itself. He pointed to information on ILGA-Europe's own website noting that more than 70 percent of the lobbying group's budget was extracted from taxpayers.

"Given the proportion of its own contribution to financing ILGA-Europe, does the Commission believe that ILGA-Europe can be described as a 'non-governmental organization' or as part of 'civil society'?" Bloom askedEuropean Commissioners, wondering whether the EU had similar NGO-accreditation rules that, like at the UN, would bar government-funded front groups. "Are there many other lobby groups that receive a similar proportion of their budget from the Commission? Or is ILGA a unique case?"

Bloom raised concerns about the potential influence of wealthy donors such as billionaire George Soros over the groups they are subsidizing, too. "Is there a risk that persons such as George Soros could 'buy' themselves one or more NGOs that are economically dependent on their donations?" he asked. "How does the Commission view the impact of this particular type of 'philanthropy' on democracy?"

Almost as soon as the concerns were raised, the homosexual lobby and its allies were on the war path. MEPs asking questions were slandered as "intolerant," "homophobic," and "bullies," while organizations such as C-Fam were derided as "ultra-conservative," "incendiary," and more. Parliamentarians who support using taxpayer money to fund the lobbying group also launched an all-out offensive.

"Mr Bloom's attempt to undermine European funding is unworthy of exposure. He should focus on the substantial question, which is equality and non-discrimination," said MEP Michael Cashman, the co-president of the European Parliament's "Intergroup on LGBT Rights." MEP Ulrike Lunacek, also co-president of the Intergroup, blasted Bloom as "a true role model for bullies around Europe."

Meanwhile, the so-called "European Court of Human Rights" recently ruled that member governments are allowed to bully and persecute anyone who expresses intolerance of pro-homosexual government propaganda. Free speech, apparently, is not to be considered a "human right" if the state disapproves.

The controversial case involved four young men in Sweden who were convicted of "agitation" against a "group" for distributing leaflets at a secondary school — a crime which can carry a penalty of up to two years in Swedish prison. The convicts said they were merely trying to spark a debate about the lack of objectivity on the issue in government schools, but Swedish courts and the European court rejected that defense.

The pamphlets about "homosexual propaganda" noted that in just a few decades, homosexuality "and other sexual deviances" had gone from being rejected by society to being embraced. "Your anti-Swedish teachers know very well that homosexuality has a morally destructive effect on the substance of society and will willingly try to put it forward as something normal and good," stated the leaflets in question, saying that homosexual lobbying groups were trying to downplay their support for pedophilia and that students should challenge the official "propaganda" by pointing out the link between homosexuality and AIDS.

The European court upheld the criminal convictions. In its ruling, it said the Swedish government undertook "legitimate and proportional interference" against free speech to protect the "reputation and rights of others," LifeSiteNews reported.
Co-Chair Martin Christensen of the EU-funded ILGA-Europe promptly celebrated the verdict, applauding the fact that individuals and organizations would no longer be allowed to criticize homosexuality by invoking the right to free speech. He also warned that the ruling sent a "serious signal" to Europeans who thought they could make "offensive statements" about homosexuality without fear of being punished.

"This is a truly important and landmark judgment," Christensen said in a press release, claiming that homosexuals have been subjected to "offensive" and "defamatory rhetoric" for decades. "For far too long those making such statement[s] were claiming their right to freedom of expression and opinion."

Chapter 15
Houston...We got a problem

One of the last articles that I wrote for the Sovereign Independent Newspapers and covers the death of the singer Whitney Houston...

There is no denying that the death of Whitney Houston is a tragedy. Sadly, her early demise was hardly a surprise. In fact I would go further still and suggest to you that her death was in reality, a tragedy just waiting to happen.

However, what does amaze me about the superstar's death, although it also comes as little or no surprise, is the outpouring of public grief en masse on social networking sites such as Facebook and Twitter.

Indeed, some of the tributes and outpouring of grief that I've read today are akin to someone losing a close family member. And it is this kind of mourning that gets me shaking my head in despair and which must beg the question; are we destined to get what we deserve in terms of the coming misery, through our own inability to put matters into perspective?

I mean, at best these tributes and outpourings of grief are pathetic and hypocritical.
Course there is no denying that Whitney Houston was without a shadow of doubt an enormous talent. But born into the lap of luxury on the 9th of August 1963, she had the kind of life most of us could only dream about.

Certainly, there are not many of us who could boast to having the likes of Aretha Franklin as a Godmother or Dionne Warwick as a cousin, that's for sure. Furthermore, you would have thought that having had all the benefits of untold wealth and moving in the same circles as the world's elite, she would have been only too well aware that drugs such as Cocaine, Crack and Heroin are going to mess you up big time.

So to first throw her career away, then her life in favour of a crack pipe, in my eyes makes her a loser, not a heroine. However, what worries me is that judging by the tributes being paid to her, the fact that she died a helpless, hopeless washed up junkie with her career in tatters makes her, in the eyes of many, a "Tormented soul".

These very same people will in all probability flick through the local newspaper tomorrow and in many cases read about the discovery of someone or others drug addled dead body being found in a high rise stairwell or a flea ridden bedsit and think to themselves "serves them right" or "good riddance to bad rubbish".

Worse still, they will do so without a thought or care as to their own hypocrisy. Yet to my mind, that dead junkie found slumped in a high rise stairwell or a filthy tenement flat is more worthy of peoples sorrow and sympathy than a spoilt, over indulged diva, too self obsessed and egotistical to appreciate all that she had going for her in life.
After all, the chances are that the stairwell junkie would have been born into a life of poverty and/or abuse and will have used drugs as a means to escape the misery and drudgery of their directionless life.

Whitney Houston cannot use those factors as an excuse. Indeed, it is a fact that it is a hell of a lot easier to overcome your addiction and rebuild your career, if indeed that is what you really want, when you're a multi millionaire than it is to do when you're just another government statistic living on state benefits.

Naturally, it's now being reported in the mainstream media that the only drugs found along with Whitney's body were those of the prescription kind. Believe that and you will believe anything.

Whitney Houston in death is by far a bigger money spinner than she has been for nearly the past 20 years... Even bigger still if she is perceived by her fans to be someone who died tragically while bravely battling her addiction.

Course, it's quite obvious that her addiction will be blamed firmly on Bobby Brown thus drawing more sympathy in her direction. And, no doubt her fans will eagerly buy into this theory rather than seeing her as the washed upped drug addict that she had become.

Mind you, it is an easy cop-out to blame bad boy, ex husband Bobby Brown for his late wife's spiral into drug addiction. However, the truth is Whitney Houston was a long way off being a star struck teenager when she first started dating the far less talented Brown. By the time she did she was already a well established, internationally renowned superstar with the world at her feet… And you certainly do not reach those dizzy heights by being a schmuck.

Yet anyone who takes Crack or Heroin these days or even back when Whitney first started her slide into drug addiction is mugging themselves off. Had Houston been of low intelligence and low self esteem, trapped in an abusive relationship with nowhere to run to, then maybe Brown could have shouldered the blame.

However, Whitney Houston was none of those things. The reality of the situation is that Houston must have known what she was getting herself in to. Her addiction is at least 20 years long and continued despite splitting from Brown over 6 years ago.

Indeed, had she wanted to quit drugs and get her life and career back on track then she certainly had the resources and access to the finest rehab clinics in the world. That all the signs point to her still being a drug addict when she died suggests that she didn't really want to get clean... And Bobby Brown cannot be held responsible for that.

It is therefore indicative of just how arse about face the average person's mindset is when there are outpourings of public grief at the death of an overindulged, fabulously wealthy prima donna, who never knew the true meaning of hardship and deserves little sympathy, while these very same people do not bat an eyelid at the death of millions of their fellow human beings who are dying on a daily basis through starvation and wars started on false pretences.

The very same warped way of thinking was afforded to Michael Jackson when he died and to a lesser, although not insignificant extent, the recent death of Sir Jimmy Savile. Now let's be very clear on this. Both Jackson and Savile were predatory paedophiles whose deaths prompted an apparently endless flood of tributes and outpouring of grief on social network sites.

Indeed, despite the mass of evidence as testimony to the pair's depraved behaviour and actions, many people simply refused to believe them guilty. Yet had these two monsters been nobody's, living on run down council estates, their neighbours, equipped with the same incriminating evidence, would have publicly lynched them both.

So, as I said at the beginning of this article, Whitney Houston's premature death at the age of 48 is a tragedy and while it may come across in this article that I didn't overly rate her much, nothing could be further from the truth.

Indeed, I think Whitney Houston was a fantastic singer. In fact so much so, that I can associate some of her songs with what I was doing at the time of their release. However, someone with the privileges and fantastic lifestyle that she was afforded, who then throws her life away in favour of the next 'high' deserves far less sympathy than a junkie, killed by the addiction that they had acquired in an effort to blot out the memories of the past.

Therefore, it has to be said that it is a truly sad and pathetic world that we live in whereby fame and fortune will get you forgiven for anything.

Chapter 16
9/11: Never Forgive. Never Forget

This was one of the first major articles that I wrote for my website
www.chrisspivey.org after I left the Sovereign independent
Newspaper - which was about to fold... No pun intended.
Since then, my website has had over 15 million views...

I would guess that with the passing of 11 years, that the majority of those people who still refuse to accept anything other than the 'official' version of events that occurred on the 11th of September 2001 in New York, Washington and Pennsylvania are by now unlikely to ever face the truth.

Whether this be through apathy, ignorance or fear is hard to say. However it is scientifically impossible for the events of that day to have happened the way that the official report says they did.
On the flip side, if the statistics are to be believed, then there are far more of us who are wise to the events of 9/11 than there are of those who buy into the official version of events.

Course, the degree to which people believe how much of a part the American government played that day varies greatly.
So, just for the record here are 10 facts concerning that day which are realistically indisputable:

1) George W Bush gave 3 different versions as to how he learned about the 'Terrorist' attacks.

2) From September 2000 – June 2001, 67 planes veered off course over America. NORAD - the US air defence system - was able to track and target all 67. Or put another way, a 100% success record. However, on 9/11 the NORAD system failed to track and intercept all 4 Aeroplanes. Or put another way, a 100% failure.

3) No high rise metal structure has ever completely collapsed through fire except the WTC Twin Towers. The towers themselves were built to withstand multiple collisions with aircrafts.

4) Jet fuel does not generate anywhere near enough heat to be able to melt steel.

5) Both towers fell at a couple of seconds off freefall speed. The law of Physics makes this impossible unless a controlled demolition took place.

6) The steel that made up the twin towers was immediately sold and shipped off to the Far East before being examined and the Pentagon crash site was buried under tons of Type 1 road stone. Since both locations were crime scenes a major crime was committed in doing so.

7) It would be physically impossible for a Boeing 757 aeroplane to have hit the Pentagon on the trajectory given in the official report. Furthermore, damage to the Pentagon building itself extended no further than 70ft. A Boeing 757 has a wingspan 2 inches short of 125 ft. If the wings sheared off before impact with the building, why is there no debris? **(See Picture 4 depicting superimposed plane flying into the Pentagon)**.

8) Despite there not being a shred of credible evidence linking Osama Bin Laden to 9/11 (*His FBI 'Wanted' poster does not even mention 9/11*), The main stream media were naming him as being responsible for the attacks less than an hour after the first tower was struck.

9) At least 7 of the alleged hijackers were subsequently found to be alive and well. Despite this fact all 7 were still named in the official 9/11 report as being responsible. Mohamed Atta, named as the hijacker's ringleader and allegedly the person to fly the hijacked American Airlines flight 11 Plane into the North Tower is subject to testimony alleging that he was spotted in lap dancing clubs and drinking vast amounts of alcohol in the week leading up to 9/11... Hardly consistent with the behaviour of a Muslim extremist.

10) The alleged crash site of the hijacked aeroplane, United Airlines flight 93 in a Pennsylvanian field is totally inconsistent with similar aircraft crash sites. Furthermore, the alleged Cell Phone, phone calls, said to have taken place from on board flight 93 and which were used to aid putting together the events which unfolded during the hijack, would have been impossible to be made at flight 93's altitude in 2001.

In regard to the official report into 9/11, the Bush Administration quite unbelievably at first refused to sanction an official enquiry. When after a year, it became obvious that the public wouldn't stand for this, the White House gave in and at first tried to appoint veteran, political heavyweight Henry Kissinger - a hugely reprehensible man to head the report.

Nevertheless, when the many conflicts of interest Kissinger's appointment heralded were pointed out to him, Kissinger stepped down to be replaced by New Jersey Governor Thomas Kean.

Indeed, the fact that the commission were only given a $14 million budget to work with compared to the $30 budget allocated to investigating the Bill Clinton- Monica Lewinsky scandal should have been enough in itself to set alarm bells ringing.

However, the report was flawed from the start not least by the fact that the commission were refused access to crucial pieces of evidence - such as the hijacked planes flight recorders. In fact it quickly became obvious that the commission were under orders to make the evidence fit the conclusion as opposed to the evidence available being used to reach a conclusion.

You see, where there could be no credible explanation for such things as the collapse of WTC Building 7 (*Which was reported on live TV by the BBC 20 minutes before the actual collapse took place*), the Commission simply and quite inexplicably omitted the events from the report.

However, the most damning evidence of all, which pointed to 9/11 being an 'inside job', was President George W Bush and Vice President Dick Cheney's point blank refusal to give evidence in front of the commission unless the following terms were met.

1) Both Bush & Cheney be allowed to give testimony together, as opposed to separately.
2) The Evidence was to take place behind closed doors.
3) Neither man would be required to do so under oath.
4) There was to be no written or recorded transcript of what they testified.

Course, the reason for Bush and Cheney refusing to give evidence separately is quite obvious and evidenced in many videos on YouTube. You see, George Bush was prone to crumble every time he was asked in interview to explain even the weakest anomaly surrounding 9/11. On the other hand, US President in all but title, Dick Cheney was a different kettle of fish altogether and as such he would have been able to hold Bush's hand throughout the ordeal.

Now although I have - in the above - already mentioned the Pentagon and Flight 93, you should be aware that I am going to concentrate this article on the WTC. However, I do intend to write articles on both the aforementioned in the not too distant future - particularly in the case of Flight 93 since some fairly new, relatively unknown evidence has surfaced proving that this Plane actually landed at Cleveland Airport, where all the passengers were safely ordered to disembark as opposed to the passengers charging, American hero style towards the hijackers, resulting in the plane crash landing.

Nevertheless, the wealth of evidence to suggest that the American Govt was complicit in the crimes committed on 9/11 is also far too great to document in a single article. I am therefore going to mainly concentrate on the newer and/or less well known facts surrounding the destruction of the WTC.

However, should anyone reading this not be at least vaguely familiar with the already well documented multitude of evidence that points to September 11th 2001 being an inside job then I can only conclude that you are either one of those who doesn't want to believe the truth or that you are desperately in need of an operation to remove your head from your rectum.

After all, there can be no doubt that both the twin towers and Building 7 (A massive skyscraper in itself) were brought down by controlled demolition involving the use of Nano Thermite. The illuminati controlled, yet supposedly impartial BBC recently tried to debunk this fact in a totally one sided programme called '9/11 Roadtrip'.

In this programme shown on BBC3, the program makers shamelessly exploited people's ignorance by stating that a lot of people believe that the towers were brought down in a controlled demolition with the use of **Thermite.** The program then proceeded to have an 'expert' pour a huge mound of Thermite onto a steel girder lying on its side. Everyone participating in the program was then theatrically moved well back for their own safety while the said Thermite was ignited. Following this impressive display in pyrotechnics, we the viewers were then shown the tiny hole that this large amount of Thermite had burned through the steel, proving beyond all doubt that Thermite could not of been responsible for bringing down the buildings… Then again, no one ever said it was…. Except the BBC of course.

Tet there can be no doubt whatsoever that the BBC are aware that it was in fact Nano-Thermite, not Thermite that was used to bring down the towers and WTC 7.

Nano Thermite is a chemically altered, hugely more powerful derivative of Thermite which cuts through steel like a hot knife cuts through butter. Therefore, the only possible conclusion for the BBC to mislead its viewers, who incidentally pay for this trash to be made, can be to aid in the cover up **(Picture 5: Steel girder cut with Nano Thermite in the midst of the tower debris)**.

Course, the evidence for the towers and building 7 being brought down by controlled demolition is overwhelming. There can be no other way that the buildings could have come down at near-on freefall speed (*A falling object with nothing in its way to slow it down*) without their central core being removed as they fell.

Moreover, there is plenty of unused testimony from credible witnesses such as Firemen in attendance that day stating that multiple explosions were heard prior to the towers coming down.

This is also consistent with photographs of the towers falling where blasts coming from well below the crumbling buildings can be seen.

Course, those who try to pour scorn on the towers being brought down by controlled demolition point out that it would take many men, many weeks to prepare the towers for such an operation to take place and for the towers to be primed for demolition, unnoticed by the buildings massive security team would be impossible... Well it would, wouldn't it?

Well no actually, it wouldn't. You see, in the months leading up to 9/11 a vacant floor in the trade centre was given over to a firm of 'Contractors'. This floor was off limits to everyone but was a hive of activity throughout the night. During the day Security guards were told that the elevators were being overhauled and from the Elevator shafts it would be very easy for the Contractors to access the towers central cores.

Further evidence to surface is testimony that in the weeks leading up to 9/11 both towers were subjected to a series of 'power downs'. However, the most compelling evidence of all is directly linked to the security company who were employed to police the WTC. You see, the company in question was called **Securacom**.

Securacom also handle the security for both Washington's Dulles Airport and American Airlines... Coincidence? Then try this for size. A 'Principal' at securacom is none other than Marvin P Bush, brother of President George W Bush.

Still not convinced? Ok let's look at who the real culprits are of these so called terrorist attacks. As I have already said, Osama Bin Laden isn't accused of anything related to 9/11 on his FBI wanted poster. Well he wouldn't be since he had nothing to do with the so called terrorist attacks. After all, the Bin Ladens and the Bush's are great friends with mutual business interests and in truth the evidence points to Jewish extremists and not as we are constantly told, Muslim Extremists.

You see, shortly after the first plane hit the South Tower a number of eyewitnesses reported seeing 2 or 3 men of student like appearance dancing in celebration on top of a large van. Despite watching an aeroplane smash into the world famous landmark. Indeed, one close-by eyewitness described the men as looking anything but shocked.

And according to Police radio transmissions and early TV news reports this van was later intercepted on the New Jersey Turnpike, which leads onto the George Washington Bridge. The occupants were promptly arrested and later handed over to the FBI. On inspection, the van was found to be packed with tons of explosives. Furthermore, New Jersey Police Officer, Scott DeCarlo, who was present when the men were arrested, testifies that one of men said *"Hey we are with you, not against you"*.

Even more ominously, a little while later, recorded Police transmissions, not once but twice, describe another suspect van as having a mural painted on one side depicting an airliner flying towards the twin towers – Well that would make it suspect alright. Two men were seen fleeing this van which they had abandoned on Kings Road, also near the George Washington Bridge. Both were quickly apprehended while the van itself subsequently blew up. Once again I ask you, Coincidence?

Therefore, in total 5 men were arrested 2 of whom have been confirmed as agents for MOSSAD. All 5 were reported on their arrest sheets as working for the '**Urban Moving Systems Incorporated**' which 2 independent CIA agents have confirmed as a 'Front Company' for MOSSAD.

Yet tellingly, all 5 suspects were quietly released, without charge after 71 days in custody and deported back to Israel. One of these men later said in a TV interview and I directly quote here; *"The fact is* *we come from a country that experiences terror daily. Our purpose was **to document the event**"*. Slip of the tongue maybe? I doubt that very much.

Course it goes without saying that anyone with advanced warning about the terrorist attacks could also make a killing on the stock market... And that is exactly what those in the know did. In fact the **San Francisco Tribune** reports that there is still $2.5 million in profits lying uncollected by investors in connection with shares relating to American Airlines. The Paper itself concludes that this money is from insider trading by people who knew what was about to take place but now fear collecting their ill gotten gains for fear of being arrested.

Furthermore, Reuters reported that '**Convar**', a firm that specialises in recovering data from damaged computers had used pioneering laser scanning technology on over 400 damaged hard drives and main frames recovered from the rubble of the towers and damaged nearby buildings. Convar found data on at least 32 hard drives to suggest that insider trading had taken place.

Reuters went on to quote Richard Wagner, a data recovery expert at Convars, as saying "Illegal transfers of more than $100 million might have been made immediately before and during the disaster" (*note he doesn't say attacks*)."There is a suspicion that some people had advanced knowledge of the approximate time of the plane crashes (*Once again, no mention of attacks*) in order to move out amounts exceeding $100 million". Reuters continue to quote Wagner as saying "They thought the transactions could not be traced after the main frames were destroyed".

What is also now coming to light is a dispute in the number of people who died on 9/11. That number was supposedly put at over 3000, but the evidence now suggests that the true figure was in fact a mere fraction of that number.

Course, we all saw on the news, the footage of photographs taped on to boards and windows around the vicinity of Ground Zero of those who supposedly perished that day. However it has now come to light that many of these photographs have in fact been photoshopped and in many cases used up to 5 or 6 times to represent a different person.

The deception ranges from changed backgrounds and flipped images to adding moustaches, darker skin tones and digitally altered features. However, when viewed side by side, there can be no doubt that you are looking at pictures of the same people.

The above is also true in the case of the 300 plus Firefighters, Police and Port Authority Officers who supposedly died that day.
That the number of victims is now thought to be greatly reduced in numbers to that of the Govt figures certainly ties in better with the evidence. Both towers were ordered to be evacuated fairly early on once the first plane had struck the South Tower. In fact many people didn't wait for the evacuation order to come, they simply up and left as soon as the plane hit the building.

The fact that even the disabled were carried down and out to safety suggests that the only civilians left inside were the few hundred or so who were trapped above the impact zones.
Furthermore, the written testimony of Chief Fire officer 'Pitch' Picciotto in his bestselling book '**Last man out**' suggests to me that the number of 1st responders killed is nowhere near that of the official figures.
Picciotto states that he and a handful of his men were the last of those to make their way down the North tower stairwell. The Fire fighters progress was slowed by the fact that they had with them a group of disabled workers and they were also checking every floor for injured or trapped survivors as they descended.

Yet despite this slow progress the group had still reached the 7th floor when the tower collapsed around them. Moreover, the building had already been evacuated of other firemen as soon as the South Tower had collapsed.

Video evidence captured by a pair of Brothers making a documentary about the NYFD, also suggests that there were only a few dozen 1st responders inside the lobby waiting to make their way up when the South tower came down. The majority of these were able to escape the collapse by running into the safer, as yet unaffected areas of the trade centre… A massive interconnecting complex in itself.

This greatly reduced death toll would account for why there is so little vocal outrage from the supposed 3000 bereaved families. They simply do not exist in anywhere near that number. After all, if, with all the evidence available you had lost a family member in the towers would you not be as vocal as possible in getting justice for your lost loved ones?

Of course you would. Therefore, does it not also make sense on behalf of those who planned the attacks to in reality keep the number of deaths to a minimum while at the same time fabricating the numbers to the maximum in order to gain public support?

So, with all this readily available evidence why has no one from within the Bush Administration been brought to justice I hear you ask? Well actually, there has in fact been numerous attempts to put George W Bush and his cronies on trial… Except none have ever been allowed to go ahead under the pretext that any court proceedings could interfere with or undermine National Security.

However, the Good news is that 11 years later, Many pressure groups such as **'Architect's and Engineer's for 9/11 truth'** and the **9/11 Truth Movement** are refusing to be silenced and continue to turn up the heat on those who should be rotting in a prison cell rather than living in the lap of luxury… To those people who's number include George W Bush, George H Bush, Dick Cheney, Donald Rumsfeld, Condoleezza Rice, Larry Silverstein and Rudolph Giuliani, to name but a few, I would say, be warned... The world knows what you did and it will not be forgotten.

On March 23rd 2012, the Sovereign Independent Newspaper published the following report:

The Obama administration touts the Navy SEALS' raid and killing of Osama bin Laden in his hideaway compound in Abbotabad, Pakistan, as one of the administration's greatest achievements. Obama even disclosed details of the raid to Hollywood for an upcoming movie.

*Given that, isn't it curious, to say the least, that **the Pentagon says it has no records — not one photo, not one video, not even an e-mail — of bin Laden's death**?*

Richard Lardner reports for the Minneapolis Star Tribune, March 15, 2012:
Government officials have openly discussed details of the mission [to kill Osama bin Laden] in speeches, interviews and television appearances, but the administration won't disclose records that would confirm their narrative of that fateful night. The Associated Press asked for files about the raid in more than 20 separate [FOIA] requests, mostly submitted the day after bin Laden's death.

The Pentagon told the AP this month it could not locate any photographs or video taken during the raid or showing bin Laden's body. It also said it could not find any images of bin Laden's body on the Navy aircraft carrier where the al-Qaida leader's body was taken. The Pentagon said it could not find any death certificate, autopsy report or results of DNA identification tests for bin Laden, or any pre-raid materials discussing how the government planned to dispose of bin Laden's body if he were killed.

It said it searched files at the Pentagon, U.S. Special Operations Command in Tampa, Fla., and the Navy command in San Diego that controls the USS Carl Vinson, the aircraft carrier used in the mission.

The Defense Department told the AP in late February it could not find any emails about the bin Laden mission or his "Geronimo" code name that were sent or received in the year before the raid by William McRaven, the three-star admiral at the Joint Special Operations Command who organized and oversaw the mission. It also could not find any emails from other senior officers who would have been involved in the mission's planning.

~~~~~~~~~~~~~~~~~

Note: WantToKnow team member Prof. David Ray Griffin, in his book Osama bin Laden: Dead or Alive?, lays out the extensive evidence that bin laden died in December 2001, and that since that time Pentagon psyops had been keeping him "alive" with fake videos and audiotapes to maintain a crucial pretext for the ever-expanding "war on terror." Could it be that the Pentagon will produce no records of its purported "death raid" because in fact it will reveal major manipulations involving bin Laden's death?

On August 6, 2011, three months after the supposed killing of bin Laden, 22 members of the exact same Navy SEALS Team 6 who had conducted the Abbotabad raid all died in a helicopter crash in Afghanistan.
Dead men don't tell tales.

** On the 24th of April 2012 Press TV reported the following:

*Washington has fabricated the raid on Osama bin Laden's compound in Pakistan to relieve political pressure on US President Barack Obama, **Press TV reports**.*

James Fetzer, American Philosopher and former Marine Corps officer, says Washington fabricated the bin Laden raid to divert public attention from "Obama not having closed Guantanamo, having stationed troops in Pakistan and having his birth certificate being subjected to minute scrutiny."

"All of that was taken off the front page by the staged fabricated attack on the compound where no one had ever seen Osama bin Laden. Indeed, how can you kill a man who died in 2001 - another time?" Fetzer said in an interview with Press TV.

Fetzer added that the idea that bin Laden was buried at sea in accordance with Muslim tradition was "preposterous."

"That's disrespectful to bodies which can be eaten by fish, sharks and other crustaceans," he added.

Obama claimed that Osama bin Laden was killed by US forces on May 1, 2011 in a hiding compound in Pakistan.

A US official later announced that bin Laden's body was abruptly buried at sea, falsely boasting that his hasty burial was in accordance with the Islamic law, requiring burial within 24 hours of death.

However, burial at sea is not an Islamic practice and Islam does not have a timeframe for burial.

"It's a shame that the United States has been reduced to one lie after another. We seem to be spending more time trying to defend lies than we are solving real problems in the world and this is, yet, one more example," he concluded.

*** On the 3rd of May 2012 the Digital Journal wrote:

Pentagon officials recently disclosed to the Associated Press (AP) that they could not find any photo or video evidence to confirm that Al Qaeda leader Osama Bin Laden was killed in the Navy Seal raid in Pakistan a year ago.

AP has submitted more than 20 requests for information surrounding the raid on Bin Laden's Abbottabad compound to the U.S. Government under the Freedom of Information Act (FOIA).

In response to the request for visual evidence of Bin Laden's death, the Pentagon stated that it could not find any pictures or video footage of the raid itself or of Bin Laden's dead body. It also told AP it could not locate any images of Bin Laden's body that were taken on the U.S.S. Carl Vinson, the Navy aircraft carrier that reportedly lowered him into the sea after his death.

In addition, the Pentagon admitted that it could not find an autopsy report, death certificate or results of a DNA identification test for Bin

Laden, in spite of claims made by President Obama and reported by CBC News that a DNA test was performed.

These admissions follow a related FOIA response by the Department of Defense in February, in which it stated that it had no emails concerning the Bin Laden raid that were sent prior to its execution.

The Atlantic Wire reported in February that the CIA claimed it had visual proof of Bin Laden's death, but the Pentagon's admission that it does not have any evidence of this kind still raises significant questions, since its jurisdiction includes the Navy Seals that conducted the raid and the Navy ship that buried Bin Laden at sea.

The latest revelation drew the suspicion of Lt. Col. Robert Bowman (ret.), the former director of Advanced Space Programs Development for the U.S. Air Force. "It makes the official story sound very fishy," Bowman said in an interview with Digital Journal. "Without proof, I'm not buying it carte blanche."

Bowman also pointed to the reports that Bin Laden died in 2001 or 2002, which have been supported by former FBI counter-terrorism chief Dale Watson, former assistant Secretary of State Steve Pieczenik, former U.S. foreign intelligence officer Angelo Codevilla and other intelligence experts. "This smacks of a cover-up," Bowman added.

Some organizations contend that the cover-up extends beyond the Bin Laden raid, including Architects and Engineers for 9/11 Truth, a group of over 1,600 technical professionals that is calling for a new 9/11 investigation. "The raid is not the only part of the Bin Laden narrative that doesn't add up," said founder Richard Gage, AIA. "It's also highly unlikely that Bin Laden and Al Qaeda had access to plant the explosives that brought down the Twin Towers and Building 7."

Chapter 17
There's Something In The Air

This was the second major article that I wrote for my website:
www.chrisspivey.org and like the rest of the articles making up this
book is now longer available to read on the interwebb.

The article takes a look at the 'nanny state' that we have become and
also focuses on how we are being conditioned to view all Muslims as
being potential terrorists. Indeed, this article could have been written
in 2018, thus proving how far we HAVEN'T come in the following six
years.

In fact to bring it up to date all that you need do is substitute the word
"Al Qaeda" with the word "ISIS"...

What is Liberty? Liberty is a concept of political philosophy and
identifies the condition in which an individual has the right to act
according to his or her own will.

"Any society that would give up a little liberty to gain a little
security will deserve neither and lose both" – *Benjamin Franklin*.

"Lock up the streets and houses, Because there's something in
the air, We've got to get together sooner or later, Because the
revolution's here, and you know it's right" - *Thunderclap*
Newman

I went to Tesco's to do some grocery shopping with my young-ish
girlfriend on Saturday morning, like you do. When we got to the
checkout my girlfriend unloaded the trolley and then walked to the
end of the conveyor belt to pack the shopping away. Being a bit tight
I stood adjacent to the checkout assistant watching her scan our
goods to see how much this was all going to cost me.

Picking up a vacuum sealed packet of 5 Tesco value table knives (*told you I was tight*), the checkout assistant turned to my girlfriend, held up the pack of knives and in an abrupt manner told her that she wasn't allowed '*these*' because she wasn't over 25 years of age... My girlfriend was in fact 24 years old although she could easily have passed for 21.

Nevertheless, in case I'd somehow become invisible, I thought that I best intervene by interrupting the Nazi-jobs-worth to tell her that I personally was over 25.

"*Are you paying for this shopping?*" Greta Snipe (*I think that was the checkout assistants name - if it wasn't it should have been*), demanded to know... And I mean demanded.

I then told Greta that I was indeed paying after which she reluctantly put the knives through the scanner. Now I don't doubt for a minute that I spoiled Greta's day, but this incident as much as any other hammered home the question; *What the fuck is going on in this country*?
I mean am I right in assuming that married couples under 25 have to eat their dinners and feed their children with their fingers? Is there an epidemic of knife wielding, respectable looking, female gangs all under the age of 25 roaming the streets looking to stab some innocent passer-by? Do only the under 25's stab people? Isn't using a Tesco knife to stab someone on a par with stabbing someone with an ice lolly stick?

Course all this nonsense with the '*Nanny State*' started in the late 1980's but really began to gain momentum after the new anti-terrorist laws were introduced in 2001.

The new anti-terrorist laws were according to our politicians supposedly brought in for our benefit to keep us safe and we as a nation fell for the con hook, line and sinker. But ask yourself this; do you feel any safer now than you did in 2001? I'll bet you don't. On the other hand, do you feel less safe because I certainly do.

So, why don't you feel safer? After all, when was the last terrorist attack that affected you? It certainly wasn't on 9/11 or 7/7. They were both 'inside jobs', organised by the US and UK government's and used as a reason to bring in the new anti terrorist laws. Course, if you still don't believe that those two attacks were 'inside jobs' despite the overwhelming evidence for both, then you may as well stop reading now and go back to watching the soaps on TV.

"Ah but!" you say, having decided to read on,"doesn't the lack of terrorist attacks prove that the anti-terrorist laws are working? After all, you hear about the security services foiling planned terrorist attacks on a regular basis, don't you?"

Well, no you don't actually. What you hear about is the security services foiling terrorist attacks that they have organised themselves... To keep you all living in fear.

I personally don't know of one thwarted terrorist attack, post 9/11 that hasn't later proved to be a 'false flag' operation planned by the US or UK security forces. The truth is, there is no terrorist threat to us unless you class the government as terrorists. There never has been. At least not since the IRA stopped their bombing campaign on mainland England anyway.

I'm old enough to remember the IRA bombing campaign unfortunately and I can tell you that there wasn't the air of oppression or wave of paranoia floating around back then like there is today. And why wasn't there? After all there is a far greater chance that you know of or are related too someone killed or maimed by an IRA bomb, than there is of you knowing someone killed or maimed by a Muslim extremists bomb.

Indeed, if proof was ever needed of the fear lurking in the back of people's minds with regards to the threat of a terrorist attack, just think back to the collective huge sigh of relief that people breathed when it was announced that Osama Bin Laden had been killed last year... Never mind that common sense should have told you that it was the second time that he had died. Then again, common sense has been on the decline for years.

The facts surrounding Bin Laden and his 1st death are all too easily available. He was one of many children born into the lap of luxury of a fantastically rich Arabian family who had *(and in all likelihood probably still have)* business dealings and a close personal friendship with the powerful and wholly corrupt Bush family. Osama Bin Laden himself was an immensely rich man and a CIA operative who died in a Saudi Arabian based American Army hospital of kidney failure in late 2001.

Yet thanks to the mainstream media's, mind control and propaganda department, people bought into the idea that Bin Laden was the devil incarnate himself, who lived in a cave and lurked around in shadows with a knife clenched between his teeth... No doubt a Tesco value table knife at that.

Meantime, the real terrorists such as Martin McGuinness who was a one time leader of the IRA and allegedly the man responsible for supplying the firearms used against British Soldiers on 'Bloody Sunday' is now the 2nd most powerful politician in Ireland. Or take the Republican politician Gerry Adams. He was another leading IRA/Sinn Fein leader who was jailed in 1972 under the prevention of terrorism act and who came from a long line of terrorists.

Get the picture yet?

No? OK let's look at the anti terrorist laws supposedly brought in to protect us from Muslim extremists, but which are in reality more to do with curtailing the rights and liberties of ordinary people.

What the anti-terrorist laws mean is that people like myself – those of us who publicly speak out against the government or *'Homeland Terrorists'* as the government likes to call us – can in theory be arrested without charge and held indefinitely without access to a legal representative. Furthermore, the authorities have no need to inform anyone of our arrest or where we are being held. Hmmm, now why does the Gestapo springs to mind?

Just this week in fact, an America army manual describing the procedure for the rounding up of '*political activists*' and detaining them in '*re-education*' camps has been exposed. Does that mean that those of us who don't agree with the Government need reprogramming until we do agree? Is free thinking no longer tolerated? The manual goes on to detail plans to make '*detainees*' carry out forced labour and for keeping 'political' prisoners locked in isolation. Hmmm, now why do Nazi concentration camps spring to mind?

And what of the so called '*War on Terror*'? An unending, illegal, corporate war centered on a bogus manhunt in and around the Middle Eastern countries. Or put another way; a war based on greed and fought for corporate gain at the cost of the lives of millions of innocent men, women and children. And that's without taking into consideration the lost lives of the apparently easily replaceable British and American servicemen and women.

Course, in order to keep this so called war on terror going, Muslims have to be portrayed to us as being the enemy, Hence the need for government propaganda relating to the threat of non-existent potential terrorist attacks. Not only do these government arranged threats allow them to rape and pillage nations that are no threat to our national security whatsoever, they also keep you living in fear and hatred of the Muslim people.

In hating these people, you become disassociated with their suffering. For instance, an over indulged, drug addled diva dies in the bath and millions upon millions of people go into mourning. Likewise a '*loony tunes*' 51 year old paedophile pop star gets given an overdose of prescription drugs and again millions of you who have never met or spoken to him are grief stricken. I even tattooed his portrait and signature on someone who was having difficulty in coming to terms with his death, yet he was an in your face kiddie fiddler. The lowest of the low for crying out loud.

On the flip side of the coin, when a few hundred thousand Muslim children are killed or maimed beyond all comprehension no one gives a damn. Why not? They are still children aren't they? Children who are Loved and cherished by their parents the same way that we love ours. How would you feel if you had to nurse your own child who'd had their arms and legs blown off courtesy of an unwanted and uninvited invading army?

Would you burn that nations flag in the street? I for one would do a lot more than that. Mind you, there is evidence to suggest that in most cases of flag burning carried out on these shore's the perpetrators are government paid agitators. Why do you think that they are never able to be got by the vast crowds of patriotic people who are inevitably around when this flag or poppy burning spectacle takes place?

The vast majority of Muslims are peaceful, decent, law abiding citizens. In fact a major survey carried out in 2010 concluded that British Muslims have a greater respect for our traditions than we do ourselves. Of course there are Muslim extremists, in the same way that we have our own right wing extremists. However, just like our extremists, theirs are also just a tiny minority of idiots who are all shout and of no real threat to anyone but themselves.

And what of the countries that we have invaded in this so called war on terror? Afghanistan, supposedly invaded for giving shelter to those cave dwelling multi millionaire terrorists. And since we are invading anyway, let's get rid of the Taliban while we are at it. That would be the Taliban who over 10 years after the invasion are now not only thriving but, according to some military strategists, unbeatable. Yes the Taliban may have had a brutal regime, but it was none of our business.

Course, had our politicians wanted rid of the Taliban for honourable reasons then maybe there could have been some justification in the invasion. Sadly, they didn't, in fact there was a far more sinister reason for wanting the Taliban removed. Course using the pretext of liberating the Afghan people gave the UK and US governments a nice cover story for their ulterior motive.

And what were their ulterior motives? Well apart from the Taliban repeatedly refusing to allow the American Government permission to run a major oil and gas pipeline throughout the length of their country and which is now in place, Afghanistan was also without a Rothschild controlled Central bank, which is also now in place.

However the staggering sums of money that the Taliban were reaping in as profits in their capacity as the world's main Heroin distributors hadn't escaped the US and UK governments attention. Since Heroin is one of the major scourge's of Western society, it would of course have made sense to stop this drug trafficking*.

That should have been no problem when you consider that the US and UK have spy satellites capable of zooming in on a single individual person, so how hard could it be to locate and burn a few large acres of Poppy field? Well according to statistics, very hard actually since there is much more Heroin coming out of the country now than there ever was under the Taliban rule.

The difference is of course, the US and the UK governments are now reaping the vast financial rewards that are to be made through this life destroying drug. In fact, the amount of money involved is so huge that the US government are thought to be using their share to prop up the American economy. So ask the Afghan people if they are better off now than they were 10 or 11 years ago. I fully expect the answer to be a resounding NO.

Course, anyone who doubts the fact that the British and American Governments are the biggest drug dealers in the world need only read the following article:

Well I guess we know who America's TOP Drug Dealers are- (CIA)The Criminal Intelligence Agency.

"WE'VE ALL HEARD THE RUMORS THAT THE CIA ARE THE REASON THAT THE UNITED STATES/CANADA IS AWASH WITH COCAINE…. IS IT TIME TO CONNECT THE DOTS NOW THAT ONE OF THEIR PLANES HAS CRASH LANDED WITH FOUR TONS OF COKE IN IT?"….

So the Arnprior OPP posted a blurb in the Guide stating "Report drug dealers". Well shouldn't we be seeking out the kingpins in Govt. namely the CIA! The most famous example of Govt. involvement in drugs (British) was the Opium war in China in the 1800's. So on the heels of that here's another extreme example of Govt. gone awry:

SEVENTEEN MONTHS AFTER AN AMERICAN-REGISTERED DC9 AIRLINER WAS BUSTED WITH 5.5 TONS OF COCAINE, A MAJOR INTERNATIONAL SCANDAL IS BREWING OVER A SECOND DRUG TRAFFICKING INCIDENT IN MEXICO'S YUCATAN INVOLVING AN AMERICAN-REGISTERED JET OWNED BY A DUMMY FRONT COMPANY OF THE KIND USUALLY ASSOCIATED WITH THE CIA.

A WEEKEND VISIT TO "DONNA BLUE AIRCRAFT INC" OF COCONUT BEACH FL., THE COMPANY WHICH FAA RECORDS SHOW OWNED THE GULFSTREAM II BUSINESS JET (N987SA) WHICH CRASH-LANDED WITH 3.7 TONS OF COCAINE ABOARD IN MEXICO'S YUCATAN TWO WEEKS AGO, HAS REVEALED THAT THE COMPANY'S LISTED ADDRESS IS AN EMPTY OFFICE SUITE WITH A BLANK SIGN OUT FRONT.

There was no sign of Donna Blue Aircraft, Inc., at the address listed at the Florida Dept. of Corporations, 4811 Lyons Technology Parkway #8 in Coconut Beach FL. …….
However, there were, oddly enough, a half-dozen unmarked police cars parked directly in front of the empty suite.
http://www.madcowprod.com/10092007.html

It seems that one of the planes logged on this list of "CIA Prison Planes" has been in a little accident – It crash landed in Mexico after running out of Jet fuel en route to the US. The authorities were more than a little surprised when they found four tons, yes you heard me right, four tons of cocaine on board.

The men flying the plane have disappeared – including one woman, the CIA refuses to comment, and the mainstream press don't want to touch the story...

And what of Iraq? That country ruled over by the feared megalomaniac, Saddam Hussein. Would that be the same Saddam Hussein that our previous governments helped to put in power? How the Iraqis must have hated him. Course, under his rule the nation didn't have to live in the most dangerous place on earth, where 1 in 3 people have either lost or had a close family member crippled. Neither were 75% of Iraqi children exhibiting signs of post traumatic stress under Saddam Hussein's rule. Are they as a Nation better off now that they have a patsy for western governments in power? Again, I fully expect the answer to be a resounding NO.

Nevertheless, whilst we are on the subject let's look at Libya? Colonel Gaddafi's gone thank god... Errr but isn't he the fella that our ex Prime minister, the Right Horrible Tony Blair used to like doing business with? Wasn't Gaddafi the fella that contributed millions of Dollars to help the criminal, Nicolas Sarkozy become the French President. Wasn't Colonel Gaddafi the one who masterminded an infrastructure that was second to none in the Middle East? Was he not the person who refused the Rothschild's permission to set up a Central Bank in the country? Was he not the one who still has millions of supporters, even now he's dead? Do the Libyan people now enjoy a better standard of living than they did under Gaddafi? I fully expect the answer to be a resounding NO.

Then there's Egypt and Syria. Both are countries with 'hostile Governments'. Have you ever noticed how our government calls those people who plant bombs, shoot soldiers & government forces, demonstrate and fight to overthrow these hostile governments, Freedom Fighters or anti government Forces. Where do you think these Freedom Fighters get all their modern weapons and ammunition from? Why, they get them from our leaders of course because we also want to rape and pillage these countries for all that they are worth**.

On the other hand, any group of people who do similar in countries with Governments which are aligned with ours are branded Terrorist Organisations. Look at how we, as a nation are condemned and vilified by our own government if we go on strike or demonstrate in this country. Look at the laws that are being constantly brought in to make it harder to demonstrate. Take away the right to demonstrate and exercise free speech and your left with a dictatorship.

Furthermore if it was about liberating people from an oppressive, tyrannical regime, why have we not invaded Saudi Arabia, a country whose human right violations are second to none? What about Bahrain? They too have an appalling record on human rights yet our sovereign, the Queen is great mates with Shaikh Hamad Bin Isa Al Khalifa, the country's King. In fact he has just accepted his invitation to the Queen's Jubilee lunch as it so happens. "*Another Gin and Tonic Ma'am*"?

Iran is the next likely target in the ongoing war on terror. Why? Well supposedly because the country poses a nuclear threat, a claim that the Iranian government categorically deny.

Course, many politicians from around the world also back Iran's denial. In fact there isn't a shred of proof that suggests Iran is a rogue nuclear power, but hell that doesn't matter. Our ex Prime Minister, Tony Blair looked us in the eye and told us we had to invade Iraq because they had weapons of mass destruction which would be used against our peace loving nation... Yet he lied through his teeth; Iraq had no WMDs as he damn well knew all along.
In truth, Iran is no threat to either our, Americas or anyone else's national security. North Korea on the other hand is a nuclear power with an appalling human rights record and far more of a potential threat to world safety than Iran ever will be. But are there invasion plans afoot for North Korea? Nah, far too risky, no oil, really not worth the effort... As of yet, but give it time.

The truth is I'm sad to say, that the UK and the USA are the real threat to world peace. Furthermore, people's civil rights and liberties are being eroded away little by little every day in both of these nations. We are told what to think, when to think it, what to do and when to do it everyday of our lives.

The Police, originally set up to protect and serve, are rapidly evolving into a privatized Army employed only to keep the population in line and in fear; not to solve crime. Our every move is tracked by CCTV camera's and our freedom of speech is all but outlawed. Moreover, once you realise where this country is really heading, you can literally feel the air of oppression and sense of doom hanging over us. Hmmm, now why does Hitler's Germany spring to mind?

* In February 2012 Press TV released the following article which proved that more heroin was coming out of Afghanistan since the Anglo/American illegal invasion of the country, than ever was under the Taliban:

Opium production by Afghan farmers rose between 2001 and 2011 from just 185 tons to a staggering 5,800 tons. Last year, levels increased by 61 percent, with more than 90 percent of heroin found on British streets being traced back to opiates cultivated in Afghanistan."

The latest UN figures indicate that the output of heroin increased by 61 percent in Afghanistan last year despite the Western claims about their will to curb the production of drugs during the invasion of the war-battered country.

Opium production by Afghan farmers rose between 2001 and 2011 from just 185 tons to a staggering 5,800 tons. Last year, levels increased by 61 percent, with more than 90 percent of heroin found on British streets being traced back to opiates cultivated in Afghanistan, according to UN figures. The UN figures make grim reading for those who backed the invasion of Afghanistan. Former British Prime Minister Tony Blair said in 2001 that a significant reason for deployment of foreign forces to Afghanistan was to curtail a flourishing heroin trade.

"The arms the Taliban are buying today are paid for by the lives of young British people buying their drugs on British streets. This is another part of their regime we should seek to destroy," he said.

However, the UN figures reveal how the outcome has been so dramatically different.
Some 15 percent of Afghanistan's gross national product now comes from drug-related exports, with the trade having a net worth of up to £1.6 billion ($2.5 billion).
UN Secretary General Ban Ki-moon told delegates at a conference in Vienna, Austria, on Thursday that Afghanistan cannot be stable while its economy depends so heavily on the drugs trade.

He noted that the problem of drug trafficking has undermined efforts to help Afghanistan emerge as a normally functioning economy.
"We cannot speak of sustainable development when opium production is the only viable economic activity in the country," Ban told delegates of the Paris Pact Ministerial Conference…

And that is still the case in 2018. Yet how can that be possible SEVENTEEN years after the illegal invasion… Especially with American satellites and spy-drones. Or are we to believe that these drones can pinpoint a man but cannot find acres upon acres of poppy fields?

Get real for fucks sake!

** On the 3rd of February 2012, the then Prime Minister, David Cameron admitted that the UK was funding Syrian Rebels. The following is from Press TV:

The UK government has acknowledged that it has provided an extra GBP 2 million to the Western-backed rebels fighting the popular government of Syrian President Bashar al-Assad.

Prime Minister David Cameron told a hearing at the House of Commons Liaison Committee on Tuesday afternoon that his government provided cash and equipment to foreign-backed rebels in Syria under such names as 'aid agencies' operating on the ground to help deliver emergency medical supplies and food.

The acknowledgement is yet another proof that the rebellion in the Middle Eastern Arab country has its root somewhere in Britain and France, where the governments of Cameron and French president Nicholas Sarkozy built the foundation of a military strike against former Libyan government of dead dictator Muammar Gaddafi.

The two European countries tabled the first draft resolution at the UN Security Council, which called for a no-fly zone over Libya and later it turned out to become an all-out war against a sovereign member of the international community.

The same scenario is being made about Syria, where David Cameron said "Britain would this week, continue to secure a United Nations Security Council resolution demanding an end to the violence and immediate humanitarian access".

The Prime Minister made three key pledges "to help Syrian citizens, promising more humanitarian assistance, to hold those responsible for slaughter to account and to bring about the political transition that would put a stop to the killing".

However, Cameron failed to mention the fact that his country's spying apparatus MI6 was the prime financier of terrorist snipers who kill people from the roofs of the buildings in some cities and towns in Syria.

He also failed to mention another fact that the UK's former police chief, assistant commissioner John Yates has been deployed to Bahrain, where the ruling family of al-Khalifa regime is brutally killing and torturing people who have come out against corruption and inequality.

John Yates resigned last year from his post at Scotland Yard in the wake of the phone-hacking scandal.

In a show of solidarity with the regime thugs, Yates said that "Bahraini police had faced extraordinary provocation during last year's turmoil".

Yates described the Bahrainis' call for free speech and an elected government as vandalism and rioting...

Now, is it not strange that our press describe these insurgents as 'Syrian Rebels' as opposed to 'Terrorists'?

After all, if there was an army of English Rebels attacking the British Government, would they not be classed as "Terrorists"? Of course they would. Therefore, the British Government was - and still is - funding terrorism.

Yet did the Anglo/American governments not invade Iraq because Saddam Hussein was supposedly funding terrorism?

Just sayin'.

Chapter 18
I Don't Like It, It's Quiet... Too Quiet

Throughout 2011, many thousands of people believed that the world would end in 2012. Course, that didn't happen and I now believe that was a conspiracy theory covertly started by the Monsters to keep the world on tenterhooks and make conspiracy theorists look stupid when nothing happened.

Moreover, in 2012 the world was once again faced with the prospect of WW3. And again this never happened. However, it is fair to say that in the six years since, not one year has gone by where we haven't been faced with the same prospect.

Nevertheless, I am much more clued up than I was six years ago and it is now obvious to me that the threat of another world war is just another means to keep us all living in fear… The people of Russia and China are not our enemies… The Monster Elite are...

I can't believe how fast this year has gone already. To be honest, with all the hype that has surrounded 2012 I was expecting the year to really drag yet we are already at the end of April.

Now, those amongst us who were sceptical about the hype surrounding 2012 will no doubt be sneering that nothing untoward has happened up to now and furthermore doesn't look likely to happen. Unfortunately, I couldn't disagree more.

The fact is, there is so much going on at the moment, it's hard to know where to start. I suppose the subject of the Police is as good as any.

I regularly read articles about Police brutality but I tend not to put them on my website since these articles are usually along the lines of an individual being shot or beaten up. And while that is unacceptable

I do tend to shy away from publishing such articles because they give the doubters the opportunity to trumpet the old adage of 'One bad Apple doesn't spoil the whole bunch'.

However, the frequency of such articles has now reached the stage where it would be wrong of me to turn a blind eye to them. I have therefore created a category on my website www.chrisspivey.org to deal solely with this matter.

You see, from 1990 to date, 1429 suspects have died while in police custody in the UK alone. Those responsible are rarely charged and when they are the powers that be are obstructive, hinder and withhold evidence from those investigating the death's. This fact was clearly highlighted earlier this year by the investigation into the shooting of Mark Duggan.
Original reports into his death claimed that armed police had been in a gunfight with Duggan which resulted in his death and a Policeman being shot.
However, we now know that was pure fiction on behalf of the MET and the truth of the matter is that an unarmed Duggan was murdered in cold blood by the police. That hasn't stopped the Police Authorities from trying to suppress the truth*.

Course, I have long been of the opinion that where the Police are concerned it's not a case of 'One bad apple', rather a case of the vast majority of Law enforcement officers being rotten to the core.

Indeed I could site instance after instance to back my view up, not just in the way they indiscriminately shoot to kill those suspected of a crime, but the unjust way in which they carry out their duties as a whole.**

However, there is much to get through in this article so I will leave it there for now. However, I can promise you now that I will highlight the activities of these corrupt, power mad, often brain dead, bully boys and girls on my website at every available opportunity.

Fukushima in Japan is another matter that I tend not to dwell on but which is now proving too big to ignore. There is growing evidence to suggest that the Earthquake that led to this nuclear disaster was deliberately triggered. For the sceptics who laugh at such a notion I suggest you do some research into H.A.A.R.P.

The radioactive fallout from the Fukushima nuclear power plant has decimated and contaminated sea life and many States in the USA are now exhibiting unsafe levels of radiation. As for the Japanese people, well they are left to live, unprotected, in a country that should by rights now be a wasteland.

Mark my words, Fukushima will ultimately prove to be a deliberate ploy in the NWO's population reduction agenda.***

Meanwhile, this population reduction agenda continues to gain momentum in the form of the Bill Gates backed mass child vaccination programme.****

And just to make sure that no child escapes this sick game of Russian roulette certain states in America are making it a criminal offence not to have your child vaccinated. I would like to elaborate on the dangers of these vaccinations but once again, it's not possible in this article as there is far too much to document.

Course, you can always do your own research. A good starting point is the unprecedented rise in Autism**** and the 1000's of child guinea pigs that have been left brain damaged or paralyzed in India and Africa after being inoculated.

And while we are on the subject of Population reduction it's worth mentioning that an avid proponent of this agenda, the Queen of England, is celebrating 60 tyrannical years on the throne this year. It's very disheartening to see so many brainwashed sheeple still willing to celebrate her jubilee. On the plus side the movement to get rid of the Monarchy continues to gain momentum.

It is disgusting that in these times of hardship, deliberately engineered by those we elected to power, that they are willing to spend millions of pounds to pay for these celebrations while people lose their livelihoods and homes on a daily basis in this country. Once again, for the skeptics I suggest you look at the unprecedented rise in soup kitchens, food parcels for the poor and the number of children now going hungry in Britain today.

And while the people of England slip into third world living conditions, the parasite who masquerades as our sovereign is more than happy to mug us off for the cost.
Think about it. She is the richest woman in the world, worth literally trillions of pounds, much of which was earned illegally, yet we are paying to celebrate the jubilee of someone who wants us dead... The phrase; mad dogs and Englishmen springs to mind.

As a footnote to this freeloader and her family of backward inbreds, it's worth mentioning that when our hard up, disgruntled people go on strike for legitimate reasons, the psychopathic Prime Minister and Rothschild puppet, David Cameron publicly denounced such action.

He berates these people and accuses them of costing the country Millions of pounds in lost revenue. Funny how the lost millions seem to count for nothing when he has so kindly declared Monday the 4th and Tuesday the 5th of June bank holidays on which to celebrate the despicable woman's jubilee. Bringing the country to a standstill for four consecutive days must surely cost the nation Billions of pounds.

"*Yes but the Queen brings in much more money in the form of tourism, than she costs the country*", I hear the skeptics cry... Don't make me laugh. Do you think Mr Kowlowski says to Mrs Kowlowski; "*Let's holiday in Enger-land this year Honey? We might see the Queen*". And of course people visit our country for our heritage but that will still be here long after Liz has been hung for treason.

In the meantime, this years Olympic Games have been exposed as something that is going to be out staged by a cataclysmic 'false flag' event. Whether this false flag operation still takes place or not, now that the cat is out of the bag remains to be seen. Certainly all the clues are there.

Once again I haven't time or space in this article to document the evidence in-depth, but if you wish to research this subject yourself I suggest you start with the location and surrounding road names of the Olympic village in Stratford and the barely concealed official Olympic 'Zion' logo. Bear in mind that Logos are one of the mainstay of the illuminati.

More tellingly still, in all this evidence is the mysterious suicide of Rik Clay, the young man who was particularly vocal about the conspiracy theory involving the Olympic Games. Rik joins the ever growing long list of 'whistleblowers' that have prematurely died under dubious circumstances.

Turning to politics, I predicted last November that Mit Romney would be chosen as the Republican nominee to challenge the corrupt Rothschild puppet, Barack Obama for the US Presidency.

Back then the equally controlled Rothschild puppet, Romney was put at around 6th place in the official opinion polls. With another 11 candidates to choose from and Romney's unremarkable campaign carrying little momentum, I wish now that I had put my money where my mouth is.

The article in which I predicted Romney's victory can be found on my website in the 'my view' section and is entitled, *Cain blunder clears the way for Romney victory, provided no one mentions whatsisname.*

The '*Whatshisname*' in question is of course Senator, Ron Paul and had the nominations not been rigged Ron Paul would have romped homed as the Republican candidate to go head to head with Obama.

Once again, there is insurmountable, conclusive evidence to support this fact. However, you only need look on YouTube for footage of the exposé at the lack of support that Romney gets at his campaign venues. He has even had to resort to making his own Placards for his small number of supporters to wave at the TV cameras. Paul on the other hand is playing to packed arenas and as such does not need to rely on underhand tactics and clever camera work to make his supporters look numerous.

Course, Ron Paul isn't the ideal candidate either. He is however the best the world could hope for at this moment in time. For that reason alone, the real powers that be will never allow him to become the President of the United States.

With regards to the predictions of WW3 breaking out this year, it appears that the immediate threat of its start is lessening now that talks are beginning to take place with the Iranian Govt.
Many will contend that the hostilities with Iran were only ever a smokescreen to take the focus away from the imminent collapse of the Euro. The collapse of the Euro would of course pave the way for the creation of the NWO.

However, I do not believe that these upcoming peace negotiations will put a stop to WW3, which will happen sometime in the future. Indeed, I believe that the lack of support in the plan to attack Iran, from a world population waking up to the real reason behind this so called 'War on Terror' has led to the globalists getting cold feet.

It is important to remember that the Elite rule from a house of cards. Alienate too many people and that house of cards will easily collapse. There was always far too much evidence readily available to support the fact that Iran is not a nuclear power intent on unleashing Armageddon on the western world to sway the general populations perspective on this matter.

Despite this fact, The Iranian Govt has done everything in its power to deflect the US and UK's disgusting attempts at Warmongering. I wholly applaud Iran's stance, as should the world as a whole. Be in no doubt that attacking Iran would be a major mistake, a mistake that would almost definitely lead to WW3 and possibly the end of the world as we know it.

Course, having said that isn't to say that WW3 will not now happen. On the contrary the very real threat still exists. The sudden, recent build up of thousands of US Marines being stationed in Australia is testament to that. Then there is the US war machine constantly rattling Pakistan's cage. The American govt would love nothing more than having an excuse to invade Pakistan since the country's location makes it an ideal place to station troops in preparation to attack China.

Russia, having now regained their status as a 'Super Power' certainly doesn't believe that the USA has revised their plans to attack and invade Iran. They continue to amass troops and artillery around the Black Sea area in readiness to thwart such an invasion.

In the meantime, the real rogue nuclear nations such as Israel continue to receive financial backing and support from both the UK and US govt's. Then again that fact is hardly surprising since both governments take their orders from Israel.

And while I'm at it, it's also worth remembering that the United States is the only country ever to use a nuclear bomb on another country. I am of course referring to the American attacks on Hiroshima and Nagasaki. History has shown that dropping the bombs was not necessary to put an end to WW2 since Japan had already agreed to surrender. Therefore, the only point in doing so was to document the devastation such an attack can cause.

As for the collapse of the Euro, the recent lack of reporting has led many to believe the situation has been brought under control. Once again nothing could be further from the truth.
I wrote last December that the Euro collapse was inevitable being as that was the plan all along. I also said that despite the IMF "Taking whatever action deemed necessary to avoid the collapse", they would in fact do nothing. They haven't.

The plan to collapse the Euro is still on track. Greece, the country used by the elite to monitor how a country's population would react

when an economy collapses, has seen a huge rise in suicides as people take their own lives rather than starve to death.
Yesterday, it emerged that the Dutch Govt was near to collapsing, paving the way for the banking cartels to seize power in much the same way as they did a couple of months ago in Italy.

Spain is in chaos with half of the youth population unemployed. Portugal's economy hangs by a thread and in reality we are not much more secure here in the UK.

Every European country is witnessing mass demonstrations by their respective populations which naturally go by and large unreported by the mainstream media. These demonstrations are quickly brought to and end by brutal, overzealous, Paramilitary police forces made up of thugs too thick to see that they and their families will also fall victim to the coming World dictatorship.

In conclusion, while things appear on the surface to be calm. Underneath the truth is very different. The world we live in continues to be as dangerous and unpredictable a place as it has ever been.

It may be nearly May already, but this year is far from over. I am in fact reminded of those cliche scenes from old cowboy films... I don't like it. It's quiet... too quiet.

* On the 26th of May 2012, Press TV released the following article on the death of Mark Duggan:

A complete inquiry may never be held into the death of black man Mark Duggan, whose death at the hands of police triggered worst unrest in the UK in a generation last summer.
The family of the 29-year-old accused the authorities, who said "sensitive information" could jeopardize the police investigation, of withholding information around his death.

A coroner holding a pre-inquest review into the death in Tottenham on August 4 said that sensitive material relating to police "decision making" meant the probe may not take place. Instead, a judge could hold an inquiry that would allow for "closed sessions" where details are kept private.

Duggan's aunt, Carole, who was accompanied to the hearing at North London coroner's court by his fiancée Semone Wilson and his brother Marlon, said they believed the news was "delaying tactics".

"We believe the IPCC are withholding information from us which is delay tactics. Maybe they think we will go away, come to terms with what has happened, but we are a grieving family and we will always grieve for Mark", she said.

Duggan was being followed by officers from Operation Trident in a covert operation when armed officers stopped the taxi he was travelling and shot him dead.
The news has prompted fears for the family that his case may echo that of Azelle Rodney who was shot dead in 2005 by police and whose family are still waiting for a public inquiry seven years later.

** On the 5th of March 2012, Press TV released the following article which also contains information about Mark Duggan:

"No police officer has been convicted over the death of the 300 people in police custody or after detention since 1998, a fact that has triggered annual demonstrations against the police atrocity and corruption."

Britain's Independent Police Complaints Commission (IPCC) says the man police shot dead in Cheshire on Saturday did not have a gun in his car after similar cases in recent months raising fears officers are given the say-so to kill citizens indiscriminately.

The Greater Manchester police earlier said on Saturday that the 36-year-old Anthony Grainger was killed in a "pre-planned" police operation but did not clarify what prompted the shooting.

Grainger's death raised speculations that he will suffer the fate of the other 300 individuals who have lost their lives in police custody or after detention since 1998.
No single officer has been convicted over the death of the 300 victims over the entire 13 years, a fact that has triggered annual demonstrations against the police atrocity and corruption.

Grainger's case was especially important, as it was at least the third such incident over the past seven months, which also included the death of the 29-year-old black man Mark Duggan.

Duggan's death is believed to have been the starting point and the trigger for the massive August unrest that was without precedence in a generation and put the country in a state of security alert.

The IPCC said on Monday that inspectors' did not find any weapons in Grainger's car and in its immediate vicinity after an "initial visual search."

"Due to the presence of CS residue in the car a full forensic examination has not yet been conducted to establish whether there are any weapons in the car," the IPCC said.
"This will take place in a controlled environment in the next few days," it added.

Grainger's' fatal shooting in "unclear" circumstances underlines fears that the police are given a free rein to kill anyone they wish while they rest assured that no trial or conviction is in the works.

The police also claimed after Duggan's murder in August that he had a gun and had shot at the officers before they fired at him.

Months later, however, the IPCC said Duggan was not even carrying a gun still less to use it to open fire on officers.
The IPCC seems to be following the same line on Grainger's case that could be the 3,181 death in police custody or after detention since 1969 for which no one has been blamed.

***On the 14th of April 2012, naturalnews.com published the following article about Fukushima:

*A Freedom of Information Act(FOIA) request filed by Friends of the Earth (FoE), Physicians for Social Responsibility (PSR), and the Nuclear Information and Resource Center (NIRS) has unearthed a shocking series of new evidence proving a deliberate, global cover-up of the true severity of the Fukushima Daiichi nuclear disaster. And the unfortunate reality is that the **mainstream media continues to blatantly ignore this colossal scandal.***

Private emails, meeting transcripts and other key documents reveal that both the Obama White House and the United States Nuclear Regulatory Commission(NRC) were well aware of just how bad things really were with Fukushima from the early days of the disaster, but did nothing to warn the public about it. In fact, NRC and the White House
purposely did not warn Americans about a massive radiation plume that struck the West Coast just days after the massive earthquake and tsunami hit Japan's eastern coast.

According to information gathered from hundreds of pages worth of private NRC emails, conference calls and secret meetings, key players in the Fukushima whitewashing campaign, including the NRC's David McIntyre and Elliot Brenner, were hard at work in the days following the disaster distracting public attention away from it. By pretending that a radioactive plume did not exist while simultaneously sending out misinformation to the media, these two, in conjunction with White House officials, actively participated in a criminal cover-up of the truth.

You can read key portions of these criminal dealings at the following link:
http://theintelhub.com

Plume-gate, the world's biggest nuclear cover-up to date

A situation that is now being dubbed "Plume-gate," this massive cover-up of critical information about Fukushima could have saved thousands of lives, including the more than 14,000 individuals, many of whom were babies, that died in the weeks following the disaster (http://www.naturalnews.com/034586_Fukushima_USA_fatalities.html).

And yet to this very day, the federal government's cozy relationship with the nuclear industry has allowed the injustice to continue, as no proper investigation into this dastardly crime has yet taken place.

"The executive branch and multiple federal agencies, agencies tasked with keeping the American public safe, did their best to hide and to cover-up information about a deadly radioactive plume and ensuing fallout that was headed for the West Coast of the United States from Japan," writes Tony Muga from The Intel Hub about the situation.

Not only did these government agencies hide the truth and deliberately deceive the public, they also used other events, including the infamous Qur'an burning in Afghanistan, as a distraction to divert public attention away from Fukushima, and away from the 104 nuclear reactors in the U.S. that are of a similar age and vulnerability as Fukushima.

*So why is the federal government getting away with all this? It is for the same reason that it gets away with most of its other crimes against humanity:**corporate fascism.**And sadly, corporate fascism is a bipartisan problem, as both Republicans and Democrats today are slaves to it, representing opposite but identical sides of the same coin.*

"It seems that the fundamental problem with what Americans are experiencing is not just radioactive fallout but Fascism, the merging of the corporate and the state," adds Muga. "In a fascist state, there is little or no responsible action from the corporations for there is little or no promotion of accountability from the state. The corporations, for all intents and purposes, control the state."...

184

Two weeks after that article appeared, naturalnews.com added a follow-up article:

Radioactive fallout from the Fukushima Daiichi nuclear disaster continues to show up at dangerously high levels in the city of Tokyo, which is located roughly 200 miles from the actual disaster site. According to an analysis of five random soil samples recently taken by nuclear expert Arnie Gundersen, the soil around Tokyo is so contaminated with Fukushima radiation that it would be considered nuclear waste here in the U.S.

During a recent trip to Tokyo, Gundersen collected soil samples from a sidewalk, a children's playground, a rooftop, a patch of moss by the side of a road, and the lawn of a judicial building. After sending those samples in for testing, it was revealed that each one had high levels of radioactive cesium-134 (CS134) and cesium-137 (CS137), while three of the samples contained high levels of cobalt-60 (CO60). One of the samples also tested positive for uranium-235 (U235).

"[W]hen I was in Tokyo, I took some samples [...] and sent them to the lab," said Gundersen in a recent video report. "And the lab determined that all of them would be qualified as radioactive waste here in the United States and would have to be shipped to Texas to be disposed of."
You can view the complete report here:
http://www.fairewinds.com

Despite the fact that radioactive plumes from Fukushima have largely drifted seaward based on wind patterns, a considerable amount of this radiation traveled southward towards Tokyo and elsewhere. The findings also confirm the reality that Fukushima radiation has likely had significant global spread as well, which confirms earlier reports of samples taken on the U.S. West Coast (http://www.naturalnews.com/035731_Fukushima_radiation_America .html).

**** On Wednesday, February 01, 2012, Natural News Staff Writer, Ethan A. Huff, wrote the following about Bill Gates and his vaccination program:

Mass vaccination is apparently not the only depopulation strategy being employed by the Bill & Melinda Gates Foundation, as new research funded by the organization has developed a way to deliberately destroy sperm using ultrasound technology.BBC News reports that the Gates Foundation awarded a grant to researchers from the University of North Carolina (UNC) to develop this new method of contraception.

For their study, the UNC team tested ultrasound on lab rats and found that two 15-minute doses "significantly reduced" both sperm counts and sperm integrity. When administered two days apart through warm salt water, ultrasound caused the rats' sperm counts to drop below ten million sperm per milliliter, which is five million less than the "sub-fertile" range, and stay that way for up to six months.

The report claims the technology is for contraceptive purposes only and not for causing sterility. However, Dr. James Tsuruta, who led the research, told reporters that it is unclear whether or not the technology can cause long-term damage, and that more research is needed to determine whether or not repeated ultrasounds cause permanent damage.

The Gates Foundation awarded 78 different research projects with $100,000 grants each as part of its "Grand Challenges in Global Health Program." Ten of these projects specifically addressed new technologies for contraception, according toTIME, including one for a pill that inhibits the growth and maturation of sperm, and another for creating chemical compounds that prevent sperm from reaching the egg (http://healthland.time.com/2010/05/14/male-birth-control-stopping-sperm-with-ultrasound/).

"We think this could provide men with up to six months of reliable, low-cost, non-hormonal contraception from a single round of treatment," wrote the researchers in their report. "Our long-term goal

is to use ultrasound ... as an inexpensive, long-term, reversible male contraceptive suitable for use in developing to first world countries." Back in 2010, Bill Gates explained to attendees at the TED Conference that year his ideas for culling the world population, one of which involved increasing vaccination rates (http://www.naturalnews.com/029911_vaccines_Bill_Gates.html).

Now, his organization is actively funding research into advanced contraceptive methods that could render individuals infertile. Coincidence?

***** On Friday, February 24, 2012, Jonathan Benson, a staff writer for naturalnews.com wrote the following in regard to Autism:

No matter how you look at it, autism research is big business. Just like the Susan G. Komen Foundation "Race for the Cure" for breast cancer, the autism industry pretends to be looking for the causes of autism and how to cure it, when in reality it is on a never-ending hunt for money to fund so-called research into the bodily changes associated with autism in order to push more profit-generating screenings and drug therapies on the public.

The worldwide propaganda campaign that continues to repeat the lie that vaccines are in no way related to autism is one great example of the medical establishment covering up one of the most obvious causes of autism. Rather than actually investigate how the body responds to vaccines, and how these responses are clearly associated with the neurological damage that is part and parcel of autism symptoms, researchers continue to churn out studies that completely avoid any investigation of this or any other likely cause of autism.

Instead, the vast majority of autism studies, which happen to be funded mostly by the pharmaceutical industry, focus solely on the physical, genetic, and chemical changes that accompany the disease, and ignore trying to identify the causes that lead to these changes in the first place. This approach is deliberate, of course, because it facilitates the development of an endless cycle of drug and behavioral therapies for autism that never get to the root of the problem, which means they will forever generate a continuous stream of new profits.

"To find a disease cause and solution to prevent disease isn't profitable," says a recent article in **Gaia Health** that addresses this important issue. "However, to find even the most miniscule physical, genetic, or chemical change in someone with an existing disease means that even more money can be squeezed out of the research funders like the National Institutes of Health (NIH) and the National Institute of Mental Health (NIMH), agencies funded by taxpayers. Anything that leads away from causes and focuses on the physicochemical effects of autism always leads to more questions and more research funds."

THE MEDICAL ESTABLISHMENT SEEKS TO DESTROY THE LIVES, CAREERS OF RESEARCHERS WHO ACTUALLY TRY TO IDENTIFY CAUSES OF, AND CURES FOR, DISEASE

On the rare occasion that an honest researcher comes along and tries to actually conduct legitimate research into the causes of autism, he or she is eventually cut off from the funding chain, and sometimes even maligned and slandered in the public eye by the medical and media establishment. This is precisely what has happened to Dr. Andrew Wakefield, whose honest research into one cause of autism led to an ongoing barrage of character and career assassination that continues to this very day (http://www.naturalnews.com/Andrew_Wakefield.html).

Be sure to take a look at the sample studies on autism analyzed by Gaia Health that show a clear disinterest by the medical establishment in actually finding causes of, or cures for, autism. These studies are clearly aimed at discovering and promoting new drug and vaccine protocols for treating autism symptoms, rather than actually trying to prevent it from developing in the first place.

Chapter 19
God bless all the little children

You won't find too much in this book about the British Royal Family simply because I intend to write a whole one on the subject in the not too distant future. Nevertheless, what follows is one of the many that I wrote about our "beloved" Queen for my website wwwchrisspivey.org

HANG THIS SATANIC PARASITE

Sometimes it is important to take a step back and look at things in perspective.

Now I imagine that you have read the text on the picture of the Queen accompanying this short article and no doubt some 'Royalists' will deem the text as treasonous.

However, I say that the text is mild. You see, while millions of people live in poverty in this country, our puppet government will squander millions of pounds to celebrate this evil woman's jubilee… Not me! I for one will celebrate when she is hanging by her scrawny neck.

The poverty that we - the Queen's subjects - suffer in this country however, is absolutely nothing in comparison to the poverty suffered by those in the so called third world countries. Course, it is from these countries that our 'beloved' sovereign made much of her wealth.

Now, there is a song that I am sure you will have heard called **'Everything is beautiful'** which opens with the line; "*God bless all the little children, all the little children of the world*". So think about that opening line and then take a look at the statistics below.

- *In the Asian, African and Latin American countries, well over 500 million people are living in what the World Bank has called "absolute poverty"*
- *Every year 15 million children die of hunger*
- *For the price of one missile, a school full of hungry children could eat lunch every day for 5 years*
- *Throughout the 1990's more than 100 million children died from illness and starvation. Those 100 million deaths could have been prevented for the price of ten Stealth bombers, or what the world spends on its military in two days!*
- *The World Health Organization estimates that one-third of the world is well-fed, one-third is under-fed one-third is starving. Over 4 million will die this year.*
- *One in twelve people worldwide is malnourished, including 160 million children under the age of 5.*
- *The Indian subcontinent has nearly half of the world's hungry people. Africa and the rest of Asia together have approximately 40%, and the remaining hungry people are found in Latin America and other parts of the world.*
- *Nearly one in four people, 1.3 billion live on less than $1 per day, while the world's 358 billionaires have assets*

exceeding the combined annual incomes of countries with 45 percent of the world's people.

- *3 billion people in the world today struggle to survive on US $2/day.*
- *In 1994 the Urban Institute in Washington DC estimated that one out of 6 elderly people in the U.S. has an inadequate diet.*
- *In the U.S. hunger and race are related. In 1991 46% of African-American children were chronically hungry, and 40% of Latino children were chronically hungry compared to 16% of white children.*
- *The infant mortality rate is closely linked to inadequate nutrition among pregnant women. The U.S. ranks 23rd among industrial nations in infant mortality. African-American infants die at nearly twice the rate of white infants.*
- *One out of every eight children under the age of twelve in the U.S. goes to bed hungry every night.*
- *Half of all children under five years of age in South Asia and one third of those in sub-Saharan Africa are malnourished.*
- *In 1997 alone, the lives of at least 300,000 young children were saved by vitamin A supplementation programmes in developing countries.*
- *Malnutrition is implicated in more than half of all child deaths worldwide - a proportion unmatched by any infectious disease since the Black Death*
- *About 183 million children weigh less than they should for their age*
- *To satisfy the world's sanitation and food requirements would cost only US$13 billion- what the people of the United States and the European Union spend on perfume each year.*
- *The assets of the world's three richest men are more than the combined GNP of all the least developed countries on the planet.*
- *Every 3.6 seconds someone dies of hunger*

- *It is estimated that some 800 million people in the world suffer from hunger and malnutrition, about 100 times as many as those who actually die from it each year.*

There is nothing beautiful about those statistics and neither is there a God blessing the children the statistics are aimed at. The Queen and others of her ilk could end that suffering today. Think about that as you wave your jubilee flags in celebration.

Chapter 20
Living In The Material World

We are told that we are 'free'. Yet that is just an illusion designed to keep us in chains...

Who are you?

Now before you go thinking that I've gone all Football hooligan on you, you ought to know that I'm posing the question in all seriousness. Furthermore, I would hazard a guess that the vast majority of the nation doesn't actually know the correct answer.

Nevertheless, I do know that the correct answer to my opening gambit will be far greater statistically than the nation as a whole. However, as was in the case of my recent article on the workings of money, I think it is important that I answer that question for those of you who have stumbled upon this site and don't know the correct answer.

To answer that question I first need you to clear your mind of the *'reality'* that you know and step out of your comfort zone. Course that's not easy to do when your brains have been deliberately programmed from the day you were born in order to get you to think a certain way – The wrong way.

Moreover, I don't doubt that most of you will not believe what I'm going to tell you. After all, the truth is often far stranger than fiction... It is the truth nevertheless.

Now apparently I fit the profile of someone able to easily process the information that I'm going to pass on to you. And as soon as I read this info I instantly knew that it was correct and for the first time I was truly able to make sense of the nonsensical.

But all the same, just for the record those most easily able to take on board what I'm going to tell you will normally be of above average intelligence yet will also have been bored and disruptive at school, often leaving without a qualification to their name. They will often feel scared, isolated or uneasy for no apparent reason. They will often read about something that is by and large accepted as fact and think to themselves *"that can't be right"*. They will be very intuitive and yet no matter how well they are doing in life, they will still harbour the thought that things are not as they should be... They would be justified in thinking that way because I promise you, things are very far from being right.

And so, with this in mind, make of the following, what you will: Everyone is - at least in theory - born equal. We are born as Human Beings not as little people. The word 'Person' is a derivative of the word 'Persona'. The nature of your persona makes up your 'personality'. All that, in theory, goes to make you the person that you perceive yourself to be.

However, the word *'Person'* also means something entirely different to what you think it does. You see, it is absolutely essential that you are a *'person'* in the eyes of the law in order to live in this make believe world that we conceive as reality.

This is because we actually exist in a fantasy world where everything is reduced to the status of a 'Company' or 'Corporation'. The UK for example is a registered company, as are all the Political Parties, every MP, every Law Court, Every Council and Every Police Force in the land.

But what is a 'Company' or a 'Corporation'? The answer to that is they are simply pieces of paper registered at 'Companies House'. They are not - contrary to what many of you may think - the buildings, employee's and stock. Those are Company assets. Therefore, in order for these companies (Pieces of paper) to do business with us as human beings (Get us to abide by their laws), we also need to be brought down to the level of a piece of paper. But how?

Well, shortly after we are born we are given a name although it is important to remember that you are not your name. In fact your names are given to you for convenience and because parents don't like to summon their child by bellowing at the top of their lungs "*Oi you*".

Course, we all have a surname aka a family name, which in my case is Spivey. This is necessary so as people who don't know me can find me or so as those who talk about me when I'm not present, are able to associate me with someone from the Spivey family.

However, since most of us all share a surname with at least one of our parents and usually our brothers & sisters etc, in order to avoid further confusion we are also give the minimum of one Christian or first name, mine being Christopher David.

Therefore, my right and proper title is: Christopher David of the family Spivey. Now it is important that you understand that this is the way your lawful name is set out. The name that appears on such places as envelopes where it is set out differently - in my case Mr Christopher David Spivey - is someone totally different.

Moreover, right up until the moment that your parents register your birth, you are a totally free, Sovereign Human Being. However, whenever you register something you transfer ownership. For instance when we register our cars we transfer the ownership of our car over to the Govt. Proof of this fact can be found by simply looking at your logbook. You are described on the logbook as the Registered Keeper.

And if a Registered Keeper was the same as an owner then why not describe that person on a log book as 'the owner'? After all, that is a lot less letters and 50% less words. Course, if you were still the owner of your car after you have registered it with the DVLA then you would not need a licence to drive it.

I mean, no one can be given licence to do something that is unlawful. Therefore any activity that is licensed must be lawful and if something is lawful then you don't need a license for it.

In fact, if you still owned the car that you have registered then you would not need to tax, MOT and insure it, unless you chose to do so. Furthermore, under common law, the Police would not have the right to confiscate it or have the authority to have it destroyed. For them to do so would be a case of them committing theft and/or at the very least criminal damage.

Therefore, It has got to be said though that this is a nice scam that the Govt have got going for them, isn't it? They trick you into giving them your car and get you to pay the upkeep. In return they generously allow you exclusive uses of the motor as long as you abide by their terms and conditions. And any profit that you make when selling their car you are allowed to keep.

Now the exact same is true in relation to your Birth Certificate. When you register your newborn baby you unwittingly transfer ownership of your pride and joy over to the state. And just like your car, the govt insists that you pay for your child's upkeep and in return they will let your child live with you for as long as you raise them in the way that they tell you or until they reach the age of consent.

That is why you have little choice in having your child vaccinated against certain diseases... If you don't, watch how you are looked at with scorn every time you take your child to the doctors. That is also why you have no choice in sending your child to school, where they are brainwashed into believing whatever the Govt choose. That is also why you cannot administer a light smack on your child. And so on and so on.

 And if the Govt don't like the way that you treat their property then they simply remove their child from your care. Once again they wouldn't be allowed to do this if the child was yours. That would be kidnapping.

Indeed, if further proof were needed then you may be surprised to learn that it is a fact that if a child is not registered then that child cannot be removed from your care, even if you knock ten bells of shit out of him/her 7 days a week. However I don't advise it because you would then be charged with assaulting a minor and even if you are lucky enough to escape a prison sentence, the said child will grow up hating you. And above all, it's not really necessary to hit kids. That makes us no better than those seeking to control us. But I digress.

Now the fact that the Govt have no claim to an unregistered child was disclosed by Torbay Council under the freedom of information act. The question was put to Torbay Council asking them directly if a child who is not registered via a birth certificate can be removed by them, from the child's parents where there are causes for concern for the child's safety. Torbay Council's reply was short and to the point. The answer is NO.

So what is a person? This is the difficult bit to explain. What happens when you register a baby is not only do you surrender your child to the Govt; the said child also becomes a 'person'. In other words the birth certificate locks that child into the system. A birth certificate is a piece of paper and as I said earlier we need to be reduced to the level of a piece of paper in order to exist in the corporate world that we perceive as reality. Your Birth Certificate therefore is what gives you the status of a 'Person'.

However, you the person is not you in the physical form. That honour belongs to you, the Human Being. You the person as I have just stated, is a piece of paper in the form of your birth certificate. And so as not to confuse 'you' the human being, with 'you' the person (your birth certificate), 'you' the person is often referred to as your 'legal fiction person'. This is because that is what a person is, nothing more than a piece of paper.

Moreover, without the creation of your legal fiction person aka your birth certificate you would not be subject to the laws of society. Therefore, in order for the Govt to hold you within their jurisdiction they have to be able to create 'joinder' between 'you' the human being and 'you' the legal fiction person.

In other words, you the human being have to be accountable for you the legal fiction person. This is because the Govt or any other law enforcement body for that matter, cannot subject us to their statute laws as human beings. Statute laws only exist within the realms of the corporate world. All Statute laws are designed to raise revenue. This is why as a human being I am known as Christopher David: of the family Spivey, but as a legal fiction person I am known in the more commonly written form as Mr Christopher David Spivey (My legal fiction person's name). The human Being and the legal fiction person are two totally different entities.

Now, only the legal fiction person (LFP) is subject to the laws of our society. The Govt however cannot get a piece of paper (Your legal fiction person) to pay income tax. It is not physically possible. Therefore they need you, the human being to take responsibility for you, the legal fiction person by way of joinder (making us one person), so as they can collect tax and any other payment for that matter, from you.

Course, it goes without saying that the Govt do not want you to know that you and your LFP are two separate entities. After all only a fool would pay tax if it was not required for them to do so. Therefore the Govt will use any skulduggery or dirty tricks to convince you that you and your LFP are one of the same.

You see, when you truly understand this information it is possible to use your LFP as a coat, that you can slip on to reap the benefits of society and then take off to avoid the negatives society offers you. If you are that way inclined that is. However, be warned, if you are not totally confident in your understanding of this and other info that I'm going to give you then you will come unstuck and end up getting your bottom smacked.

It is therefore important to understand the very many different ways that the Govt will use to trick you into believing that you are your LFP.

They even go as far as using a different language to ours in order to bamboozle us.

This language is often referred to as being called 'Legalese'. The clever, yet no less devious trick with legalese is that you don't even know that it is a different language. This is because legalese uses the same words as we do yet they can have very different meanings.

That is why when you read a legal document you can read the words but you don't have the foggiest idea what the document says. To make matters even trickier, the-powers-that-be are constantly changing the meanings of words. Does that sound far fetched? Do you think I'm talking rubbish? I don't blame you but consider this. If Legalese was the same language as ours then why does it have its own dictionary?

The legalese dictionary is called the 'Black's law Dictionary'. However, ask a solicitor to borrow a copy and they will be outraged. Now if legalese wasn't a separate language to ours, ask yourself this; why don't they use the oxford dictionary or the Collins dictionary like the rest of us? After all the Oxford, Collins & Cambridge dictionaries etc all contain the same words with the same meanings despite the fact that they come from different publishers. And I can guarantee you that you will never see a person who needs to speak legalese with anything other than Black's law Dictionary (BLD).

Furthermore BLD is on its ninth edition. Now, where as the Oxford dictionary will get a revised edition every once in a while, usually due to new words coming into common use, this isn't the case with the BLD which is regularly updated due to the need to change the meaning of words.

Needless to say, one of the BLD's most important definitions is that of a 'Person' which it describes as thus: *A person, a group of people, a company or corporation, a group of companies or corporations...* Concrete proof then that a person is a company in the eyes of the law.

Now check on the Oxford dictionaries definition of a person and without me even looking I can guarantee that it won't be anything like the BLD's version. I will however come to the BLD's reason for their strange definition later.

Now to understand the lengths that the-powers-that-be will go to in order to confuse, trick and manipulate us and also as an indication of how on the ball you need to be in order to out manoeuvre them, consider this:
The word '*IS*', is a two letter word we use literally 100's of times a day. So if I was to ask you to define the word 'IS' to me, you would have no problem doing so would you?... I said, would you?

Not so easy is it?

Okay, with that in mind you may be surprised to know that BLD reportedly has no less than 18 different meanings for the word 'IS'... Yet you will struggle to give one meaning of the word!

And as a footnote to legalese and also as an example of the contempt the-powers-that-be hold us in, the BLD describes a '*Human Being*' as a '*non person*' or a '*Thing*'. How quaint. You should also bear in mind that now the illuminati have us well and truly hoodwinked, they will fight tooth and nail to keep us that way.

Now, an interesting way in which you are tricked into creating joinder with your Legal fiction Person is by the use of the legalese word, '*Understand*'. For instance if you have ever been arrested, the police will try to get you to create joinder from the offset. The simplest way that they do this is by asking you your name. And as soon as you identify yourself via your name you have automatically created legal joinder and as such are now responsible for any punishment handed down on your legal fiction person via a law court. However, it is also important to remember that the Police, like us, are not privy to this info. Indeed, as far as they are aware, they are just doing their job.

Course, if you refuse to reveal your name you will more than likely be arrested and read your rights. On completion of this you will be asked if you 'understand'. And anyone who does not know any different will naturally assume that the police officer is simply asking you if you "understand" what he has just told you in regard to your rights under the law.

For example: "*you do not have to say anything but anything you do say blah, blah, blah*"...

And by affirming that you 'understand' you have once again been tricked into creating legal joinder. This is because you are not in fact affirming that you understand the caution you have just been read. You are in fact, in law agreeing to STAND UNDER the terms of statute law and stand as surety for any punishment that your LFP may incur. And these little tricks continue right the way up to the law courts until they have achieved their goal. The goal is to get your money, keep you poor, and keep you working hard for the 'Company'.

In fact every day you inadvertently take responsibility for your LFP without even knowing it. Yet if we were all to one day stop wearing the coat that is our LFP we would all be able to enjoy a far more rewarding, pleasurable not to mention beneficial life.

You see, the Corporate world exists entirely for the benefit of a few. It is a make believe world designed to keep the masses enslaved. The phrase '*working for the rat race*', springs to mind.

And until we rid ourselves of our LFP's we merely exist. We are all born free... Real life is about staying free.

Chapter 21
Terrorism: A modern day fairy tale

First published on my website on the 21st of June 2012... The contents of which are self explanatory...

Are you all sitting comfortably? Good,then I shall begin...

Once upon a time, long long ago in a far away land called Muslim, a baby Devil was born in a cave. However, it was a very big cave, because the baby devil's Mummy & Daddy were very rich. And, the cave needed to be big because the baby devil already had many, many brother and sister devils running around.

However, This was no ordinary baby devil, for as the baby devil's parents already knew; their baby was a gift from Allah ,The great God of Evil.

Now, as with all baby devils born in the evil land of Muslim, the baby devils Father, Natas, immediately took his new born son to dangle him by the ankles over the fires of Hell. In keeping with this centuries old tradition, as soon as the baby devil began to scream in the searing heat of hells fire, Natas called out the words *"Praise yee, oh evil Allah, for blessing us with a son. He shall be known from this moment forward as... Osama of the family Bin Laden"*.

Meanwhile, barely 11 years earlier in a land far away from Muslim, a good Christian man sat in a massive mansion staring at his own new born son. And on the face of it the man should have been happy. After all, he had a lovely big house, Millions of Dollars in the bank and on this day, July 6, 1946 AD, his beautiful wife Barbara had just presented him - George Herbert Bush - with a son and heir.

However, the mansion & money meant little to 'Herbie'. After all, pretty much all of the God fearing white men born here, in the country known as America (*The home of the Brave and the land of the free*), had position and wealth. And so, even the birth of his 1st born son, soon to be named George Walker Bush, couldn't lift 'Herbies' spirits.

Nevertheless, as he sat, lovingly cradling his new born son, he looked upwards, with a mournful yet resigned-to-his-fate, look on his face. "*If it be thy will oh lord, then so be it*", Herbie said softly to his creator up in heaven. For God - the one true God - had spoken to Herbie and laid him open to his plans.

This was because God - being all seeing and all knowing - had foreseen the coming of the Antichrist and in readiness for the ultimate battle between good and evil, had sent his own son to Earth; the very same son that Herbie now sat cradling in his arms.

And so, as Herbie asked God for guidance a big beam of light shot through the window engulfing everything in the nursery in a beautiful, warm, Golden light.

In the very same instant Herbie heard God's voice: *"Look after my son well Herbie. School him well in the teachings of the righteous. Make him a man amongst men. Fore I cannot tell you the exact timing of the Antichrist's coming. All that I can tell you is that when he arrives he shall be the epitome of all that is evil and he will be born into wealth, to cave dwellers in the district of Al Qaeda in the land of Muslim"*.

"But how will our son know when it's time Lord?" Herbie asked.

"I will send Three Kings to Guide him" God answered. *"They shall be known by the names of Dick Cheney, Donald Rumsfeld and Condoleezza Rice"*.

Herbie's brow furrowed. *"But surely Condoleezza Rice is a woman?"* Herbie protested.

"Some would say Herbie, Some would say", replied God.

"Then so be it Lord" Herbie said, bowing his head.

With God having outlined his plans, Herbie, in the time honoured tradition of the west looked up to heaven and said,"*And what's in it for me Lord?"*.

Meanwhile, eleven years onwards, time passed quickly in the evil land of Muslim and Osama Bin Laden, although dogged with ill health, grew both tall and beardy.

Course, like all devils in the evil land of Muslim, Osama had attended the local Primary school as soon as the 1st signs of bum fluff appeared. It was here, that he - *like all Muslims* - learned the art of jealousy. Once jealousy was mastered, usually by around the age of 11, Muslim devils are sent to the local comp where they are taught to channel their jealousy into outright hatred for Democracy.

And so it is that by the age of 14, the average Muslim devil will leave school, provided that he can demonstrate that he is capable of growing a six inch long beard and setting up a market stall selling bland, flowerpot type vessels.

However, for the Elite Muslims such as Osama Bin Laden, They attend the prestigious University of Al Qaeda.
Here Students are expected to grow beards to a minimum length of 8 inches and attend lectures on how to destroy Democracy and obviously, the main focus of these lectures centres around the Democratic Republic of America.

Having graduated from the UOAQ with honours, Osama was ready to begin formulating his master plan. And having been presented with a top of the range Donkey, as a graduation present from his proud father Natas , Osama quickly set about the task of opening a chain of Terrorist Training Schools. From these schools Osama would invite the 'creme dela creme' to come and work with him.

And soon enough, Osama had assembled a terrifying army; The Army he nostalgically liked to call after his old University: Al Qaeda.

The day of reckoning for Democracy was now finally drawing near.

That day came on September 11 2001. George W Bush, in accordance to his destiny had by now become the President of America. However, the attack, when it came that day was a total surprise to President Bush, the three Kings and the population of America as a whole.

After all - as George Bush said himself - no one could of predicted that 19 aeroplane hijackers, acting on the instructions of Osama Bin Laden, would use stolen airliners as missiles... Could they?

Nevertheless, once the safe, but deadly dust particles had dispersed, George Bush immediately flew to New York to inspect the devastation caused by the hijackers. Incensed by the loss of life Bush, backed by God and the full military might of America, fearlessly Lead his troops into war against the Axis of Evil - from the safety of the White House.

However, it would be nearly a further full 10 years before Osama Bin Laden, would finally be brought to justice and in doing so, put an end to Al-Qaeda. And by then America would have a new President, while George W Bush would be busy doing God's work elsewhere.

But there is not a man alive today who can deny that they don't owe President George Walker Bush a big thank you for replacing freedom with security.
Thank you Mr President, Thank you very much indeed.

The End...#

Don't you just love a good fairy tale? And to be fair, as fairy tales go, that ones a cracker.
Mind you, the truly frightening thing is, that the way things are going those are more or less the exact words that our great, great Grandchildren will be having drummed into their young minds in the future.

In fact, the more aware that you become of what's happening around us right now, then the easier it becomes to predict the school history lessons of the future. Course, by that time, even if there is anyone still alive able to pour scorn on the story, the level of fear imposed on the masses by the state will be such that those people will keep silent.

That is unless the vast majority of people very quickly wise up and do something to stop it. The only problem with that is that the masses are more likely to believe the unbelievable rather than the believable.

A typical example of this was demonstrated on Facebook just last week. You see, a computer nerd somewhere, whose world probably ends at his bedroom door, posted a status declaring that Facebook was about to start charging people to use it.

He added to this statement, a series of tariffs and the instruction for readers to Copy & Paste and within days it was global news on Facebook; not to mention widely accepted as fact.

Indeed, this belief in the nerd's status led to the threat of mass boycotts of the networking site by its members. Others still were saying that charging to use FB was bound to happen sooner or later. Yet none of those who reposted the status had bothered to check on its authenticity.

Not that it should have been necessary to do so in the first place. I mean had these sheeple taken a moment to think about it logically then they would have realised that not only would it have been a disaster for Facebook to start charging; it also wouldn't have been workable for the simple fact that many people - especially the young - don't have credit cards to pay online subscriptions.

Moreover, even if Mark Zuckerberg was silly enough to start charging, I think he would have announced the decision himself, rather than let a computer nerd with too much time on his hands do it.

And therein lies the problem. You see, rather than think for themselves, people are prepared to believe the unbelievable.

So okay, maybe my fairy tale is a bit tongue in cheek, but it's still pretty close to the official version of events surrounding 9/11.

It is in fact quite fair to say, bearing in mind the various means available for mass communication these days, that there shouldn't be anyone on earth who, in possession of more than 2 brain cells, still buys into the official version of events surrounding 9/11 and Osama Bin Laden.

Yet the vast majority of people do, despite the official version being a lot more unbelievable than the truth. And as if proof of this mindset was necessary, someone recently said to me that although the Government version of 9/11 was full of holes, the said Government couldn't be behind the attacks because they would know that they would never get away with it.

Yet it is precisely that kind of warped logic that allows our Governments to get away with it. Wasn't it Hitler's propaganda minister, Joseph Goebbels who said; "*The bigger the lie, the more it will be believed"?*

This fact was again clearly demonstrated on May 2nd 2011, the day that Bin Laden finally (According to the American Government) met his maker. The only thing that surprised me about that day is that it wasn't henceforth declared a world holiday. You could in fact, almost feel the Earth sag as it let out a collective, huge sigh of relief now that the Devil incarnate was finally dead.

Yet the fact that Bin Laden was a highly paid CIA agent, who according to a Government source actually died in late 2001 from kidney failure, seemingly counts for nothing. Neither did the fact that despite there not being a shred of evidence to link Bin Laden with 9/11, it didn't stop the BBC, ITV or any other news station for that matter, broadcasting him as being the brains behind the attacks.

The fact that they did was nothing short of slander. After all, even The FBI were not brazen enough to actually accuse him of being responsible for 9/11. At least not on their 'most wanted' poster, which while mentioning the many crimes that he's wanted for, does not mention 9/11 as being one of them.

Therefore the fact that the BBC did name him as being responsible, while supposedly being an impartial, unbiased TV network, is justification alone to stop paying the TV licence fee. That is if you are one of those people still silly enough to be paying it. The truth is that on May 2nd 2011, the masses were sold another fairy tale, one that they were only too eager to believe and one that; had they sat and thought about it logically, they would have seen it for what it is.

For starters, the American President, Barack Obama - with his support rating at an all time low - needed a popularity boost, especially with the 2012 election looming.

So, in order to boost his ratings (*which worked spectacularly in the short term*) the pentagon had us believe that after 10 years of frantic searching for Bin Laden in caves, nooks and crannies in and around the Middle East and with the best tracking equipment known to man, the Terrorist leader was finally located in a large luxury compound in Abbottabad in Pakistan.

Then, having finally found him and without bothering to inform the Pakistani Government, we are told that Navy SEALS in conjunction with CIA operatives, stormed the compound in a covert operation which ended in the death of Bin Laden... Or should that have been Bin Had?

Now can you Imagine the uproar from the US Govt, if that scenario had been the other way round?

We are then told that, despite Obama and his top Government Cronies supposedly watching this operation taking place live, via satellite pictures (*beats watching a John Wayne DVD I suppose*), all of the initial news reports on the operation were still confusing, conflicting and totally wrong.

In fact all of those early bulletins led us to believe that a fierce firefight had taken place between the Navy SEALS and Bin Laden's bodyguards, who supposedly put up massive resistance.

The yarn then went on to tell us that once those bodyguards had been dispensed with, the SEALS then allegedly located a heavily armed Bin Laden who was finally killed only after bullets had been exchanged by both sides.

Course, whether Bin Laden's "*You'll never take me alive*" last stand made the 'Terrorist' sound too heroic for Obama and Co's liking isn't known. Nevertheless, for one reason or another, the TV and Radio news reports on the operation quickly changed scenarios and we were in fact, now being told that Bin Laden was found unguarded.

Yet reports had it that he was still heavily armed himself while watching TV with his wife... Plausible. After all, isn't it common practice for all terrorists to watch Coronation Street with one arm around the wife and the other around a submachine gun?

However, I digress.
Now, when the SEALS entered his home, a gun battle ensued with Bin Laden, who we are told immediately used his wife as a human shield... Pat on the backs for the White-House spin doctors since Bin Laden was now made to sound like a bit of a coward.

Fast forward a few more hours and the White House press office were still not totally happy. This led to a further improved, final version of events that now had the Navy SEALS storming the unguarded compound where an unarmed Bin Laden was found watching TV with his wife and who In a bid to escape, got his comeuppance.

However, before meeting his maker, Bin Laden had grabbed hold of his wife to use her as a human shield and then pathetically begged for his life while screaming and crying like a frightened schoolgirl. If in doing so Bin Laden was hoping to be spared then his ploy failed miserably because the SEALS shot him anyway.

Now, that being the case, am I the only one left thinking that this means Bin Laden was murdered in cold blood? I mean, does the law not say that everyone, regardless of race, colour, creed or crime is entitled to a fair trial? Apparently not, at least according to the way the American Government defines justice. But as usual, I once again digress.

Bin Laden's bullet ridden body was then supposedly photographed... Although it was later admitted by the Pentagon that no such photos exist. The [non] photo session was then swiftly followed by a quick search of his house, after which the SEALS - along with Bin Laden's body - quickly evacuated the scene of the crime.

Bin Laden's body was then, or so we are informed, quickly buried at sea. This was despite him not having or coming from a Naval background. No details of the funeral were given, but under the circumstances I can't imagine that it was a very dignified send off.

Yet having now paid the ultimate price for his supposed crimes, was the man not entitled to a decent funeral? Was his family not entitled to say their goodbyes? Once again, apparently not.

We are told that one of the reasons for the quick burial was out of respect for Muslims whose faith requires that their dead to be buried within 24 hrs. Strangely enough, no mention was made of the Muslim Cleric who presided over this Muslim funeral. Presumably there was one? Then again, once more, perhaps not.

The other reason given for the quick burial at sea was apparently to stop Bin Laden's grave becoming a shrine for fundamental extremists. This again is nonsense. I mean when the Child murderer Myra Hindley died, such was the hatred directed towards her from a still angry public that the home office had great difficulty finding an undertaker willing to carry out a funeral. Nevertheless, one was found and her funeral took place late at night, in a secret location.

Furthermore, the worlds press soon got wind of this secret location but the funeral still, nevertheless, went ahead. Hindleys body was immediately cremated and her ashes scattered at a secret location of her own choosing. So, if we in the UK can do it and with the location of the body already known, then why couldn't the Americans do it with a body that could have been anywhere for all that the press knew?

Moreover, the American Government assured us that DNA samples taken from Bin Laden's body proved that the man they allegedly shot dead was indeed who he was meant to be. The fact that this was confirmed before it was scientifically possible to obtain DNA results - given the time frame and location of his death - apparently mattered not one iota to the worlds press.

We were further told that evidence taken from his house proved that Bin Laden was still a threat to world safety and still very much the top man in the Al Qaeda terrorist organisation. At the same time, the Pentagon contradicted themselves by telling the world that Bin Laden was a pathetic shadow of his former self who spent his days watching old Videos of himself taunting the West and bragging about his exploits.

Presumably these videos of long gone glory days that this frail, tired old man watched, were the ones which had over the course of the 10 year manhunt, subsequently been proven as being CIA fakes.

Nevertheless, the Powers that be in their haste to humiliate Bin Laden further, released a tape (*allegedly also found at his compound*) showing him sat in front of a small TV (*Hardly the type of TV that a multi millionaire living it up in the lap of luxury would have*) watching his glory days.

We are further lead to believe that this taped footage is a home movie which being the case, is most strange and surely begs the question; *who takes a home movie but only films the subject from behind, never once giving the viewer a clear shot of the subjects face?*

We are also told that Bin Laden's body was photographed after he'd been murdered. The world population then held their breath while the US Government agonised over whether or not to release these Photos to further prove beyond all doubt that it was indeed Bin Laden who was killed that night. Finally and very predictably it was decided that the Photographs were far too gruesome for people to see… Although as I say, it was later stated that no such photos exist.

Nevertheless, presumably the top brass in Washington DC have never heard of Heaven666.com whose website shows the most gruesome film footage and photographs known to man.

Likewise, they must neither have heard of the book Author, Bernard O'Mahoney, whose website will allow you to view extremely graphic autopsy photographs of 3 Essex Gangsters, all shot twice in the head at point blank range with a shotgun. Perhaps Bin Laden's head exploded differently to these 3 gangsters heads which are seen in these easily accessible photos?

Are you starting to get the feeling that you are being mugged off yet? No?
Okay try this for size. After 10 years of fighting the so called war on terror, the Taliban recently scored what was by far their greatest victory after managing to shoot down a US Chinook helicopter using a hand held surface to air rocket launcher. That fete alone would have qualified as being their greatest hit so to speak.

However, the fact that the helicopter allegedly had on board the Navy SEAL'S who had supposedly murdered Osama Bin Laden, lifted the strike to the heights of which fairy tales are truly made of.

Course, the death of Bin Laden twice in the space of 10 years presented the USA with another problem in the form of people wanting to know as to whether his death would now mean an end to the war on terror. And so, in a near state of panic at that prospect, the White House moved quickly to dispel such talk. Indeed, statements were quickly prepared in order to clarify that whilst Bin Laden was indeed dead, Al Qaeda in fact remained a very real threat to world safety.

We were also further informed that because of the Al Qaeda's leader's death, we were now all in grave danger of being blown to kingdom come in revenge attacks. Now, while it's all very well convincing the general public that they are still at risk, if there are no bombs going off that threat becomes an empty one.

So, in order to keep the public living in fear, the FBI were called into action. As a result we were informed via the world media of all manner of terrorist plots being thwarted thanks to the hard working undercover FBI agents*.

What the media neglected to mention however, was that these hard working undercover agents were targeting street gangs and promising them vast fortunes in return for planting bombs at locations of the FBI's choosing. Course, your average street gang has limited access to bombs and weapons, but no problem because the FBI provided them also.

Then, just before these street gangs could carry out the FBI's orders, they were all arrested. Unfortunately there are only so many times that the Feds can plan a terrorist attack, finance it , provide the means to carry it out and then arrest those that they have coerced into doing it.

Furthermore, a thwarted terrorist attack actually means very little to Joe Public.
Enter Anwar al-Awlaki, the new public enemy number 1. Yes, just as things were finally beginning to quieten down the US Government proudly announced their latest victory in the war on terror. This victory came in the form of the death of Al Qaeda's new top man , Anwar al-Awlaki. The Pentagon claim that his death came about by American air strikes after he had been located hiding in the Yemen.

And in order to further appease the sceptics, the Americans then had the Yemeni Defence Ministry back their claim. That ought to have been an end to it had it not been for the fact that like Bin Laden before himself, al-Awlaki was also a CIA agent with high ranking friends in the American government.

Mind you, the coincidences don't end there either, because just like Bin Laden, al-Awlaki had already died once before - prior to his second death. Furthermore, as coincidence would have it, al-Awlaki's first demise in December 2009 had happened in pretty much the same way as his second death had.

Still, you have to hand it to the American government, they are nothing if not consistent. So after putting their heads together they come up with 'Haqqanis'... Who?

Exactly... Now according to 'whistle blower' Paul Craig Roberts, a former assistant secretary of the US treasury as well as the former associate editor of the Wall Street Journal, Haqqanis are a terrorist organisation, far deadlier than Al Qaeda.

Strange then that practically nobody outside of military intelligence has ever heard of them before. Having said that, pretty much nobody had ever heard of Al Qaeda prior to 9/11. That is except for the CIA and the Mujahideen, for whom Al Qaeda, meaning 'The Base', was a code word used by both during the Afghanistan- Russian war.

Nevertheless, this sudden emergence of Haqqanis was brought about to serve two purposes, the first of which was to scare the public now that Al Qaeda had passed their sell by date. The second purpose, according to Paul Craig Roberts was far more sinister and could eventually lead to Armageddon.

Now there can be no doubt that the USA has been trying to provoke Pakistan for some time. This fact was clearly demonstrated in the alleged covert operation to assassinate Bin Laden. So, with that in mind it comes as no surprise then that Haqqanis supposedly hail from Pakistan, where as Al Qaeda wasn't tied to any specific country.

Moreover, the Chairman of the US joint Chiefs of Staff, Admiral Mike mullen claims that Haqqanis are tied to the Pakistani intelligence service, ISI and it was on their orders that Haqqanis attacked the American Embassy in Kabul, Afghanistan on Sept 13th 2011, along with a US Military base in Wadak Province.

These attacks lead Warmongering US Senator Lindsey Graham, a member of the Armed Services Committee to declare that there was "*broad bipartisan support*" within Congress for a military attack on Pakistan. Add this to the usual verbal diarrhoea banded about by US politicians that Pakistan is an unstable Nuclear Power and gives shelter to anti American Factions and it is not so much a question of will America invade Pakistan but more a question of When?

The Pakistani Prime Minister,Yousuf Raza Gilani certainly seems to think so anyway. He recently called his Foreign Minister home from talks in Washington and ordered an emergency meeting of the Government to assess the prospect of an American Invasion.

However, according to some Knowledgeable analysts, the real reason behind any US invasion of Pakistan would be more to do with the country's location than the perceived threat from Haqqanis. You see, Pakistan borders with China and as such is the ideal place to launch WW3.

Certainly now would be the right time to do it what with the financial meltdown looking inevitable, Russia in disarray and China preoccupied with dealing with the problems associated with their rapid economic growth. An American invasion of Pakistan on this basis is certainly more plausible than an invasion because of a terrorist organisation. Particularly so if the Foreign Minister of Pakistan, Hina Rabbani Khar is to be believed. He claims that for many years Haqqanis were the Blue eyed boys of the CIA.

You really couldn't make it up y'know.

*On the 14th of May 2012, naturalnews.com released the following article:

If it seems as though the FBI is making a large number of terror busts these days, maybe it's because the agency itself is at least partly responsible for hatching the plots. That has some political observers wondering if the FBI's strategies are making the best use of the nation's limited counterterrorist resources.

In recent months, FBI agents have arrested suspects who were planning a range of terrorist attacks, from shooting Stinger missiles at military aircraft to driving van loads of explosives into crowded events. But these amazing cases might not have ever been made if the FBI itself wasn't themselves planning the attacks.

A number of these cases were profiled recently in a New York Times op-ed column, which noted that the so-called plots were devised by an agency that seems to be operating as if the nation is so devoid of legitimate threats that it needs to manufacture some in order to seem relevant.

Withstanding legal scrutiny, but still questionable
*Consider the case of Oregon college student Mohamed Osman Mohamud. He thought about using a car bomb to attack a well-attended, festive Christmas tree-lighting ceremony in Portland. The FBI gave him a van packed with **inert** explosives consisting of some real, but inactive, detonators and six 55-gallon drums, along with a gallon of diesel fuel. **An FBI agent even drove the van.** When Mohamud called the cell phone number that was supposed to trigger the explosion, nothing explosive happened, except that he got arrested.*

Was Mohamud seriously considering such an attack prior to the FBI involvement? If so, could he have put it together by himself? Was he working with someone else the FBI doesn't know about who is more of a legitimate threat?

216

It's hard to say. Obviously Mohamud was at least having bad thoughts, and that's disconcerting in and of itself (though not criminal). But if the FBI had not manufactured an attack, would he have gone through with anything?

Mohamud's case is far from the only one manufactured by the FBI, and it is certainly not the only one that has held up in court. In fact, such operations are not only legal but they are a common counterterrorism tactic employed by the agency in the post-9/11 world. Terror defendants most often try to claim entrapment, but they also most often lose because the law says as long as they showed at least some intent to commit a terrorist act, even if tempted to do so by undercover agents, they are guilty.

Using even the weak-minded to make a case

"Many times," says Dean Boyd, a Justice Department spokesman, "suspects are warned about the seriousness of their plots and given opportunities to back out." But, the Times report indicates recorded conversations show that the warning is not always given, and that in some cases suspects are even encouraged to continue.

Inventing such cases isn't as easy as, say, manufacturing a sting operation where an alleged drug dealer or arms trafficker sells to an undercover agent. That's because those kinds of crimes occur regularly in the United States.

But David Raskin, a former federal prosecutor told the Times, "There isn't a business of terrorism in the United States, thank God."

"You're not going to be able to go to a street corner and find somebody who's already blown something up," he said. "So the goal is to find someone who isn't engaged in terrorism yet but is looking for a real terrorist who could provide them with an opportunity."

You can sometimes get the impression that maybe the FBI is operating off of some sort of counterterrorism quota. Consider one of the most recent cases of thwarting a planned attack:

*Of five so-called anarchists who were arrested for ostensibly planning to destroy a bridge in Ohio in late April, three of them had documented mental health issues. One was even talked out of committing suicide in February,***right before he was enticed to join in the plot by an FBI informant.**

Chapter 22
MONEY MADE EASY

This was the first of many articles that I have written on the money-scam employed by the Monster Elite in order to keep us down at heel...

♫I work all night, I work all day, to pay the bills I have to pay♫
Ain't it sad
And still there never seems to be a single penny left for me.♫
♫That's too bad
In my dreams I have a plan
If I got me a wealthy man
♫I wouldn't have to work at all, I'd fool around and have a ball♫...
Money, money, money♫
Must be funny
♫In the rich man's world
Money, money, money
Always sunny♫
In the rich man's world
Aha-ahaaa
♫All the things I could do
If I had a little money
♫It's a rich man's world ♫
...*MONEY, MONEY, MONEY - ABBA song 1976.*

I wonder if Benny Andersson and Bjorn Ulvaeus, the composers of the above song were aware that when they penned the hit record 36 years ago, that there is much more to be derived from the lyrics than is first obvious... Of course they were.

Course, back in 1976 nowhere near as many people as today were aware of the global money scam, although even now those numbers are still nowhere near enough to put a halt to it.

Therefore the purpose of this article is to try and educate those that don't know.

Now, there can be no doubt in anyone's mind that it is indeed a rich man's world. However, truly accurate figures as to how much of a rich man's world planet earth is are few and far between, but if you work on the widely agreed estimate that 85% of the world's wealth is in the hands of 6% of the world's population, then you won't be far off target.

Mind you, exactly how rich that small minority is, it is impossible to say. In all probability these parasites – *for that is what they are* – are so rich, they probably don't know themselves.

However it is grossly obscene that their wealth can be estimated as being in the trillions when there are over a billion people in the world - a large percentage of whom are babies and small children - dying for want of Food, Water and/or Shelter.
Course, the more research you do on the ruling elite, the more obvious it becomes that those poor starving babies etc, are all dying needlessly and the reason for that all boils down to the needs of these rich psychopaths to control us all.

This control is exercised via the money scam which ultimately allows them to impose their will on us. Indeed, it is a fact that there are more than enough resources and space available to ensure that no one amongst the 7 Billion of us need go without the essential food, water and shelter needed in order for a person to survive. And the fact that those three necessities are deprived to some is nothing short of murder by design.

Nevertheless, once you understand the way that the monetary system works it quickly becomes obvious that it is a scam. It is for this very reason that the monetary system is deliberately designed to appear complicated. That way the vast majority of us believe that we will never be able to fathom out the complexities of money and thus make no effort whatsoever to understand it.

Moreover, that fact doesn't just apply to your average Joe. It also applies, albeit to a lesser degree, to financial consultants, Bank Managers and even those so called 'money experts' who appear on our TV's to explain what the latest hike in interest rates means to us all, while at the same time being totally oblivious to the money scam.

In fact, the global elite depend on this ignorance in order to make the scam work. However, the fact that we are being scammed, despite the many smoke screens put in place to hide the fact, just goes to show how pathetic we really are as a species.

Indeed it is bad enough that the scam works on the basis that money is worthless and between 80-90% of money in circulation doesn't actually exist. Furthermore it's almost unbelievable that the scam has been used since the 1700's and is imposed on us as a means of control and enslavement, while at the same time bringing extraordinary wealth and power to those in control.

But what really galls me the most is the fact that we are all so conditioned, controlled, apathetic and gullible that those in the know and who benefit from the scam are so egotistical and hold us in such contempt, that they openly tell us that we are being fleeced!

Two very good examples of this can be seen in the following, famous quotes...

"It is well enough that people of the nation do not understand our banking and monetary system, for if they did, I believe there would be a revolution before tomorrow morning" - **Henry Ford**.

"Give me control of a nation's money and i care not who makes her laws" – **Mayer Amschel Rothschild**.

Now in regard to that first quote given to us by the motor car magnate, Henry Ford, the inference that we are being scammed is blatantly obvious; along with the serious implications as to the nation's reaction should the scam be uncovered.

The second quote is given to us by Mayer Rothschild, the founder of the modern banking system and therefore chief architect of the money scam. So successful is the scam that it is the Rothschild family who now rule the world. What Mayer Rothschild is saying in his quote is that if he had control of the money supply (The printing and issue of currency), which he & his family did and still do, then they are the real owners of the world… And as I say it is they who wield the real power and control over nearly every single nation in the world.

However, before I explain the way that money works and how it is used to control us, which I shall attempt to do in a way that can be understood by all, you should be aware that the scam isn't a con without end.

You see, the purpose of the scam is and always was to transfer the world's wealth into the hands of a few and enslave the rest of the world's population. The scam is now nearing its conclusion I'm afraid to say and boy, when it does are we and our children going to suffer for our and our ancestor's inertia.

Now, we all like to think we know the value of money. Unfortunately the truth is that most of us don't. This is because money is worthless. For example, get a £5 note, a £10 note and a £20 note and look at them. There isn't much difference in size and printed content, so how can a £20 note be worth twice as much as a £10 note and four times as much as a £5 note?

It can't. The truth is all bank notes are printed en masse and cost pence - if that - to produce.
Course, our banknotes were once backed by our country's Gold reserves. This basically meant that the amount of money in circulation was equal to the amount of Gold that the country had. That's why the words '*I promise to pay the bearer...*' are printed on every single one of our bank notes.

Now what those words mean in theory is that you can take your £20 note to the Bank of England and exchange it for £20 worth of Gold.

However in 1931 *(although it could have been as late as 1935)* our banknotes stopped being backed by gold or anything else for that matter. In doing so, they became valueless, thus those printed words, '*I promise to pay the bearer the sum of*' are now a promise without foundation. This means that our banknotes are nothing more than fancy IOU's... And an IOU is a debt.

Therefore our economy is run on debt. But how does money come into being? Or put another way, how does money get into circulation? I mean we know how it circulates. You go to work, get paid a wage, and spend that money in shops or at the pub. Those shops and pubs in turn spend that money on replenishing stocks and so on and so on... But that is only how the *'money go round'* works.

What I want you to ask yourself is; how does new money get into the system? After all, there isn't a man on every street corner with a pot full of cash; handing out brand new £20 notes to anyone walking passed him is there?... No... But new money has to come into circulation somehow doesn't it? ...Yes.

And the way that money comes into circulation is through debt. Now that isn't as confusing as it sounds. What it means is that every time someone takes out a loan or Mortgage, that money is new money.

Course, this is where the banking scam begins. You see, what happens when you go to a bank for a mortgage or a Loan Company for say a car loan is that the money you are leant is not the banks or the loan companies. And it isn't actually leant to you either, because it is new money that you have created out of thin air, via your signature.

However, I can imagine that there are a few readers scratching their heads right now, which is fine. After all, I did the very same thing the first time I heard that. Mind you, it really is quite straightforward though.

You see, what I am saying is that the company who you believe that you are borrowing money from, be it a Bank or Loan company does not lend you a penny of their own or anyone one else's money... The law - for all intents and purposes - forbids it for a start.

Instead, what happens is that your signature allows the Bank of England to type the figure you want to borrow onto a computer and add interest to it (More on that added interest later).

And that money, which is no more than numbers on a computer screen, is now in circulation. Yet the Bank or Loan Company didn't create that money. You did, via your signature that you scribbled at the bottom of the contract. This Money - which only exists on a computer screen - is then paid into your bank account or the bank account of the people you are buying the house or car from.

However, being as that money is only numbers on a computer screen, you will hopefully now have a better understanding as to how 80-90% of money in circulation doesn't actually exist. In fact, if everybody went to their bank at 10 AM in the morning and tried to draw all their money out, the banks would have to lock their doors within minutes - having quickly run out of banknotes.

The scam doesn't end there though. You see, as soon as that nonexistent money that you created - *the bank or loan company certainly didn't create it* - is in your bank account, the bank or loan company who brokered your loan tell you that you have to start paying them that money back... Despite the fact it is your money in the first place.

More unbelievably still, they tell you that you have to pay them your money back with added interest; just too really extract the urine from you... How's that for sheer arrogance, front and greed?

What's more, if you default on paying back that money that never existed in the first place, the bank will legally seize the very real assets from under your feet that you used the nonexistent money to buy them with.

However, you haven't heard anything yet though. That is just the start because not only are you paying your own money back with added interest, under the rules of Fractional Reserve Banking (*And all high street and central banks operate on this system*), the money that you created is doubled by the bank between 10 and 30 times, which they are allowed to pocket for themselves.

Put simply, say you borrow £1000. Now although that £1000 is created by you and as such is your money not the banks, you are made to pay back the £1000 plus interest. Course interest rates vary, so for arguments sake, let's say that the interest comes to £250. That being the case, you needlessly pay back the bank or loan company £1250.

But as I just told you, under Fractional Reserve Banking that money can be doubled up to 30 times. That means that your £1000 has lost you that sum in the belief that it isn't your money, then cost you £1250 to pay the bank back and earned the bank £31,250, just by getting you to sign a piece of paper.

Now imagine hundreds of thousands of people taking out loans everyday for £50,000 or £60,000 a time and you begin to understand where the term '*greedy bankers*' comes from.

The same rules apply to the Government, except they cut out the middle man so to speak and go directly to the bank of England for their loans. Now I want to make this very clear to you that what I am about to say is the one and only reason that this country and virtually every other country in the world is in a mess.

You see, this is the big boy scam if you like. The one that has an ultimate goal, which as you may or may not be aware, has collapsed the Economies of Southern Ireland, Iceland and Greece.

Spain, Italy and Portugal are also very close to collapse and the rest of the world, the UK and the USA included are not far behind them. Therefore, be under no illusions that it is a foregone conclusion that the world economy will collapse at some point in the future and no amount of hot air and bullshit from the likes of our world's leaders and the IMF is going to save us.

Be very aware also, that all our leaders and the IMF along with many other organisations - supposedly there to benefit mankind - are in on the scam. They are puppets put into power by the global elite. And the big-boy-scam was engineered to end in global economic collapse, where at that point, the global elite will have the whole of the world in their pockets.

Indeed, when the collapse finally happens many of us will die as a result of food prices rocketing as the world sinks into a depression, the likes of which has never been seen before.
Then, when enough human misery has been caused and many millions have died, the global elite will step in, wipe off the world's debt and form a one world government - with them as our Lords and masters. Those lucky enough to survive will then become the slaves of the ruling elite.

However, if you doubt any of what I've just divulged then just ask yourself this: Why are countries once rich and prosperous now on the brink of collapse? And if you don't know the answer then I will tell you. It is all because of their and our National Debts.

Think about it? 30 or 40 years ago, a couple would get married, the husband would go out to work and the wife would stay at home raising the kids and they would manage quite nicely on the husband's salary. Nowadays, hardly anyone amongst the working class can survive on one wage. Not only that, look at the cuts to our services. 40 yrs ago you got your dustbins emptied once a week by dustmen who would walk around to your back garden, hoist the metal dustbin over their shoulder, walk it to the dustbin lorry to empty, then return the bin back to your back garden.

There was no talk back then of switching street lighting off after midnight in order to save a few bob on the electricity bill. Neither did you get charged an arm and a leg to park your car… Indeed; it was possible to afford to run a car back then.

Small retail shops also thrived back in the day, whereas now the high streets are deserted waste lands. Neither did the Government have to rely on ever increasing fines, from petty new laws to help balance the books.

Back then, the Police were there to protect us against real crime, not there to rigorously enforce the new petty laws which have reduced them to the status of Revenue Collectors - aggressive, intolerant ones at that.

The NHS is dying on its feet because it is staffed by inexperienced, overworked, underpaid junior doctors or under skilled, cheap foreign doctors. Why? Well basically because of the continual cuts in the NHS budget, that's why.

Yet in reality, the technological age should have meant that we are all better off, so why are we not? The IMF said in November 2011 that they would take whatever steps necessary to save Europe from collapse. I said at the time that they would do nothing and they have done exactly that.

People are dying, in this country through lack of the basics and to my way of thinking that is a gross national outrage and can only be due to government corruption. I could go on and on at the many ways that things are not as they should be, but this article is about money and I think I've given you enough food for thought for now.

I will however just add that while we all get continually poorer, our corrupt, egotistical, self serving MP's think nothing of taking our hard earned money and using it to decorate their 2nd houses while we often struggle to pay the rent on one overcrowded small flat.

The Queen, a wholly unsavoury woman, is another who people pledge their support to yet she just so happens to be the richest woman in the world (estimates put her as a multi trillion air), who thinks nothing of having us pick up the tab for her Grandsons wedding.

Our MP's do not give tuppence for our plight. They are not working for us; they are self serving puppets who are controlled from behind the scenes by the global elite. I will however provide you with unarguable proof of that fact at the end of this article.

Now, before I get back on track, some more quotes are called for:

"I am one of those who do not believe the national debt is a national blessing... it is calculated to raise around the administration a moneyed aristocracy dangerous to the liberties of the country"... 7th US President Andrew Jackson letter to L. H. Coleman of Warrenton, N.C., 29 April 1824

"The drive of the Rockefellers and their allies is to create a one-world government combining supercapitalism and Communism under the same tent, all under their control... Do I mean conspiracy? Yes, I do. I am convinced there is such a plot, international in scope, generations old in planning, and incredibly evil in intent"...Congressman Larry MacDonald.

"The real truth of the matter is, as you and I know, that a financial element in the larger centres has owned the Government ever since the days of Andrew Jackson"...32nd US President Franklin D. Roosevelt, letter to Col. Edward Mandell House (21 November 1933)

"If the American people ever allow private banks to control the issue of their currency, first by inflation and then by deflation, the banks and corporations that will grow up around them will deprive the people of all property until their children wake up homeless on the continent their fathers conquered"...3rd US President Thomas Jefferson 1816.

"I am a most unhappy man. I have unwittingly ruined my country. A great industrial nation is controlled by a system of credit. Our system of credit is concentrated. The growth of the nation, therefore, and all our activities are in the hands of a few

men. We have come to be one of the worst ruled, one of the most completely controlled and dominated governments in the civilized world. No longer a government by free opinion, No longer a government by conviction and the vote of the majority, but a Government by the duress of a small group of dominant men"....28th US President Woodrow Wilson. 1916.

"The world is governed by very different personages from what is imagined by those who are not behind the scenes"...UK Prime Minister Benjamin Disraeli. 1844...

So there you have it, quotes from powerful men telling it like it really is. Now at this point I would ask you to keep the Thomas Jefferson quote at the forefront of your mind. That quote is paramount to what I am about to tell you and take no notice of the fact that Jefferson was talking about America when he made the quote. You see, the exact same applies to every government who allows a private central bank to issue their nations currency. And as I write, there are only 3 countries that don't do that...They are however in the firing line of the USA and the UK.

So what happens when our government needs money that they haven't got? The simple answer is that just like us, they borrow it of course. However, every penny that the Government borrows is supposedly on our behalf and as such we are responsible for paying it back which we do via our taxes.

This borrowed money is what is commonly known as the National Debt, and as I'm sure you all know, it is - according to our government - the size of our National Debt that is to blame for the severe cuts in services that we now have to endure. David *"we're all in this together"* Cameron has said that the national debt has to be reduced at all costs in order for us to have a brighter future… I would therefore now suggest to you that he is an out and out bare faced liar.

Indeed, if it was a case of merely reducing the national debt then why do the cuts have to be so severe? I mean it would make political and common sense to increase the time frame of the reduction and by doing so the cuts to services wouldn't have to be so harsh. This would make it easier on the nation and make him much more popular, which as we know is vital for re-election.

However, the real reason for the severity of cuts in services is because the country is having difficulty making the interest repayments on the national debt. And as long as the interest repayments are being met the country can continue to operate. Course, once we default on the interest repayments the central bank will call in their loans and our economy will collapse.

And that is for all intents and purposes what has happened in Southern Ireland, Greece and Iceland*. Course, they are lucky because they are receiving bailouts from the rest of us. Unfortunately when the rest of the world's economies collapse, there will be no countries left to receive bailouts from.

Not that the cuts have done us any good. In fact far from reducing the National Debt, it has in fact increased and is now for the first time in UK history into the Trillions of pounds. Have you got a Plan B Mr Cameron? No he hasn't... Why not? Because he doesn't need one.

You see, Plan A is working perfectly. The whole idea is to collapse the economy. Yes you read that right but I will repeat it anyway. The whole idea is that the economy will collapse because that is what the bank scam has been working up to.

Course the government, for obvious reasons has to be seen to be trying to prevent this happening but it is a foregone conclusion and here is why: Every time the government goes to the Bank of England (*Our country's central bank*) for a loan, every penny that has been borrowed has interest added on to it. It is for this reason that the national debt can never be paid off and will in fact, on the contrary keep growing until we can no longer afford the interest repayments.

To help you better understand what I mean, here is a very simplified example...

Imagine that there is a village that runs on a barter system. And all is fine until people start getting into debt with one another. This means that the barter system breaks down and needs to be replaced by a monetary system. But there is no money in existence in the village, so I as the village leader go and borrow a thousand pounds from a money lender on the village's behalf. The lender is of course happy to lend me £1000 but he adds interest to it meaning we owe him £1250. I agree to the terms and take the £1000 which I spread around the village so as everyone can pay their debts off and buy food and other essentials. The villagers in turn are going to pay me £5 a week each in tax from their share of the money so as I can pay the loan back. And with the £1000 now in circulation, everyone's happy. But no matter how you look at it, the village still owes £1250 and with only £1000 in circulation it can never be fully paid back. This means eventually that the money is going to be used up, paying back the village debt and I am therefore going to have to borrow more money to keep the village economy going, thus incurring more un-payable interest while at the same time adding more to the village debt...

And this is what has happened to nearly every country in the world but on a much larger scale. Every time our govt borrows money from the central bank, another nail is banged into the UK's coffin...
Course, we are not meant to realise this which gives our chancellor, George Osborne who, it has to be said is another thoroughly despicable character, the confidence to shaft us all while at the same time making him appear to be doing his job.

In fact the term quantitative easing (QE) seems to be the Chancellor of the Exchequer, George Osborne's favourite mantra at the moment. This is a perfect example of those in power deliberately making the money system sound unfathomable to us minions in the hope that we will leave them alone to get on with the job of destroying the country.

Course, there will always be some who are not so easily fobbed off and for this reason Osborne's policy has to be seen to have a purpose. So, on the face of it QE does have some short term benefits, but the long term consequences are dire. Now the reason for this is that QE is really nothing more than putting a lump sum of money into circulation, very much in the same way as I did in the village story.

And the more money that is in circulation the stronger the economy is in terms of growth. However, to simplify that for you look at it as the more money you have in your pocket the more that you can do. Nevertheless, the downside of QE is that the cash injection has to come from somewhere, and that somewhere is the central bank, adding further to the national debt and incurring more interest which can never be paid back.

What is really laughable however, yet not many seemed to have latched onto is that Osborne recently announced that he would need to borrow over £11 Billion more that he had envisaged borrowing (All with un-payable added interest don't forget) to invest in an economy that by his own admission is in dire straits with no immediate signs of recovery.

This policy is on a par with you buying a car without an engine or wheels then borrowing money, way beyond your means, to put an engine in your wheeless car. It makes no financially or common sense whatsoever. Worse still, while the cretin Osborne is borrowing Billions to shore up our failing economy he is giving away more than he's borrowing in foreign aid.

And if you need a comparison for that, it is equivalent to you spending all of your money on food, then giving it all away to a tramp that actually doesn't really need it, and then putting yourself in debt to buy yourself more food albeit less than what you need...Madness.

Now surely you're not naive enough to believe that Cameron, Osborne and all the other loathsome puppets that make up the government, including the opposition parties are not aware of this fact?

And while we are on the subject of failing economies, I would imagine that you are under the misguided notion that we are in recession because *"recessions happen from time to time"*. But believe me; nothing happens in this world without careful planning.

Now, because the central bank is responsible for the money in circulation, which as I have said gets into the system via loans, those who really run the country from behind the scenes are able to control prosperity and depression.

You see, it works like this; the more loans that the banks make, the more money there is in circulation which creates a 'boom'. This is done by lowering interest rates, thus making loans more affordable… And a boom will be purposely created to get people in debt with the bank… Think about it, your jobs going well, the economy is healthy, you have spare cash in your pocket, what better time then than for 1st time house buyers or those looking for a bigger house to take the plunge?

However, once the banks have enough people in their debt they will inevitably raise the interest rates on one pretext or another and at the same time reduce the number of loans that they make. This takes money out of circulation, causing a depression.

And so, with less money now in their pocket and increased repayments due to the raised interest rates people begin defaulting on their loans left right and centre, leaving the banks legally entitled to snatch their assets… And all accomplished by lending money that never existed in the first place.

The same is true for the Stock- Market with stock brokers moving trillions of dollars a day around the financial and banking markets. This gives those with clout the power to decide what stocks go up and what stocks go down, which ones soar and which ones crash. But stock market crashes don't just happen, they are crashed by design. This is what happened in the great American depression of the 1930's. The market was purposely crashed leaving those not in the know bankrupt and ruined, many of whom committed suicide. Meanwhile, those in the inner circle such as Joseph Kennedy, Father of assassinated US President, John F Kennedy made untold fortunes out of people's misery.

That then in a nutshell is how money works and how it is used to control us. This just leaves me the job of revealing to you the indisputable proof that our politicians are corrupt to their core and no more than puppet front men for the global elite.

You see, the way things stand the outcome of the banking scam can only end in a global economic crash, as country after country defaults on their national debt. When this happens, the great depression of the 1930's will look like a picnic compared to the depression that will follow the collapse of the world economy. And all because our leaders borrow money from a central bank. I would now draw your attention back to the earlier quote from Thomas Jefferson.

"If the American – or any other - people ever allow private banks to control the issue of their currency, first by inflation and then by deflation, the banks and corporations that will grow up around them will deprive the people of all property until their children wake up homeless on the continent their fathers conquered"...

You see, never a truer word was spoken. And the proof that this is indeed now the case is all around us, should you just engage your brain, take a break from watching Eastenders or Coronation Street and look at what is unfolding.

But it doesn't have to be this way because a country's government is quite entitled to print its own currency and put it into circulation without added interest. Should this be done, prices right across the board would tumble, creating a boom the likes of which have never been seen before?

Therefore, if our government were truly working for us and had our best interests at the forefront of their minds, that is what they would do. In fact Abraham Lincoln, the 16th US President did this in direct conflict with the American Central Bank rather than pay their interest charges on the money that he needed to borrow to fight the American civil war.

This move cost him his life when he was assassinated by John Wilkes Booth, an assassin funded by the central bank shareholders. And the same can be said for assassinated US President John F Kennedy, who had also put into motion, plans to start printing interest free currency.

Course, assassinations are no longer necessary because it is now the global elite who decide who is to be manoeuvred into Downing Street or the White House, long before the chosen one becomes a household name.

In fact don't ever be fooled into thinking that it is you who decides who is in charge by putting your X on a slip of paper before popping it into a ballot box... Because believe me, you couldn't be more wrong.

*On the 20th of June 2012, the following article was published on itmakessense.com:

Since the 1900's the vast majority of the American population has dreamed about saying "NO" to the Unconstitutional, corrupt, Rothschild/Rockefeller banking criminals, but no one has dared to do so.

Why? If just half of our Nation, and the "1%", who pay the majority of the taxes, just said NO MORE! Our Gov't would literally change over night. Why is it so hard, for some people to understand, that by simply NOT giving your money, to large Corporations, who then send jobs, Intellectual Property, etc. offshore and promote anti-Constitutional rights... You will accomplish more, than if you used violence. In other words... RESEARCH WHERE YOU ARE SENDING EVERY SINGLE PENNY!!! Is that so hard?

The truth of the matter is… No one, except the Icelanders, have to date been the only culture on the planet to carry out this successfully. Not only have they been successful, at overthrowing the corrupt Gov't, they've drafted a Constitution, that will stop this from happening ever again.

That's not the best part… The best part, is that they have arrested ALL Rothschild/Rockefeller banking puppets, responsible for the Country's economic Chaos and meltdown.

Last week 9 people were arrested in London and Reykjavik for their possible responsibility for Iceland's financial collapse in 2008, a deep crisis which developed into an unprecedented public reaction that is changing the country's direction.

It has been a revolution without weapons in Iceland, the country that hosts the world's oldest democracy (since 930), and whose citizens have managed to effect change by going on demonstrations and banging pots and pans. Why have the rest of the Western countries not even heard about it?

Pressure from Icelandic citizens' has managed not only to bring down a government, but also begin the drafting of a new constitution (in process) and is seeking to put in jail those bankers responsible for the financial crisis in the country. As the saying goes, if you ask for things politely it is much easier to get them.

This quiet revolutionary process has its origins in 2008 when the Icelandic government decided to nationalise the three largest banks, Landsbanki, Kaupthing and Glitnir, whose clients were mainly British, and North and South American.

After the State took over, the official currency (krona) plummeted and the stock market suspended its activity after a 76% collapse. Iceland was becoming bankrupt and to save the situation, the International Monetary Fund (IMF) injected U.S. $ 2,100 million and the Nordic countries helped with another 2,500 million.

Great little victories of ordinary people

While banks and local and foreign authorities were desperately seeking economic solutions, the Icelandic people took to the streets and their persistent daily demonstrations outside parliament in Reykjavik prompted the resignation of the conservative Prime Minister Geir H. Haarde and his entire government.

Citizens demanded, in addition, to convene early elections, and they succeeded. In April a coalition government was elected, formed by the Social Democratic Alliance and the Left Green Movement, headed by a new Prime Minister, Jóhanna Sigurðardóttir.

Throughout 2009 the Icelandic economy continued to be in a precarious situation (at the end of the year the GDP had dropped by 7%) but, despite this, the Parliament proposed to repay the debt to Britain and the Netherlands with a payment of 3,500 million Euros, a sum to be paid every month by Icelandic families for 15 years at 5.5% interest.

The move sparked anger again in the Icelanders, who returned to the streets demanding that, at least, that decision was put to a referendum. Another big small victory for the street protests: in March 2010 that vote was held and an overwhelming 93% of the population refused to repay the debt, at least with those conditions.

This forced the creditors to rethink the deal and improve it, offering 3% interest and payment over 37 years. Not even that was enough. The current president, on seeing that Parliament approved the agreement by a narrow margin, decided last month not to approve it and to call on the Icelandic people to vote in a referendum so that they would have the last word.
The bankers are fleeing in fear

Returning to the tense situation in 2010, while the Icelanders were refusing to pay a debt incurred by financial sharks without consultation, the coalition government had launched an investigation to determine legal responsibilities for the fatal economic crisis and

had already arrested several bankers and top executives closely linked to high risk operations.
Interpol, meanwhile, had issued an international arrest warrant against Sigurdur Einarsson, former president of one of the banks. This situation led scared bankers and executives to leave the country en masse.

In this context of crisis, an assembly was elected to draft a new constitution that would reflect the lessons learned and replace the current one, inspired by the Danish constitution.
To do this, instead of calling experts and politicians, Iceland decided to appeal directly to the people, after all they have sovereign power over the law. More than 500 Icelanders presented themselves as candidates to participate in this exercise in direct democracy and write a new constitution. 25 of them, without party affiliations, including lawyers, students, journalists, farmers and trade union representatives were elected.

Among other developments, this constitution will call for the protection, like no other, of freedom of information and expression in the so-called Icelandic Modern Media Initiative, in a bill that aims to make the country a safe haven for investigative journalism and freedom of information, where sources, journalists and Internet providers that host news reporting are protected.

The people, for once, will decide the future of the country while bankers and politicians witness the transformation of a nation from the sidelines.

Chapter 23
Never in the field of human conflict was so much owed by so many to so few - Winston Churchill... He wasn't fucking lying, dontcha know

This article takes a look at democracy & hypocrisy...

We supposedly live in a Democracy don't we?

Well yes we do, but we don't... Well not really anyway.
That is unless you describe a Democracy as a country that gives you the illusion of choice whereby you can cast a vote that will realistically allow one of two political parties - who given the majority of these votes - the power to form a Government.

But that is where the Democracy ends and as I have just stated; your vote is an illusion of choice - Nothing more.
I mean ask yourself this; *"Has any political party in government ever made a real difference to your standard of living"*? And no doubt some of you will say "yes" and point to Maggie Thatcher's Tory Govt of the 1980's.

And to be fair, strictly speaking, I suppose for some of you that could be said to be true. However, I doubt it was to a life changing extent. Furthermore, Maggie's reign was put in place to create that false boom. Indeed, it would have been the same type of boom no matter who was at the helm of the Conservative party at the time.

Now I was one of those people working while Maggie in power although personally, I actually earned a lot more money while the Corpse masquerading as John Major was the Prime Mincer. And that was only through my own hard work because there was actually a major recession on at the time (no pun intended).

Furthermore - and as Maggie knew all too well - the prosperity of the "*Loadsa Money*" 1980's was brought about at the vast cost to future generations. You see, what Maggie Fuctcher actually did was deliberately take away the power and rights of the the working man, in what was then, the beginning of an agenda to strip future generations of their basic civil liberties - An agenda that has not only worked to perfection, but has also still gone pretty much unnoticed by the vast majority of the dumbed down UK population; a population who are too preoccupied with modern gadgets and propaganda TV programs to even notice or care.

Course, in order to do so she had to fool the nation into thinking that she was the greatest leader since the war time Rothschild puppet, Winston Churchill - Another corrupt, depraved politician who to this day is still unbelievably hailed as a hero... He wasn't, he was in fact corrupt to the core.

So, what better way to fool a gullible population then, than giving them the illusion that they were well off?

Nevertheless, the truth is that there isn't a choice in our democracy. The Conservative Party is the Labour Party is The Liberal Party is the UK Independence Party. Choosing which one to vote for is no different from choosing whether to shop in Tesco, Sainsbury's, Morrisons or Asda... They all sell the same packages at the same price.

Furthermore, until the population as a whole wake up nothing will ever change. Britain is governed by Europe who in turn is governed by the Corporations and Banksters via elitist groups such as Bilderberg.

Course, if you are still under the delusion that our government are working for us, just ask yourself this question: "*Why do the Government continue to borrow £billions on a daily basis from a*

Central Bank, when that borrowed money is lent with added interest"?

Did you know that our corrupt, puppet leaders are entitled to print their own currency - with no added interest? ... But they don't.
Did you know that if they did exercise that right to print their own currency, prices would go into free fall for literally everything from food and clothing right through to houses and cars... But still they don't.

Furthermore, if the Government turned around and flatly refused to pay off the National Debt - a debt deliberately acquired through corruption and stealth - your income tax would be a tiny fraction of what it is now... If anything at all... But they won't.

In fact our Government - which ever Political flag they masquerade behind - has the ability to give us a lifestyle that we can only dream about. In fact, all of the Governments of the world have that power... But they won't.

You see, they won't adhere to any of the above because the government are not working for us. In fact, by voting them into power we are actually contributing to our own misery... And we are supposedly the most intelligent life on Earth. Really? We don't sound very intelligent to me.

So once we have exercised our 'democratic right' to vote in a Government, that in theory may be the choice of just over half of the population, any sort of democracy that we imagine we had, promptly disappears.

Indeed, promises that elected these carefully pre-selected politicians to power are quickly broken with excuses like "*We couldn't possibly have foreseen....* " or "*We find ourselves unable to make good on our promise to Blah Blah Blah, because of the mess that the last Government left us to clear up*".
They are then free to spend the next 3-5 years doing what the hell they please. Course you can be sure that in doing so, they are not

serving us or looking after our interests... Not by any stretch of the imagination. For instance:

Would you choose to give away borrowed Billions - With added interest - in foreign aid, to superpowers such as India?

Would you choose to give away borrowed Billions - With added interest - to prop up a currency that is nothing to do with us and which we opted out of joining?

Would you choose to add to the decline of our country's crumbling economy - An economy that by our own Chancellor of the Exchequer's admission can expect to see negative growth over the next 5 years - by injecting billions of pounds, borrowed with added interest in the form of 'Quantitative Easing'? Especially while at the same time knowing that in doing so, you will cause further problems in the not too distant future?

I strongly suspect not.
And who benefits from the above? We the people certainly don't...
But the Central Bankers do... Oh don't they just. So you tell me;
Where is the Democracy?

In fact it is this corrupt, unnecessary borrowing that has led to our Trillion Pound and rising National Debt. A debt that can never be repaid because of the added interest... Unless of course our Queen does the noble thing and pays it off for us... She could... But she wont.

Course, a Trillion Pound is just a figure as far as the apathetic population of the UK is concerned. I mean have you ever given a thought to just how much a Trillion Pound is?
A trillion Pounds = £1,000,000,000,000. That's 12 zeroes to the left of the decimal point. A trillion is a million million Pounds.

And by way of an example; if your take home pay after taxes was £10,000 per hour and you worked 8 hours a day, 50 weeks a year (2 weeks off for good behaviour), You would have to work 50,000 years to earn one trillion Pounds.

Yet that is the extent of the National debt run up by those supposedly acting in our best interests. And if you believe that they are then you will believe anything. Our Government are merely front men for those who really hold power.

In fact, the depths that our puppet government leaders are prepared to sink to in order to gain a pat on the head from their masters is absolutely breathtaking.

For instance yesterday, without the merest hint of shame and seemingly totally oblivious to his own hypocrisy, David Cameron, a pampered, smarmy public schoolboy, publicly slammed Comedian Jimmy Carr for daring to legally save himself a few quid in taxes. And what do we pay our Taxes for?

Well, the majority of our tax payments go towards paying the interest repayments on a National Debt which as I have just said, is now over a Trillion Pounds.

A National debt that despite tough austerity measures is still rising.

A National debt that Criminals like Cameron and his equally corrupt chancellor George Osborne add to on a daily basis by borrowing Billions of pounds - with added interest - from the Central Bank, whether we like it or not.

Take Greece, a prime example of what happens when you can't afford to pay the interest on your national debt. Unemployment there is rife, wages have been slashed to below poverty levels. Basic amenities such as Gas, Electric and running water are no longer guaranteed.

Suicide rates have gone through the roof. People are queueing in their thousands for free food handouts - handouts by those more fortunate I hasten to add, not by the Greek government. And worst of all, children are being abandoned by families who are no longer able to feed them - Economic Collapse, coming to a country near you sooner than you think.

Course, you won't hear any government say that the problem was caused by the central bank scam... Ohhh no.
You will however hear the likes of IMF chief Christine Lagarde - The Central Banks pet puppet - blame the Greeks for bringing the problem on themselves for... Wait for it... Not paying their taxes.

Taxes that would have gone towards making the interests repayments on their National debt... That was created through the Greek Government borrowing from the Central bank instead of printing their own currency.

In fact there is only one word that I can use to describe Christine Lagarde and that word is Cunt. And while that word may offend some readers, answer me this; What do you call a person who sits in judgement of others for not paying their taxes while earning a tax free yearly salary of £298,675 topped up with a tax free allowance of £83,760, payable without justification?

A Cunt perhaps?

Finally, let's have a look at our Prime Ministers breathtaking hypocrisy that I made mention of earlier. Below is just one of the many articles published yesterday in the Corporate owned mainstream media giving details about Cameron's condemnation of Jimmy Carr.
Immediately below that article is another article published in the Guardian in April of this year, the contents of which are self explanatory... You really couldn't make it up, don't cha know.

DAVID CAMERON SLAMS COMEDIAN JIMMY CARR'S 'MORALLY WRONG' TAX ARRANGEMENT.

244

20/6/12

Prime Minister David Cameron today branded comedian Jimmy Carr "morally wrong" for seeking to avoid taxes.
In an interview with ITV News, he said reports of Carr's tax arrangements suggested that he was involved in "straightforward tax avoidance".

And he said it was unfair on the people who pay to watch the comic perform that he is not paying his taxes in the same way that they do. Speaking during a round of TV interviews during his trip to Mexico, the PM said: "I think some of these schemes - and I think particularly of the Jimmy Carr scheme - I have had time to read about and I just think this is completely wrong.

"People work hard, they pay their taxes, they save up to go to one of his shows. They buy the tickets. He is taking the money from those tickets and he, as far as I can see, is putting all of that into some very dodgy tax avoiding schemes.

"That is wrong. There is nothing wrong with people planning their tax affairs to invest in their pension and plan for their retirement - that sort of tax management is fine.
"But some of these schemes we have seen are quite frankly morally wrong.
"The Government is acting by looking at a general anti avoidance law but we do need to make progress on this.

"It is not fair on hard working people who do the right thing and pay their taxes to see these sorts of scams taking place."
Mr Cameron said he had not had time to look at allegations relating to singer Gary Barlow, who has also been subject to newspaper investigations.
It comes after Mr Carr broke his silence over claims that he dodged tax, insisting: "I pay what I have to and not a penny more."

The funnyman is said to have used an aggressive - but legal - tax-avoidance scheme which enables members to pay income tax rates as low as 1%.

Carr, who has famously lampooned fat cat bankers, reportedly protects some £3.3 million a year by channelling cash through Jersey-based company K2 which then returns the money in the form of a loan. This is not subject to income tax.

He spoke out last night amid claims that members of Take That - Gary Barlow, Howard Donald, Mark Owen and their manager Jonathan Wild - invested at least £26 million in another scheme run by Icebreaker Management Services.

Carr was confronted over his own financial arrangements during a show in Tunbridge Wells, in Kent.

Challenged by a member of the audience who told him "You don't pay tax", he replied: "I pay what I have to and not a penny more", The Times reported.

It came after he appeared to make light of the furore surrounding his payments to HM Revenue and Customs (HMRC).

He asked: "Got through the papers? I haven't really been through the papers today. The Murdochs are after me..."

Carr is said to be one of more than 1,000 beneficiaries who shelter some £168 million from the taxman each year using K2.

Fellow comic Frankie Boyle took to Twitter in apparent condemnation of his alleged tax-avoidance.

He wrote: "It's ok to avoid tax providing every time you do a joke about a town being s*** you add 'Partly down to me I'm afraid' under your breath."

Carr courted controversy last year after making a joke about a car crash in the wake of a pile-up on the M5 that claimed seven lives. Writing on Twitter, he said: "An (sic) couple married for 66 yrs died within 3 days of each other.

"That's nothing. My grandparents died on exactly the same day.... car crash."

He later apologised, insisting his remarks did not relate to the accident in Somerset.

Barlow, Donald, Owen and Wild are among almost 1,000 people who contributed £480 million to 62 partnerships in music industry investment schemes, The Times reported.

A Revenue and Customs spokesman said it had successfully challenged an avoidance scheme run by Icebreaker 1 LLP, winning on the main arguments in the tribunals.

The spokesman said: "This type of scheme will fail where there is circular borrowing which serves no economic purpose or which cannot, in fact, be used in a trade.

"We are now preparing to litigate Icebreaker 2 but for legal reasons cannot say more at this time.

"We examine the implementation of avoidance schemes in detail and will not let any aspect of these cases go unchallenged."

HMRC said the K2 scheme was already under investigation.

THE GUARDIAN

CAMERON FAMILY FORTUNE MADE IN TAX HAVENS

20/4/12

David Cameron's father set up offshore investment funds which explicitly boasted of their ability to remain outside UK tax jurisdiction. Photograph: Dan Kitwood/PA

David Cameron*'s father ran a network of offshore investment funds to help build the family fortune that paid for the prime minister's inheritance, the Guardian can reveal.*

Though entirely legal, the funds were set up in tax havens such as Panama City and Geneva, and explicitly boasted of their ability to remain outside UK tax jurisdiction.

At the time of his death in late 2010, Ian Cameron left a fortune of £2.74m in his will, from which David Cameron received the sum of £300,000.

Cameron and other cabinet members have recently suggested that they would be willing to disclose their personal tax filings amid growing scrutiny following the budget, but this would only shed light on annual sources of income rather than accumulated wealth or inheritance.

The structure employed by Cameron senior is now commonplace among modern hedge funds, which argue that offshore status can help attract international investors. UK residents would ordinarily have to pay tax on any profits they repatriated, and there is nothing to suggest the Camerons did not.

Nevertheless, the dramatic growth of such offshore financial activity has raised concerns that national tax authorities are struggling to pin down the world's super-rich.

Ian Cameron took advantage of a new climate of investment after all capital controls were abolished in 1979, making it legal to take any sum of money out of the country without it being taxed or controlled by the UK government.

Not long after the change, brought in by Margaret Thatcher after her first month in power, Ian Cameron began setting up and directing investment funds in tax havens around the world.

Leaving his full-time role as a City stockbroker, Ian Cameron went on to act as chairman of Close International Asset management, a multimillion-pound investment fund based in Jersey; as a senior director of Blairmore Holdings Inc, registered in Panama City and currently worth £25m; and he was also a shareholder in Blairmore Asset Management based in Geneva.

However, the family will – a public document seen by the Guardian – only details the assets of Ian Cameron's estate in England and Wales. Offshore investments would only be listed in submissions to HMRC for inheritance tax purposes. It is unclear what those assets – if any – are worth and which family member owns them.

In 2009 the compilers of the Sunday Times Rich List estimated Ian Cameron's wealth at £10m.

He was survived by his wife, Mary Fleur Cameron, who as his spouse would not have had to pay inheritance tax on sums transferred between them.

In 2006 Ian's eldest son, Alexander, became the sole owner of the family's £2.5m house in Newbury, Berkshire, where David had been brought up.

Another family home in Kensington, London, worth £1m, passed to his two daughters in equal share.

Cameron's father was "instrumental" in setting up the Panamanian company, Blairmore Holdings, in 1982, which was exempt from UK tax, when David was a pupil at Eton aged 16.

The fund shares its name with the family's ancestral home in Aberdeenshire, Blairmore House, in which Ian Cameron was born in 1932 but which the family no longer owns.

A lengthy prospectus for Blairmore Holdings written in 2006 and meant to attract high net worth "sophisticated" investors, with at least $100,000 to buy shares, is explicit about how the fund sought to avoid UK tax. At the time more than half of the fund's 11 directors were UK nationals.

Under Panamanian law the fund was excluded from taxation derived from other parts of the world.

"The fund is not liable to taxation on its income or capital gains as long as such income or capital gains are not derived from sources allocated within the territory of the Republic of Panama," the 2006 prospectus reads.

"The Directors intend that the affairs on the Fund should be managed and conducted so that it does not become resident in the United Kingdom for UK taxation purposes. Accordingly ... the Fund will not be subject to United Kingdom corporation tax or income tax on its profits," the prospectus continues.

The investor document also credits Ian Cameron as a founder member of Blairmore Holdings and states that as an adviser he would be paid $20,000 a year – the highest paid director – whatever profits were realised.

In fact, the long-term Panamanian investment fund performed above market rate over many years averaging a 116% return from 2002-2007. Today many of the fund's largest holdings are in blue-chip stocks such as Apple, Unilever and Coca Cola.
Before his death, aged 77, Ian Cameron was also chairman and shareholder of Close International Equity Growth Fund Ltd, registered in Jersey and worth £9m according to papers filed in 2005. In that year just under half of the fund's holdings were in UK listed stocks.

A third fund set up in Geneva, Switzerland, had a shorter life span and finally dissolved in 2007 but had many of the same registered shareholders as the Panamanian outfit. These included a number of former employees of Panmure Gordon, the stockbroking firm where Ian Cameron spent much of his career and those from Smith and Williamson investment management where Cameron senior was a consultant.

One notable investor into the Panama fund was a charity established by Tory peer Lord Vinson. Accounts from 2009 show that a charitable trust set up under his own name invested £82,000 into the fund – almost one quarter of its investments in shares.
Vinson's trust that year went on to donate tens of thousands of pounds to rightwing think tanks including the Institute of Economic Affairs and Civitas.

David Cameron has recently remarked on companies who have taken advantage of offshoring to legally avoid tax. Speaking at the start of the year to small business leaders in Maidenhead, he said:
"With the large companies, that have the fancy corporate lawyers and the rest of it, I think we need a tougher approach.
"One of the things that we are going to be looking at this year is whether there should be a general anti-avoidance power that HMRC

can use, particularly with very wealthy individuals and with the bigger companies, to make sure they pay their fair share."

The row also comes as the top rate of tax was lowered in last month's budget from 50p to 45p and the rate of corporation tax continue to drop to achieve the chancellor's ambition of giving the UK one of the lowest rates of corporation tax in the G7.
Responding to opposition criticisms over the lowering of the top tax rate, Cameron said: "The cut in the 50p tax rate is going to be paid five times over by the richest people in our country."

Downing Street said it did not want to comment on what was a private matter for the Cameron family.

A spokesperson added: "The government's tax reforms are about making sure that some of the richest people in the country pay a decent share of income tax."
The investment managers Smith and Williamson, for whom Ian Cameron worked, chose not to comment.

Chapter 24
Drills of the Dead: Maine Prepares for Zombie Attack

First published on the 26th of June 2012…

Over the past couple of months I have been reading more and more about isolated incidents of what the mainstream media have been calling '*Zombie Attacks*'. However, I have somewhat shied away from reproducing these articles because as I say, they have been isolated incidents and to be frank, the general public as a whole more or less dismiss the existence of the so called Reptilians, so they are definitely not going to buy into the idea of Zombies inhabiting the world.

Nevertheless, it has now got to the stage where Emergency Drills and training exercises are being carried out by the Emergency services (*which therefore follows that they are being done so with the backing or on the orders of the security services*), with the scenario being that of a Zombie attack.

Course. the fact that these isolated incidents and now this training exercises have all been reported in the media means that I can no longer continue to ignore them.
Indeed, I firmly believe that even those people who don't buy into the NWO and the many possible ways in which it is meant to be brought about (e.g *UFO attack/ Nuclear bomb*), have a underlying sense of unease about the future, albeit they don't know why.

Now, one of those ways in which the NWO was meant to be put in place was via an alien attack, which was scheduled to take place during the Olympics. And with that in mind, is a Zombie attack any less plausible? To my mind a Zombie attack, started by a released virus is every bit as likely as that of an attack on Earth from outer space.

Furthermore, it is without doubt that the Elites like to give us clues as to their plans via Hollywood blockbusters (Alien attack, war, 9/11) and they further like us to get used to the idea and that the said idea is plausible via the gradual increase in reports via the Mainstream media (*UN have appointed a minister for space, Egypt, Libya, Syria being next etc, etc*).

It is also true to say that there has been, within the passed 10 years, a huge increase in big budget Zombie type movies (Day/ Dawn/ Night of the dead and Zombieland to name but a few) and then there are those films that have the world threatened by the release of a top secret biological weapon (The Fog) or via a virus (Resident evil, I am legend, both of which see the people who are lucky enough to survive attacked by Zombies). That begs the question: Coincidence or deliberate?

Which ever it may be, the increase in Zombie type news reports are now at a level where I can no longer dismiss them, regardless of how ludicrous they may sound to the majority of people. Below is the latest Zombie news.

RT News
26/6/12

Emergency officials in Maine have taken part in a training exercise in preparation for a zombie apocalypse. This comes just weeks after the federal government publicly denied the existence of zombies.

Around 100 emergency responders from eight different counties participated in the event in the quiet city of Bangor.

The premise: an unknown virus originating from Jamaica has reached Maine, turning the infected into zombies. Once infected, the virus quickly spreads to the brain, and turns the host into a full-fledged zombie, who has only one thing on its mind: biting other people.

The officials were armed with two would-be vaccines – one to prevent the infection from reaching the brain, and one to bring the zombies back to life.

"We have identified in several states, particularly Texas, New York, Illinois outbreaks of these civil disturbances and biting," one official said. "And in conjunction with that there are also widespread power outages."

The event may have been a staged act, with locals playing zombies, but it gave emergency responders an opportunity to prepare for a real life epidemic.

"This gives us the opportunity to do something a little bit different, but it still has the same principles that would apply in a real situation," Kathy Knight, director of the Northeastern Maine Regional Resource Center told the Bangor Daily News. Emergency workers "need to figure out what they need, how they're going to respond and how they are going to share their resources to respond to the disaster. They need to know who to go to outside their community to find the resources they don't have, so it's a different twist."

The training exercise comes just several weeks after the US Center for Disease Control <u>*publicly denied the existence of zombies*</u>*.*

Rumors of a "zombie apocalypse" have been on the rise after a series of disturbing incidents.
In Florida, police caught a naked man chewing on the face of another person. They eventually shot him dead after unsuccessfully trying to push him away from the victim.
In Maryland, an engineering student allegedly stabbed a man to death and ate his heart and brain.

In Canada, a porn actor was detained on charges that he had killed and dismembered his lover. He is alleged to have recorded a video of himself copulating with some of the body parts, and consuming others. He is also suspected of sending the limbs of the victim to the headquarters of political parties, as well as two schools in Vancouver.

254

Chapter 25
Facebook: The Devil's Playground For Social Misfits

Now just to avoid any confusion, I should explain that when I wrote this my main income was still coming from my job as a Tattoo Artist as opposed to a writer.
Nevertheless, this post was written to demonstrate the huge drop in moral standards...

Do I have Facebook? Yes, of course I do, who doesn't?
Well, some of the older generation may not, I suppose, but apart from them, pretty much everyone else does.
Facebook (FB), as I'm sure I do not need to tell you is a Social Networking Site. I personally associate the words 'Social' & 'Networking' as meaning 'mixing with other people in order to further a common goal.

This is why my FB is geared up around promoting my work and myself in my capacity as a Tattoo Artist & Body Piercer. Furthermore, with 99% of my business now coming via my FB, it has to be said that as a networking site, Facebook works.

Now obviously, it goes without saying that I also use my FB to keep in contact and up to date with my friends. However, out of the 884 'friends' on my FB, there are only about 20 or 30 who I can really say are my actual friends. The other 850 or so are either customers or potential customers and to my way of thinking, that is what a networking site is all about.
Now, pushing FB to one side for a moment, I should explain that I am what you would call a people watcher. I listen to what they have to say and watch how they act. So, fair to say then that people fascinate me.

Moreover, while not wishing to brag I have always been very perceptive about people and I am quite proud of the fact that 9 times out of 10, I am right in how I perceive them. Indeed, it is in fact not untrue to say that; in the majority of cases I can get a measure on someone within 15 minutes or so of first meeting them.

Having said that, those of you who know me will know that I make no secret of the 'downer' that I have on people. You see, I deal with the public on a one to one basis daily in my job and I have reached the conclusion that people are becoming needier & more self obsessed than ever before.

I do in fact find it both annoying and frustrating that people - *or should that be sheeple* – refuse to think for themselves, take blame for their actions and refuse to see what is staring them straight in the face. And by that, I am of course referring to what is going on in this country and indeed, the world.

However, it is pleasing to note that a significant number of people are now slowly becoming a lot more aware of what is going on. Unfortunately, the fact still remains that the vast majority of people are still so mind controlled and deeply embedded into 'the system', that they simply are unable to see the direction that our government is steering us and the pitfalls that await us, once we get there.

In my recent article, **Monsters Inc,** I did attribute some of this social blindness to people's natural inbuilt coping mechanism. This mechanism, which Psychologists' say is triggered when a person is forced to step outside of their comfort zone, does not allow that person to accept any truth other than his or her own. Sadly, these people are the ones who will never learn. That is to say, they won't until it is too late to change things.

You also have the type of person who knows that things are far from how they should be, but are of the opinion that there is nothing that they can do to change the situation... So they do exactly that; nothing.

Others, commonly known as the 'timid sheeple', are just too scared to object for fear of what the consequences will be if they do. These sheeple, whose aim in life appears to stop at having the ability to lose themselves among the flock - *where they feel safe* - are the worst offenders in my book. Their apathy will not make the situation go away. On the contrary, it will hasten the process. These people need to wake up and realise that it is the Government who are meant to be afraid of the people - not the people who are afraid of the Government.

This type of person is the kind that our corrupt government thrive on. It was in fact this type of person who submissively walked into the Nazi gas chambers during WW2. And there were allegedly at least 6 million of them... Although that is highly doubtful, but that is another story.

But what does all this have to do with FB, I hear you ask? Good question.

You see, as I said earlier, I have around 850 people on my FB friends list who are not my friends in the true sense of the word. It is in fact safe to say that I don't actually know the vast majority of these people from Adam. That said, I have spoken to nearly every one of them on at least one occasion. After all, these people add me because they want a tattoo done so they normally speak to me at least once.

And whenever anyone adds me, unless I am already aware of who they are, I tend to have a nosy at their profile info and photos, etc. I do so in part because as I have said, I am a people watcher. However, I do so in the main as a means of safeguarding myself since a lot of those who add me tend to be under 18 (*the legal age in the UK for a tattoo is 18*).

Course, these days, tattoos are now so mainstream that you cannot bracket the type of person to have one. I have in fact, to my knowledge tattooed: Policemen, Firemen, Paramedics, Nurses, Bank staff, Accountants, MacDonald employees, Builders, Models and drunken yobs, to name but a few.

So, it is fairly safe to assume that the 850 people or so currently on my FB friends list, and who are not real friends, will be made up from a cross section of society.

And as an aside, I do not think that I need to dwell too long on how closely the government's security service's monitor us here on FB. In fact I will take it as read that you are already aware of that fact.

However, this wide range in diversity amongst those who use FB is certainly one of the reasons for the government doing so, allowing them to gain an insight into the mood of the country.

Another of their reasons for spying on us is to keep an eye on how their various human agendas are panning out. These agendas range from how dumbed down the nation has become, through to causing racial disharmony via the [nonexistent] terrorist threat (*in order to keep us divided*).

Indeed, you have to remember that the only way that they can keep us from becoming a threat to their corrupt reign of power is by having us divided and at each other's throat. I mean Dog forbid we should ever get together as one and see these greedy, corrupt psychopaths for what they really are.

Course, having said that, it is worth noting that some of us are monitored a lot closer than others. This is so as when the shit hits the fan - which it will do - the government will know exactly whose houses they need to dispatch their goons off to. But that is also a different story.

So, of my 850 'friends' who aren't really my friends, I would estimate that roughly 15 - 20% of them never post anything on FB. A similar percentage will only post game scores etc. I tend to hide postings made by these people being as their game postings are just an irritation and tend to clog up the news feed... But I digress... As usual.

A further 20 - 25% or so are made up of those who will post maybe once, or twice a day- occasionally more. Others within that 20 - 25% bracket will often only post once or twice a week. These posts, although not always interesting to me, will be valid, well thought out, intelligent, and have significance.

However, it is the remaining 35-45% that concerns me. These people would appear to have extremely narcissistic tendencies. And the fact that they are so obviously transparent does not alter the fact that if FB is representative of a nation, then 35-45% equates to around 20 - 30 million adults (16+) in the UK alone.

Moreover, all of these remaining people can be bracketed into one social category or another, none of which instill me with much hope that one day we will all wise up, turn around, and say enough is enough.

However, before I list the various categories that these people fit into, I ought to point out that everyone gets a little down now and again. Likewise, everyone gets ill and feels sorry for their self once in a while. When these and other lousy things happen, there is nothing wrong with sharing it on FB. I personally have a genuine empathy with people who are suffering through no fault of their own.

Nevertheless, it is people who continually seek sympathy, kudos or an ego boost without deserving it that fit into these social categories. You can in fact gain a huge insight into what a person is like by the type of status that they regularly post. Furthermore, over a period of time you begin to notice a reoccurring theme building up among these people.

So, if I - *in my capacity as an amateur people watcher* - can gain an insight into what these people are like, the government analysts must be having a field day. It is therefore little wonder that the authorities so openly take the piss out of us. They have no reason to do so covertly when so many people are so wrapped up within their own little worlds that anything else ceases to matter.

Now, as it happens not many of my FB friends take an interest in this site or what I have to say and as such, I doubt many will even read this. After all, why would they? They are my FB friends through their interest in tattoos; not with political matters.

Having said that, I still wouldn't moderate what I have to say for fear of upsetting anyone anyway. After all, sometimes being blunt is the only way to get through to people and while it pains me to say it; many people really do need a kick up the backside.

Mind you, strangely enough I am often described as *"being a blunt"*... At least that is what I think they say about me. Then again, I am a little deaf. Certainly, I have in the past noticed in this site's statistics that on two occasions; someone has typed into Google the words 'big mouth' and then been directed here.

So with that in mind, I feel that I should point out to anyone on my FB friends list who does happen to read this and thinks that they may be one of those people listed in the following categories, the chances are you are probably right.

The categories then are as follows:

The Munchhausen.

These are the people who continually broadcast that they have a "Migraine" or that they have "the Flu".

And I used to suffer from Cluster Migraines and I can promise you that if you have a real Migraine, the last thing you would want to do is look at a bright computer screen or squint at a mobile phone.

I also count myself as being fortunate to only have had the Flu once in my life. On that occasion I was totally wiped out and bed ridden for three days. Yet despite this one bout of Flu being pre-computer days, had it not been, I certainly wouldn't have been in any fit state to announce how ill I felt on FB.

Course, if you are going to post a status on FB along the lines of: "*I have never been in so much pain in all my life*", while in reality you have just woken up with a slight fuzzy headache, brought on by too much sleep, then you can only be posting such a statement in order to gain sympathy or because you are a total wimp and believe me, wimps number many. In fact I meet an awful lot of them in my job.

Now to my way of thinking, to make these migraine/flu claims when you have nothing more than a minor headache or a slight cold is self obsession at its worst and stinks of *"poor me, poor me"*.

Moreover, the majority of the time, these very same people will post a status half an hour later saying how they are out having a great time shopping or working out down the gym.
Furthermore, there also happens to be an offshoot branch of the Munchhausen. And following on with the medical theme, I call This branch: *'The Munchausen by proxy'*. These people will try to draw attention to themselves and solicit sympathy by posting messages about how ill their children are.

Course, for their children to be that ill and that often makes you wonder why the sympathy givers do not contact the social services rather than pander to the needy.
And worse still, in my opinion it is because of this type of person who inevitably spends a great deal of time at the doctors, that I and others struggle to get a appointment when we need one. Therefore, these hypochondriacs really need to Man up.

The Happy Clapper.
These people are almost exclusively all women and are fooling no one but themselves. They will proceed to tell you almost every time that they post, how happy they are. Course, there is nothing wrong with being happy. In fact, there is nothing wrong with posting a status, saying so. What I question is why they need to constantly tell people? It is almost as if they repeat it enough times then they themselves will start to believe it.

Now I have noticed that the majority of these women who post these, *"such a happy Girl today"* type notifications will have recently come out of a relationship or are desperate for one.

However, having spent 18 years dealing daily on a one to one basis with the public, many of whom have just come out of a relationship *(i.e people who come to me to have their ex's name covered)* and drawing on my own experience with relationship break ups; if you're genuinely glad that the relationship is over, then you do not feel the need to tell everyone how happy you are with your life.

In fact my overall impression of these people is that they are far from happy. Certainly, they conjure up images in my mind of a village idiot going up to strangers and saying "*I'm happy*", with a big vacant smile on their face. These people need to learn that happiness is a state of mind, not something that they can force on themselves by continually repeating it.

However, what these *Happy Clappers* need to address is why they need to convince people of their 'happiness'... Although ironically I suspect that depression has a lot to do with it.
Nevertheless, there is also another type of Happy Clapper. And again, they will all be almost exclusively women. They will also all be very overweight - and i'm talking obese here not carrying a few extra pounds.

These women appear to have an obsessive need to convince people that they are comfortable with their weight by posting how happy they are with life. This is why fat people are usually said to be '*bubbly*'. Yet in reality they are filled with self loathing and are anything but happy.

I mean how can anyone be happy being enormously fat? Being fat doesn't look good on a person (unless you are in the fat fetish minority). Moreover, being fat also hinders a person's mobility and their ability to enjoy themselves... And it will most certainly end your life a lot quicker than if you are slim.

Now I am obviously aware that I may come across as sounding judgmental here but this really is not the case at all. What I am doing is pointing out the pitfalls associated with being very overweight.

I therefore ask you, why would a person purposely want to restrict what they can and can't do in return for a body that will shorten their life? In fact if proof were needed it is true to say that I have never

ever heard someone who was once very fat, having now lost the weight, say that they were happier the way they was before.

Course, it is easy to put weight on, but a lot harder to lose it and being very overweight is usually a vicious cycle of hating being fat and comfort eating junk food to feel better about the fact. And ultimately, laziness also plays a large part in obesity.

Nevertheless, be it laziness, lack of motivation or living off nervous energy, it cannot be considered constructive or helpful to society. Inevitably, these kinds of people are needy, self obsessed and easily bought or manipulated. They certainly crave love and attention. And as I say; being genuinely happy is a state of mind and shouldn't need broadcasting. If you are happy then your happiness will soon shine through unaided.

The Faithful Sheepbooker.

These people will copy & paste a post on request without checking the contents accuracy first. Now while this might sound as if I am just being intolerant towards people who may have a genuine desire to promote worthy causes, you have to look at the bigger picture. You see, to my way of thinking, if they will blindly Copy & Paste anything just because they have been asked to do so, does it not follow that they will also do this in all aspects of their lives?
In fact as far as I am concerned, anyone who does something without question is dangerous. Indeed, if more people questioned the government or said "No" they are not going to do something that isn't right, then we wouldn't be in this mess.

That fact aside, the vast majority of these Copy & Paste things actually cheapen the cause that they are supposed to be championing. For instance, the ones that read something like the following, I find particularly distasteful:

"Stupid Cancer... We all wish for different things... A new car, a new TV, or an iPhone. But people with Cancer only wish for one thing... To get better... If you know someone who has died, is

fighting or has recovered from cancer, copy & paste this... 93% of my friends wont. I think I know the 7% who will".

How condescending is that?

Cancer is an awful disease that wreaks havoc on the sufferer and their family. In fact I know from very close quarters how people with cancer react. That's why I find crap like this so insulting. For a start, Cancer sufferers don't wallow about in self pity *"wishing for a cure"*. They get on with life because they have no choice in the matter. Moreover, any doctor will tell you that positive mental attitude is of major benefit to a cancer sufferer. And just for the record, I can categorically state that sufferers also have the same wishes and dreams as anyone else does... I know because I have had cancer.

However, even more insulting is the made up statistics that you invariably find at the end of these copy and paste posts. You see, these statistics are inevitably plucked out of thin air by the tiny minded idiot who wrote the status in the first place just so as hundreds and thousands of unthinking sheeple can blindly re-post and in doing so, pander to his or her hugely inflated ego.

Moreover and beyond contempt are the Sheeple who blindly re-post the ones that have just been re-hashed - Same wording, different disease. Therefore, my advice to these twats is; if you're going to insult someone who has a life changing illness at least insult him or her with something that is original.

Indeed, what these sycophants should really be promoting is the fact that all the evidence points to diseases like cancer being curable. Unfortunately, we as part of the so called 99% are not in general privy to the cure.

However, ask yourself this: If the statistic for people suffering from cancer is correct, then 1 in every 3 of us will be a sufferer. Yet when was the last time that you saw a member of the British Royal Family catching cancer. Philip, Elizabeth, Charles, Camilla, Ann, Tim, Andrew, His paedophile Boyfriend, Edward Sophie & their kids,

William, Harry, Andrew's two daughters whatever their names are, Zara, Peter... And there you have the names of the Queen, her husband, her children & their partners as well as her grandchildren. Eighteen people in all, yet not one case of cancer.

Now if the statistic for us was the same as the immediate royal family's (and don't forget that there are many more of the parasites, all cancer free), imagine how many millions more lives would be spared this awful disease.

Unfortunately, I feel that these people don't 'copy and paste' out of a desire to champion a worthy cause. You see, in reality I believe that they do so out of a need to be part of the pack. They certainly don't do any research before they copy and paste - that much is obvious.

The same can be said about the Copy & Paste posts that start with: *"Its Sister/Brother/uncle/Aunt week... If you have a sister/Brother/uncle/Aunt who has always been there for you, etc, etc, etc".*

Now how pathetic are these things... No! It is not Sister week or anyone else's week for crying out loud. Yet people post this crap repeatedly, either out of a desire to appear 'Caring' or to endear themselves to the person that they copied & pasted from.

I mean, if you genuinely want to honour someone or pay tribute to him or her then fine. But be original and do it because you want to, not because you feel that you have to.
However, whilst the aforementioned C&P posts are just mainly embarrassing, to my mind some are bordering on being dangerous. I am of course referring to the ones that tell of children being abducted or molested, usually outside a shop or supermarket. Sometimes they will name a specific make of car and give its registration number or name a supermarket where the child was supposedly molested in the toilets - usually by Eastern Europeans.

Mind you, the Government must have loved the introduction of Eastern Europeans being brought into play... Never mind that there wasn't a shred of truth in it. The seed was planted in these idiots minds and from that point on, literally thousands of people became suspicious of everyone who spoke with a foreign accent.

What's more, nine times out of ten the author will try to add further validation to the status by proclaiming that the information was on 'Fox News at 5' or some other media source. Then, before you can blink, this old bollocks has in those brown-noser's tiny minds also become fact.

Now, on the face of it, many will view these C&P posts as being harmless. But what happens if one day a child really is snatched? I mean there has been that many hoax C&P's on FB that no one outside of these sycophants will take any notice!

I am in fact literally gob-smacked by people's willingness to believe anything, no matter how implausible the scenario may be, without asking questions or verifying the facts for themselves. Worse still, they do so just because one of their 'friends' says it's true.

Indeed, it wasn't so long ago that everyone was up in arms because someone had posted a C&P status saying that FB was about to start charging. And I still can't believe that it went viral! After all, you can just imagine Mark Zuckerberg chairing a board meeting and saying; "*I think we ought to start charging our subscribers... Get on to that little cranky kid, y'know, the one that has no mates, and tell him to announce the charges*".

I can only put the gullibility of those who fell for it down to the fluoride in our drinking water taking affect... Madness.

The Billy Liars.
These people are the kinds who think everyone but himself or herself have the memory of a goldfish... And to some extent, they may have a point I suppose... But I digress... Again.
These people will post a status saying something along the lines of "*I'm getting my new Car next week*" or "*Can't wait to move into my new flat*", so as someone will ask them about it.

Those examples would be absolutely fine as a status, should they have any foundation to them. However, the people that I'm referring to don't have a hope in hell of achieving whatever it is that they are bragging about.

Now I personally refuse to pander to the person's ego by even questioning the wisdom behind their claim, yet others do in their droves. In doing so, they give the sad sack who wrote the status their five minutes of glory while pandering to their ego at the same time. However when the Job, Car, House, Rich Boyfriend, etc, etc, fail to materialize, those who took the time to ask about the new car - *or whatever it was* - don't bother to take the Billy Liar to task.

In fact it is usually the person who inquired about the last fantasy, who will be the person to ask about the next one. And the process starts all over again.
Now once again, it could be asked why these type of people bother me. And the answer to that is for various reasons. Obviously, those telling the lies about their lives either do so out of low self esteem, a need to be liked, or a yearning to make others jealous. But it is not reality. We live in an illusionary world as it is, forced upon us by the elites without our own kind taking it a step further.

It bothers me that people are so quick to believe anything except the truth, the truth being that if they don't wake up soon, they are going to be very, very sorry. The coming NWO is not a game. These monsters will not go away.

Furthermore, one of my pet hates is liars and another is people mugging other people off. A lie is a lie and if someone buys into the lie, then they are being mugged off. It is through the corrupt Government liars that we find ourselves at this dangerous point in history. A small lie today can become a big lie tomorrow. By encouraging the sad sack in their fantasy world, is only encouraging them to lie all the more.

If on the other hand, the person swallowing the lie is doing so because they do not have the intelligence to see through it, then they are being made a fool of or being used to further the liar's agenda. This is a form of Mind Control and we all know where that leads. What this country needs are more people who can think logically and see through the implausibility of a lie. In the event that they do fall for it, confront the liar about it when their boast fails to materialize. Attitudes need to change and until people who constantly lie are challenged, standards will continue to decline.

The clever brain dead.

These are the people who continually bombard the news feed with pictures that have profound words with a deep meaning attached (memes). And if it was only now and then that these clever brain dead people were posting these things then fine.

But it isn't! In fact they continually post them as if by doing so somehow qualifies them as being the author. I actually see people commenting on these post's saying "*Oh John/Jane you are funny*" just as if John/Jane had actually written the words on the picture or taken the funny photo themselves.

Once again, this annoys me because people buy into it, instead of realising that the person who posted the meme has no imagination of their own. I mean, if I want to look at funny pictures or read poignant words then I will go find them for myself. I certainly do not need them shoved down my throat by someone so lacking in imagination that they are not capable of thinking for themselves.

Then there is the other kind of picture that is usually blunt and has '*attitude*' or is sickly sweet in its content. The people who post these things will have picked the chosen wording as supposedly being a representation of themselves. The message will inevitably be either caring or feisty. One example is: *"Don't like me... Deal with it... Don't like what I say... Delete me"*.

These people are supposedly adults yet they post pictures, designed to '*big themselves up*' just like school children do. Course, what they fail to recognise is that they are in fact so lacking in imagination that the message they are trying to get across is anything but a true representation of themselves.

Grow up and think for yourself. If you are a caring person say what is in your heart, not what is on a picture. If you are a feisty person, then why do you need to use other people's words to get your message across? Moreover, why do you want people to perceive you as being feisty anyway?

The Badaman.
Now nine out of Ten times the Badaman will be young, male, and White and although their posts are in English, they will make no sense whatsoever to anyone over the age of 25. However, what little you can make sense of, will usually be aggressive.

The Badaman will inevitably talk like a Jamaican Yardie and will be in desperate need of his trousers being pulled up. Sadly, this kind of person will have no respect for anyone or anything.

They will however, hypocritically demand respect for themselves and their property. Unable to claim benefits yet totally unemployable, the Badaman will carve out a living by selling dope and stolen goods.

The Govt absolutely love these young fellas as they can be used as a an excuse to bring in new revenue raising laws and assist in the further progression of the 'Nanny State'.

The amateur dramatics society.
The ADS brigade is a particularly needy lot who thrive on drama. They will post a status that demands a comment should the reader be half interested. They thrive off life's gossips and nosy-parkers, but in the process also reel in a few good Samaritans along the way.

A typical ADS status will read something along the lines of: "*If you think you can mug me off , give it your best shot*" or "*I can't believe you would do that to me*".The first example is for those who thrive on gossip and the only way to find out what the status is about is to ask via a comment. In doing so they give the author the attention they crave.

The second example is aimed at those more caring or sycophant, who will feel compelled to comment.

Course the more experienced of this group, and by that I mean those who add to their friends list in the 1000's, won't bother with typing such long drawn out updates as the two examples I have given. For the ADS 'Dons', a simple; *"Grrr WTF "* will suffice and get them the attention that they thrive upon in double quick time.

The Grateful Brain-dead
This last category is proof, if any were needed, that there is an active government agenda in place, to dumb down the nation. It has become increasingly obvious to me over the years that kids are leaving school in ever increasing numbers unable to read or write properly.
These semi-literate people will post status after status all totally devoid of any punctuation. Well, I say devoid of any, but the more astute of the Grateful Brain-Dead may insert the odd '*lol*' as a stand in for a full stop. This lack of punctuation makes deciphering what these people are trying to say extremely difficult at times.

Moreover, trying to read their status - already devoid of punctuation - is further hampered by the Grateful Brain-Dead's poor grasp of the English language. For example, these people can never work out if they should use the word '*there*' for "*their*", "*here*" for "*hear*", "*who's*" for "*whose*" or "*aloud*" for "*allowed*", etc, etc.

Worse still, some difficult to spell often used words appear to have been totally replaced by a revamped version. For instance, '*Gorgeous*' has now become '*Gawjus*'.

The same can be said for words that do not make sense without an apostrophe. A good example of this would be "*he's*" which sounds like '*hez*' when the apostrophe is left out. To combat this problem The GBD have simply replaced "*he's*" with '*his*'. This means we no longer

have sentences such as "*He's at the shops*". Instead, we now have;
"*His at the shops*"...

Now, having categorised these people, I can quite well imagine that
this article reads like a rant. And to be fair, I have had a little sound
off. Furthermore, I suppose that some will accuse me of being overly
'picky' but I can assure you that I am not.

However, the point is this: If we continue to allow ourselves to be so
easily led or taken in without thinking for ourselves or if we continue
to encourage liars to lie and bullshitters to spout bullshit (*which then
becomes fact*), we are playing the game in exactly the way that the
establishment want us to play it.

Furthermore, a drop in standards - social or otherwise - will only lead
to a further increase in the Nanny state mentality. Moreover, if the
government feel the need to monitor FB, then you can guarantee that
they are using that information as a yardstick to dictate policy.

So, the way that I see it is, if 30% of the population or 15 million
people are so gullible, needy, or easily led, then we really are in
trouble. We need to use our brains and think for ourselves. The more
we do, the easier learning becomes. A sloppy, apathetic, uneducated
public, is an easily manipulated, public that will allow a democracy to
become a dictatorship. I don't think any of us, no matter how needy
wants that to happen, do we?

Just sayin'.

Chapter 26
Fukushima

*My reports on the Fukushima Nuclear Power Plant disaster were
what began to first get me noticed, especially in the Far East.
However, it has become increasingly clear to me over the following
years that the earthquake that triggered the disaster was no accident.
Nevertheless, what follows is the first of many articles that I wrote on
the subject...*

Last week I was contacted out of the blue by a lady named Pia
Christina Jensen who happened to have stumbled across this site.
Pia has been following the Fukushima Nuclear power plant 'accident'
in Japan from the beginning and has immense knowledge on the
subject.

In her communication she sent me some links to information
regarding Fukushima, that you will not read in the mainstream media.
I was of course already aware that the Japanese authorities were
doing nowhere near enough to safeguard the lives of their fellow
countrymen. Indeed, the accident was so serious that apart from
evacuating the whole country (Obviously not practical), there was not
that much that they could do to guarantee the safety of their citizens.

However, it is becoming abundantly clear that the Japanese
government(JG) could have done an awful lot more. In fact, from
what I am reading now, the American and Brazilian governments
could have also done more (The fallout effects are now impacting on
both countries). Instead, the Japanese government have embarked
on a wide scale cover up, releasing little information about the extent
of the danger that Japan's citizens are facing.

What little information they are releasing is at best incorrect and
misleading and at worst blatant lies. Certainly, the JG are lying about
what the safe level of radiation is before evacuation becomes

necessary. As such they are going to be directly responsible for many thousands of death's through radiation poisoning. You can bet your life that the Japanese elite are not eating the contaminated food or drinking the contaminated water that the rest of the Japanese population are having to survive on.

Following the publication yesterday on this site, of one of the articles Pia sent me a link for, I was contacted in the early hours of this morning by the author. The article was in the form of a medical report detailing the ever increasing number of people becoming sick with radiation poisoning.

The Author **Yuri Hiranuma,** pointed out in his communication to me that the medical report dated back to January 2012. He told me that since the release of that report, he has not had the time to release an update. The following is lifted directly from his message to me and details exactly why no update has been forthcoming:

" *We have not had a chance to do more reports simply due to an overwhelming number of reported cases. In other words, current situations in Japan are worse than in this report. In addition, medical information in Fukushima is sealed, which means we have no idea what is truly going on there. What's in our report is from the rest of the country* ".

At this stage, I do not want to bombard you with too many facts until I have had a chance to read the reports I have been sent. However, it is now crystal clear that Fukushima is no longer a Japanese problem. It is a global problem. I would like to thank both Yuri and Pia for the information that they have sent me links for.

* *THE FOLLOWING IS AN ARTICLE FROM **ENFORMABLE NUCLEAR NEWS** RELEASED ON THE 25TH OF AUGUST 2012:*

Almost a month after reports surfaced that workers at the damaged Fukushima Daiichi nuclear power plant were told to use lead covers in order to hide unsafe radiation levels, a team of Japanese researchers has published an article in the Journal of the American

Medical association, revealing that 47% of participants having taken a survey given to workers at Fukushima Daiichi had experienced severe psychological distress.

The team lead by Jun Shigemura, M.D., Ph.D., from the National Defense Medical College in Saitama, Japan, had studied the psychological status of Fukushima workers 2 to 3 months after the disaster for symptoms of general psychological distress (nervousness, hopelessness and depression), including posttraumatic stress response (PTSR), and included all full-time workers from the Daiichi plant. Just under one-third of Daiichi workers had symptoms of post-traumatic stress disorder, or PTSD.

The biggest reason for the feelings of mental anguish was verbal or physical abuse, such as receiving strong insults and being targeted by thrown objects, according to the report.
A separate report in the August 15th issue of JAMA lead by Masaharu Tsubokura, M.D., of the University of Tokyo, researchers studied the amount of internal radiation exposure among residents of Minamisoma, a city north of the Fukushima Daiichi power plant. In total, 3,286 individuals (or 34.6%) had detectable levels of cesium, including 235 children (16.4%) and 3,051 adults (37.8%). In children, the concentration ranged from 2.8 to 57.9 Bq per kg, while for adults the range was 2.3 to 196.5 Bq per kg.

The tests were done between September 2011 and March 2012. The researchers note that partially due to the voluntary nature of the screenings, and also because this screening program started 6 months after the nuclear power plant disaster, higher exposure levels might have been detected earlier.

** The following is from FRCSR and was released the day after the above:

FRCSR *collects, through the Internet, reports of physical changes people have been experiencing since the Fukushima nuclear accident after March 11, 2011. The extent of radiation contamination is extremely serious, and we receive many inquiries from overseas.*

We will extract important points from applicable news articles, and translate it into English. Our intention is to share with you the recognition and understanding of the reality of radiation contamination in real time as much as possible.

SUNDAY, AUGUST 19, 2012

In the last ten days, there were multiple reports of changes in white blood cell counts. In Fukushima-city, 60 kilometers from ground zero, a five-year-old child is already hospitalized with leukemia. At a Tokyo private medical clinic 250 kilometers from ground zero, it is reported that 700 children have had leukopenia since last April. This constitutes 80% of children who were seen at this clinic. There is no end to occurrences of infectious diseases, especially rubella, and reported cases are triple what was reported last year and previous years, according to a summary by Japan's National Institute of Infectious Diseases.

Reports from members of the general public:

My legs are badly swollen, so I thought I was taking in too much water, but I don't feel it so much even though the heat is intense. I have more moles. I had thyroid cyst aspiration done. My uterine fibroid is a little worse and anemia is a little worse. When I begin to list these issues, I feel that I am slowly being done in. My doctors tell me these are due to aging and menopause. I had tests done at a fairly large public hospital, but they hardly gave me any data from my tests and told me I was "okay." I went to a trustworthy private practitioner in Kodaira for re-examination and follow-up. I am considering a move to an area less contaminated.

I found out yesterday that a five-year-old son of my acquaintance is already hospitalized with leukemia. He and his divorced mother lived in Fukushima and now live in Ibaraki. They began his treatment with one cycle being 2 years. The acquaintance said, "I never imagined this would happen to my own child!".

My children (ages 7 and 3) had blood tests at the end of June, and their white blood cell counts are slightly low. In addition, it was pointed out that their neutrophils are low. My elder child has lower white blood cell and neutrophil counts. Seven-year-old boy: WBC over 10,000 with 43% neutrophils in January 2012, but WBC was 6,300 with 25% neutrophils in June 2012. Three-year-old boy: WBC over 10,000 with 28% neutrophils in October 2010 and WBC 7,300 with 28% neutrophils in June 2012. I heard at the hospital that children living in places which are not hot spots in the Kanto region have shown the same tendency since March 2012. The results for both of my children were frightening to me. We are getting ready to move soon.

I am a counselor. Four women from central Tokyo who came for counseling last month had abortions and another woman had a baby who weighed less than 1,000 grams: this baby was later found to have a hole in heart.

My high school age daughter and I both have decreased white blood cell counts. She is 16. She is thin to begin with, but she lost over 2 kg in the last 18 months. Blood tests from November 2011 showed decreased WBC, platelets and RBC, and high CK, GPT, ALP and lymphocytes. She had urinary frequency in the fall of 2011. She also had proteinuria and diffuse goiter, but she already had enlarged thyroid before 311. We are taking maximum precautionary measures with food, but I extremely regret that she was outside on March 15, 2012. She has irregular menstrual periods with hypomenorrhea and shortened cycles. Ambient radiation level is 0.07 to 0.10 µSv/h inside and outside the house. We are considering a move, including our daughter withdrawing from school, but we are having difficulty making a decision.

I was asked by a cashier how much my purchase was, and I thought, "Okay, so it's so-and-so yen," but at the instant I was trying to get the money from my purse I forgot how much it was. I had no idea if a 1,000 yen bill was sufficient or a 10,000 bill was sufficient. My head was totally blank. After a few moments, I remembered the total amount, and I was able to pay.

Since this spring, I have hardly been able to do complicated paperwork from government offices and my children's schools. As soon as I read documents or hear explanations from clerks, I forget what I just read or heard. I have to take notes on the spot so I can maintain my daily routine. I can't remember nouns. I was in a western city in Tokyo until the end of last year. It wasn't contaminated that much there. I was giving safe food to my child. I was being careful with food. I don't have any decrease in motor ability. Another symptom that bothers me is menstrual irregularity. By the way, my 6-year-old daughter had decreased WBC when she had blood tests done in June 2011. She had no weight gain from April 2011 to August 2011 and from September 2011 to December 2011.

*** The following was released by Newsquest Online also on the 26th of August 2012:

The ongoing series of crises at Japanese nuclear power plants is spreading the fear of radiation sickness not only in the island nation but worldwide.

According to an expert quoted in an article appearing in "Scientific American," acute radiation sickness usually gains traction after a full-body dose of radiation that is at least 3,000 times greater than what is considered an annual safe dose.
With the situation on the ground in Japan changing by the minute, it is unknown what the exact radiation level is.

What are the symptoms associated with radiation sickness?
The sickness first presents itself with nausea, vomiting, rashes and diarrhea, says the U.S. Centers for Disease Control and Prevention (CDC). The symptoms may follow just minutes or even days after exposure.

A time of serious illness – marked by the loss of appetite, fever, and extreme fatigue – can be relatively brief or continue for a long period of time.

Death is often the final outcome.

Potassium iodide is the recommended treatment that is used to protect the thyroid gland from being damaged by radioactive iodine. Thyroid damage is irreversible.
The substance, which can only protect the thyroid gland, should be taken as soon as possible after exposure to radiation. One dose lasts 24 hours.

Experts agree that it is safe for a pregnant woman to take potassium iodide when instructed to do so by a doctor. The dosage apparently also protects the thyroid of the fetus.
There are reports of panic buying of potassium iodide pills on the U.S. West Coast and elsewhere.

****The following was published by truthout.org on the 29th of August 2012:

Experts say acknowledging the threat would call into question the safety of dozens of identically designed nuclear power plants in the U.S.

More than a year after the triple meltdown at the Fukushima Daiichi power plant, the Japanese government, Tokyo Electric Power Company (Tepco) and the U.S. Nuclear Regulatory Commission (NRC) present similar assurances of the site's current state: challenges remain but everything is under control. The worst is over.

But nuclear waste experts say the Japanese are literally playing with fire in the way nuclear spent fuel continues to be stored onsite, especially in reactor 4, which contains the most irradiated fuel -- 10 times the deadly cesium-137 released during the 1986 Chernobyl nuclear accident. These experts also charge that the NRC is letting this threat fester because acknowledging it would call into question safety at dozens of identically designed nuclear power plants around the U.S., which contain exceedingly higher volumes of spent fuel in similar elevated pools outside of reinforced containment.

Reactor 4: The Most Imminent Threat

The spent fuel in the hobbled unit 4 at Fukushima Daiichi not only sits in an elevated pool outside the reactor core's reinforced containment, in a high-consequence earthquake zone adjacent to the ocean -- just as nearly all the spent fuel at the nuclear site is stored -- but it's also open to the elements because a hydrogen explosion blew off the roof during the early days of the accident and sent the building into a list.

Alarmed by the precarious nature of spent fuel storage during his recent tour of the Fukushima Daiichi site, Sen. Ron Wyden, D-Oregon, subsequently fired off letters to Secretary of State Hillary Clinton, Secretary of Energy Steven Chu, NRC Chairman Gregory Jaczko and Japanese ambassador to the U.S. Ichiro Fujisaki. He implored all parties to work together and with the international community to address this situation as swiftly as possible.
A press release issued after his visit said that Wyden, a senior member of the U.S. Senate Committee on Energy and Natural Resources who is highly experienced with nuclear waste storage issues, believes the situation is "worse than reported," with "spent fuel rods currently being stored in unsound structures immediately adjacent to the ocean." The press release also noted the structures' high susceptibility to earthquakes and that "the only protection from a future tsunami, Wyden observed, is a small, makeshift sea wall erected out of bags of rock."

As opposed to units 1-3 at Fukushima Daiichi, where the meltdowns occurred, unit 4's reactor core, like units 5 and 6, was not in operation when the earthquake struck last year. But unlike units 5 and 6, it had recently uploaded highly radioactive spent fuel into its storage pool before the disaster struck.

Robert Alvarez, a nuclear waste expert and former senior adviser to the Secretary of Energy during the Clinton administration, has crunched the numbers pertaining to the spent fuel pool threat based on information he obtained from sources such as Tepco, the U.S. Department of Energy, Japanese academic presentations and the Institute of Nuclear Power Operations (INPO), the U.S. organization created by the nuclear power industry in the wake of the 1979 Three Mile Island accident.

What he found, which has been corroborated by other experts interviewed by AlterNet, is an astounding amount of vulnerably stored spent fuel, also known as irradiated fuel, at the Fukushima Daiichi site. His immediate focus is on the fuel stored in the damaged unit 4's pool, which contains the single largest inventory of highly radioactive spent fuel of any of the pools in the damaged reactors.

Alvarez warns that if there is another large earthquake or event that causes this pool to drain of water, which keeps the fuel rods from overheating and igniting, it could cause a catastrophic fire releasing 10 times more cesium-137 than was released at Chernobyl.
That scenario alone would cause an unprecedented spread of radioactivity, far greater than what occurred last year, depositing enormous amounts of radioactive materials over thousands of miles and causing the evacuation of Tokyo.

Nuclear experts noted that other lethal radioactive isotopes would also be released in such a fire, but that the focus is on cesium-137 because it easily volatilizes and spreads pervasively, as it did during the Chernobyl accident and again after the disaster at Fukushima Daiichi last year.

With a half-life of 30 years, it gives off penetrating radiation as it decays and can remain dangerous for hundreds of years. Once in the environment, it mimics potassium as it accumulates in the food chain; when it enters the human body, about 75 percent lodges in muscle tissue, including the heart.

The Threat Not Just to Japan But to the U.S. and the World
An even more catastrophic worst-case scenario follows that a fire in the pool at unit 4 could then spread, igniting the irradiated fuel throughout the nuclear site and releasing an amount of cesium-137 equaling a doomsday-like load, roughly 85 times more than the release at Chernobyl.

It's a scenario that would literally threaten Japan's annihilation and civilization at large, with widespread worldwide environmental radioactive contamination.

"Japan would suffer the worst, but it would be a global catastrophe," said Kevin Kamps, nuclear waste expert at the watchdog group Beyond Nuclear. "It already is, it already has been, but it would dwarf what's already happened."

Kamps noted that these pool fires were the beginning of the worst-case analysis envisioned by the Japanese government in the early days of the disaster, as reportedby the New York Times in February. "Not only three reactor meltdowns but seven pool fires at Fukushima Daiichi," Kamps said. "If the site had to be abandoned by all workers, then everything would come loose. The end result of that was the evacuation of Tokyo."

In an interview with AlterNet, Alvarez, who is a senior scholar at the Institute for Policy Studies, said that the Japanese government, Tepco and the U.S. NRC are reluctant to say anything publicly about the spent fuel threat because "there is a tendency to want to provide reassurance that everything is fine."

He was quick to note, "The cores are still a problem, make no mistake, and there will be some very bad things happening if they don't maintain their temperatures at some sort of stable level and make sure this stuff doesn't eat down through the concrete mats." But he said that privately "they're probably more scared shitless about the pools than they are about the cores. They know they're really risky and dangerous."

AlterNet asked the NRC if it is concerned about the vulnerability of the spent fuel at Fukushima Daiichi and what, if anything, it had expressed to the Japanese government and Tepco on the matter. "All the available information continues to show the situation at Fukushima Dai-ichi is stable, both for the reactors and the spent fuel pools," NRC spokesman Scott Burnell replied via email. "The available information indicates that Spent Fuel Pool #4 has been reinforced."

But nuclear experts, including Arnie Gundersen, a former nuclear industry senior vice president who coordinated projects at 70 U.S. nuclear power plants, and warned days after the disaster at Fukushima last year of a "Chernobyl on steroids" if the spent fuel pools were to ignite, strongly disagreed with this assessment.

"It is true that in May and June the floor of the U4 SFP [spent fuel pool] was 'reinforced,' but not as strong as it was originally," Gundersen noted in an email to AlterNet. "The entire building however has not been reinforced and is damaged by the explosion in both 4 and 3. So structurally U4 is not as strong as its original design required."

Gundersen, who is chief engineer at the consulting firm Fairewinds Associates, added that the spent fuel pool at unit 4 "remains the single biggest concern since about the second week of the accident. It can still create 'Chernobyl on steroids.'"

Alvarez said that even if the unit 4 structure has been tentatively stabilized, it doesn't change the fact "it sits in a structurally damaged building, is about 100 feet above the ground and is exposed to the atmosphere, in a high-consequence earthquake zone."
He also said that the urgency of the situation is underscored by the ongoing seismic activity around northeast Japan, in which 13 earthquakes of magnitude 4.0 to 5.7 have occurred off the northeast coast of Honshu between April 14 and April 17.
"This has been the norm since 3/11/11 and larger quakes are expected closer to the power plant," Alvarez added.

A recent study published in the journal Solid Earth, which used data from over 6,000 earthquakes, confirms the expectation of larger quakes in closer proximity to the Fukushima Daiichi site. In part, this conclusion is predicated on the discovery that the earthquake that initiated last year's disaster caused a seismic fault close to the nuclear plant to reactivate.
"There are a few active faults in the nuclear power plant area, and our results show the existence of similar structural anomalies under

both the Iwaki and the Fukushima Daiichi areas," lead researcher Dapeng Zhao, a geophysics professor at Japan's Tohoku University, said in a press release. "Given that a large earthquake occurred in Iwaki not long ago, we think it is possible for a similarly strong earthquake to happen in Fukushima."

AlterNet asked Sen. Wyden if he considers the spent fuel at Fukushima Daiichi a national security threat.

In a statement released by his office, Wyden replied, "The radiation caused by the failure of the spent fuel pools in the event of another earthquake could reach the West Coast within days. That absolutely makes the safe containment and protection of this spent fuel a security issue for the United States."

Alvarez agrees, saying, "My major concern is that this effort to get that spent fuel out of there is not something you should be doing casually and taking your time on."
Yet Tepco's current plans are to hold the majority of this spent fuel onsite for years in the same elevated, uncontained storage pools, only transferring some of the fuel into more secure, hardened dry casks when the common pool reaches capacity.

For the moment, though, and for the foreseeable future -- unless the international community substantively comes to Japan's aid -- Tepco couldn't transfer the irradiated fuel from the damaged reactor units into dry cask storage even if it wanted to because the equipment to do so, such as the crane support infrastructure, was destroyed during the initial disaster.
"That's kind of shocking," said Paul Gunter of Beyond Nuclear. "But that's why we're still sitting on this gamble that there won't be another earthquake that could topple a very precarious unit 4."

Gunter is concerned that even a minor earthquake or a subsidence in the earth under unit 4 could cause its collapse.
"I think we're all on pins and needles every day with regard to unit 4," he said. "I mean there's any number of things that could happen. Nobody really knows."

Gunter added, "Right now its seismic rating should be zero."

Alvarez echoed Wyden's letters to the Japanese ambassador and U.S. officials.
"It really requires a major effort," he said. "The United States and other countries should begin to get involved and try to help the Japanese government to expedite the removal of that spent fuel and to put it into dry, hardened storage as soon as possible."

Same Spent Fuel Pool Designs at Dozens of U.S. Nuclear Sites
So why isn't the NRC and the Obama administration doing more to shed light on the extreme vulnerability of these irradiated fuel pools at Fukushima Daiichi, which threaten not only Japan but the U.S. and the world?

Nuclear waste experts say it would expose the fact that the same design flaw lies in wait -- and has been for decades -- at dozens of U.S. nuclear facilities. And that's not something the NRC, which is routinely accused of promoting the nuclear industry rather than adequately regulating it, nor the pro-nuclear Obama administration, want to broadcast to the American public.

"The U.S. government right now is engaged in its own kabuki theatre to protect the U.S. industry from the real costs of the lessons at Fukushima," Gunter said. "The NRC and its champions in the White House and on Capitol Hill are looking to obfuscate the real threats and the necessary policy changes to address the risk."

There are 31 G.E. Mark I and Mark II boiling water reactors (BRWs) in the U.S., the type used at Fukushima. All of these reactors, which comprise just under a third of all nuclear reactors in the U.S., store their spent fuel in elevated pools located outside the primary, or reinforced, containment that protects the reactor core. Thus, the outside structure, the building ostensibly protecting the storage pools, is much weaker, in most cases about as sturdy, experts describe in interviews with AlterNet, as a structure one would find housing a car dealership or a Wal-Mart.

Not what Americans might expect to find safeguarding nuclear material that is more highly radioactive than what resides in the reactor core.

The outer containments surrounding these spent fuel pools in these U.S. reactors patently fail to meet the NRC's own *"defense in-depth"* nuclear safety requirements.
But these reactors don't merely suffer from the same storage design flaw as those at Fukushima Daiichi.

In the U.S., the nuclear industry has been allowed to store incredible volumes of spent fuel for decades in high-density pools that were not only originally designed to retain about one-fourth or one-fifth of what they now hold but were intended to be temporary storage facilities. No more than five years. That was before the idea of reprocessing irradiated fuel in this country failed to gain a foothold over 30 years ago. Once that happened, starting in the early 1980s, the NRC allowed high-density storage in fuel pools on the false assumption that a high-level waste repository would be opened by 1998. But subsequent efforts to gain support for storing nuclear waste at Yucca Mountain in Nevada have also been scrapped.
More recently, the NRC arbitrarily concluded these pools could store this spent fuel safely for 120 years.

"Our pools are more crammed to the gills than the unit 4 pool at Fukushima Daiichi, much more so," noted Kamps of Beyond Nuclear. "It's kind of like a very thick forest that's waiting for a wildfire. It would take extraordinary measures to prevent nuclear chain reactions in our pools because the waste is so closely packed in there."

Experts say the only near-term answer to better protect our nation's existing spent nuclear fuel is dry cask storage. But there's one catch: the nuclear industry doesn't want to incur the expense, which is about $1 million per cask.

"So now they're stuck," said Alvarez, "The NRC has made this policy decision, which the industry is very violently opposed to changing because it saves them a ton of money. And if they have to go to dry *hardened storage onsite, they're going to have to fork over several hundred million dollars per reactor to do this."*

He also pointed out that the contents of the nine dry casks at the Fukushima Daiichi site were undamaged by the disaster.
"Nobody paid much attention to that fact," Alvarez said. "I've never seen anybody at Tepco or anyone [at the NRC or in the nuclear industry] saying, 'Well, thank god for the dry casks. They were untouched.' They don't say a word about it."

The NRC declined to comment directly to accusations it's reluctant to draw attention to the spent fuel vulnerability at Fukushima Daiichi because it would bring more awareness to the dangers of irradiated storage here in the U.S. But the agency did respond to a question about what it has done to address the vulnerability of spent nuclear fuel storage at U.S. nuclear sites with the Mark I and II designs.

"All U.S. spent nuclear fuel is stored safely and securely, regardless of reactor type," NRC spokesman Burnell replied in an email. "Every spent fuel pool is an inherently robust combination of reinforced concrete and steel, capable of safely withstanding the same type and variety of severe events that reactors are designed for."

He continued, "After 9/11, the NRC required U.S. nuclear power plants to obtain additional equipment for maintaining reactor and spent fuel pool safety in the event of any situation that could disable large areas of the plant. This 'B5b' equipment and related procedures include ensuring spent fuel pools have adequate water levels. The B5b measures are in place at every U.S. plant and have been inspected multiple times, including shortly after the accident at Fukushima.

"The NRC continues to conclude the combination of installed safety equipment and B5b measures can protect the public if extreme events impact a U.S. nuclear power plant."
But nuclear experts told AlterNet that the majority of Burnell's response could've been made prior to the disaster at Fukushima. In fact, Ed Lyman, senior staff scientist at the Union of Concerned

Scientists, investigated these so-called "B5b" safety measures the NRC ordered post-9/11 and published his findings in a May 2011 *Bulletin of the Atomic Scientists* article.

Directly reflecting Burnell's response to AlterNet, Lyman wrote that after the Fukushima disaster, "the NRC and the industry invoked the mysterious requirements known as 'B5b' as a cure-all for the kinds of problems that led to the Fukushima crisis.

"Even though the B5b strategies were specifically developed to cope with fires and explosions, the NRC now argues that they could be used for any event that causes severe damage to equipment and infrastructure, including Fukushima-scale earthquakes and floods."

But contrary to these NRC assurances, then and now, Lyman's report found B5b requirements inadequate, containing flaws in safety assumptions that suggest the NRC has not applied the major lessons learned from the Fukushima disaster. Additionally, he revealed emails showing that the NRC's own staff members questioned the plausibility of these procedures to effectively respond to extreme weather events like floods, earthquakes and concomitant blackouts.

Burnell sent a follow-up email, noting, "I also should have mentioned the NRC issued an order in March to all U.S. plants to install enhanced spent fuel pool instrumentation, so that plant operators will have a clearer understanding of SFP status during a severe event." This is a curiously roundabout way of saying that spent fuel pools at U.S. reactors currently have no built-in instrumentation to gauge radiation, temperature or pressure levels.

Kamps also pointed out that the NRC commissioners voted 4 to 1, with Chairman Gregory Jaczko in dissent, to not require such requested safety upgrades to U.S. reactors until the end of 2016.

He added, "Burnell's flippant, false assurances prove that pool risks, despite being potentially catastrophic, are largely ignored by not only industry, but even NRC itself, even in the aftermath of Fukushima."

Chapter 27
It's never Harry's fault, is it?

I wrote this article after Prince Harry was photographed in the tabloids, naked and cavorting with two young ladies. However, I should point out that during the course of the article I mention that both Prince Charles and his father, Prince Philip had a hand in Princess Diana's death… A fact that I now know not to be true…

So, I see that Prince Harry has once again made the front pages of newspapers across the world this past week. And once again, it is for all the wrong reasons.

On this occasion, the Prince has been caught with his pants down, after being photographed naked in a Las Vegas hotel room. The Prince was snapped playing Strip Billiards with his friends and two young ladies, whom were picked up just hours before in a Las Vegas nightclub.

One of the poor quality snaps involves the royal bachelor cupping his "crown jewels" while one of the women is behind him. Another of similar poor quality shows the prince bear-hugging a naked woman - who is presumably, one of the two girls in question.
However, seemingly not content with just the two women, the Prince and his chums are said to have hosted a second vodka-fueled pool party with a dozen '*randomly recruited*' girls Just seven and a half hours later .

Following the leaking of the snaps, taken on a mobile phone last week, Harry has been ordered by the Palace to delete his Facebook account which he operated under the pseudonym of Spike Wells.

Harry's private secretary Jamie Lowther-Pinkerton, who is heading an inquiry into the Prince's trip to Las Vegas, has also asked Harry's two friends who joined him on the jaunt, Tom 'Skippy' Inskip, 25 and

Arthur Landon, 30 to do likewise. Both have complied. Mind you, it doesn't make for a safe future to disobey the Palace, don't cha know.

However, the photographs – *which have largely gone unpublished by the mainstream media in there uncensored form* - appear to be just the tip of the Iceberg in this latest Royal scandal. At least that is, according to the 'Mail on Sunday'. In fact the Newspaper quoted a source used by the celebrity blogger, norm Clark as saying: *'Something pretty gigantic' is involved; something more serious than 'strip billiards'.*

The newspaper then went on to say the following about the 3rd in line to the throne:
"The latest comment to surface surrounding the 27-year-old's antics has no implicit context, but could be linked to concerns raised by the Prince following the US publication of the derobed heir.
The Prince was said to be 'terrified' further damaging images might emerge and his concerns intensified after photos of an 'even wilder' week in the British Virgin Islands on Sir Richard Branson's private island of Necker, shortly before the Vegas weekend, were leaked to a newspaper".

Nevertheless, it appears that the great British public - *seemingly accepting of anything that the social elite do* - are making light of the scandal and dismissing the incident as being no more than *"what all young men of his age get up to"*.

Personally, I myself in no way share that opinion and find that sort of attitude rather sycophantic, not to mention pathetic, to be honest . After all, most young men of Harry's age are not the 3rd in line to the throne. Indeed, the fact that Hooray Henry (Henry being his real name) is third in succession, in my view, carries with it a certain code of conduct.

The same should also apply to the people Harry associates with in private. The person who took the snaps reportedly sold them to WMZ Magazine for £10,000 - a relatively small amount of money which suggests that the photos were sold for ulterior motives rather than financial gain.

Naturally, the Palace controlled BBC tried to deflect the blame away from Harry by transferring it on to his Bodyguards. What an insult! Harry is nearly 28 years old. He is not a child or even a headstrong, immature teenager so to blame the bodyguards is a cop out.

However, I suspect that the Royal household are more upset with the fact that Harry's antics made the headlines rather than with the deed itself. After all, from what I have read the Royal family - both past and present - see no wrong whatsoever in wandering around naked at parties.

Indeed, it has been alleged that Harry's Great, Great Uncle, Edward VIII was at one party being pushed around in a pram by his slut wife, Wallis Simpson. Worse still, Edward - who abdicated the throne - was said to have been dressed in nothing more than a baby's nappy. Another example is a party given by Harry's Great Aunt, Princess Margaret who was allegedly photographed cavorting with three naked men. One of the three was reportedly the married princess's lover *Roddy Llewellyn...* Llewellyn, 17 years Margaret's junior was at the time her landscape gardener.

Unfortunately, this is far from the first time that Harry's behavior has been called into question. You see, as a teenager, Harry found himself splattered across the British tabloids with reports of him smoking Cannabis and drinking alcohol. St. James Palace later confirmed that Harry "*[had] experimented with the drug on several occasions*".

Course, the fact that he was prone to the odd 'joint' or two, is not really shocking in its self. After all, millions upon millions of people also indulge. In fact, Cannabis has many, many benefits to it – As I am sure the Royal family are aware.

However, the fact that it is a prohibited Class B drug *(sometimes Class C – It changes according to the views of whichever idiot is running the country at the time*) means that the Prince should have at the very least, been more discreet.

It was then claimed that Harry was later sent to rehab for his 'problem'. However, I find that hard to believe. And if he did, then it was no more than a public relations exercise.

Then there is the question of HRH's volatile temper. One incident happened at Pangaea - *a top London nightclub* - where Harry attacked a press photographer. The photographer later claimed that Harry:

"burst out of the car and lunged towards me as I was still taking pictures. He lashed out and then deliberately pushed my camera into my face. The base of the camera struck me and cut my bottom lip".

Hmmm, not exactly the behaviour or temperament becoming of someone who's career involves learning to fly Apache helicopters. In fact, had that assault been by an ordinary member of the public then they would have found themselves arrested and hauled into court.

However, not only does Harry show a complete lack of discipline, his judgement is also repeatedly being called into question.

This fact was clearly demonstrated in 2005 when the Ginger haired firebrand attended a 'costume ball' dressed in a Nazi uniform. The prince later said that:

"It was a very stupid thing to do and I've learned my lesson, simple as that really".

However, the truth is Harry has not learned his lesson. Especially in regards to being caught. I also suggest that his decision to go to a party dressed in Nazi regalia was a lot more than *"a very stupid thing to do".*

But once again, I doubt that the backlash from his relatives was anything near as bad as the newspapers reported. In fact, after the initial tongue lashing for being caught, I feel sure that Harry's Grandad, the Duck of Edinburgh (no typo) would probably have remarked on how smart & dashing Harry had looked in the uniform.

You see, you have to remember that Phillip and the vast majority of the Royal household are at best Nazi sympathizers. However, being caught dressed as one is a Royal 'No-no'. I mean Phil & Co might have no respect whatsoever for our war dead, but it certainly doesn't do to let the Nation know it.

Prince Harry - He certainly has the traits of a Windsor

would also imagine that racism has been etched into Harry's personality from an early age. Prince Phillip is a notorious racist, so much so that the in-breed cannot even keep his bigoted thoughts to himself.

This would explain why Harry famously referred to a colleague in his Army platoon as "Our little Paki friend...Ahmed".
At the time, the Royal Family released a statement saying that the term "Paki" was a nickname for a friend in his platoon. However, I strongly disbelieve that explanation and see it as just another example of the mugs this parasite family take us for.

Indeed, you only have to look at the way Harry worded the sentence to see that he was being abhorrently racist. And had the Palace's lame excuse had any truth to it, Harry would have been heard to say "My little friend; Paki", not "Our little Paki friend...Ahmed".
Moreover, I cannot imagine that anyone of Asian origin would readily answer to, or even accept the nickname 'Paki'.

Other evidence of racist incidents include the video given to the 'News of the World' showing a British soldier with a cloth over his head. On the tape Prince Harry's voice can be clearly heard in the background saying,"Fuck me, you look like a raghead".
And once again, St. James's Palace responded to the remark by saying that; "Prince Harry used the term 'raghead' to mean Taliban or Iraqi insurgent". Bollocks did he! You go and ask your local EDL thug exactly what the term "Raghead" means and the context that it is used in.

Course, it can come as little surprise that Harry has turned out the way he has. He is a spoilt brat who learned from an early age that he has no need to respect anyone or anything as long as he doesn't attract the attention of the press. You see, it isn't the deed, it is the getting caught that angers the palace.

There are other factors of course that will undoubtedly have messed with Harry's head. For instance, he has to live with the knowledge that the public believe his biological Father more likely to be James Hewitt rather than Prince Charles. The following is an extract taken from my article 'Monsters Inc':

A longtime employee of Harry's mother Princess Diana told IUC that the Royal Family was involved in a massive cover up to hide the fact that Diana's ex lover James Hewitt is in fact Harry's real father. According to the source Prince Philip threatened Hewitt's life if he didn't go along with the cover up. "They made him lie about the timeline," the source told IUC. "Prince Philip told Hewitt he would destroy him if it ever leaked out. It's impossible that Charles is Harry's real father. Hewitt was on the scene as Diana's lover two years before Harry was born. Diana stopped having sex with Charles years before Harry was born. Harry looks exactly like Hewitt":

Likewise, the fact that the evidence, (*the real evidence, not that fiction put out by the mainstream media to suggest otherwise*) points to both Harry's 'father' & 'Grandfather' having a hand in his mother's death, cannot be easy to live with.

However, neither of the above factors can be used to justify Harry's behaviour. As a senior member of the Royal family his conduct should be beyond reproach. Once again, this inept, in-bred, parasitic family have embarrassed the nation in the eyes of the world. The quicker that we get rid of them, the better off we will be.

Below, is the Photograph that the mainstream media dare not print. Both the above article and the photo below are copyright of the author.

Phillip: "*Oh for pity's sake... Don't look now but that awful bounder Spivey has just turned up. He really does get everywhere*".

Harry: *'Fucking Hell! Get rid of him Daddy. He's stealing my thunder. Get rid of him right now or i'll squeam and squeam till I'm sick'.*

Charles: *'Ding bloody dong... Errr, hang on now son. Lets not errr be too errrr bloody hasty. And don't call me errr Daddy. Errr call me Big Chaz'.*

Chapter 28
The True Axis Of Evil: 9/11 remembered

This was my third major article about the government orchestrated 9/11 and was written on the 11th anniversary of the event…

In the 11 years since the attacks of September the 11th, I cannot recall seeing many sicker sights than that of George Wanker Bush (*that is what the 'W' stands for isn't it?*), Standing atop a pile of debris left by the collapsed WTC towers, with a protective arm, casually draped around an ageing fire fighters shoulders.

Bush, megaphone in hand and looking like he had just won an Olympic gold medal was at Ground Zero, in what was a shameless display specifically designed to whip up patriotism and anti Middle Eastern sentiment amongst a shell shocked American - nay, World - population.

Looking extremely, smarmy and self satisfied, the Monster - revelling in the applause that he was receiving - began to speak:

"I can hear you... The World can hear you... And pretty soon the people who knocked down these buildings will be hearing from all of us".

What a Cunt!

The man – and I use the term extremely loosely – stood there like some kind of Wild West hero, basking in his own sense of self worth, while at the same time knowing full well that he and his bunch of reprobates were responsible for all of the lives lost that day.

What a sick Cunt!

Sick C***.

.

This sadistic display took place on September 14th 2001, just three days after the attacks. Course, the choking air had cleared of dust by then and all work had been halted to avoid creating more.

In fact that would be the same choking air that the abomination masquerading as Condoleezza Rice knew all too well was dangerous to work in, but nevertheless still withheld the information.

That would also be the same choking air about which - the then - EPA Administrator, Christine Todd Whitman said on the 18th of September 2001:
"Given the scope of the tragedy from last week, I am glad to reassure the people of New York and Washington, DC that their air is safe to breathe and their water is safe to drink".

Perhaps Ms Todd Whitman wouldn't have been so "**glad to reassure the people of New York and Washington, DC"** that everything was hunky-dory had she been made to work in an area where the air, according to air pollution expert, Professor Emeritus Thomas Cahill contained dust that was in his own words; *"wildly toxic"*.
Professor Cahill concluded that:

The thousands of tons of toxic debris resulting from the collapse of the Twin Towers consisted of more than 2,500 contaminants, more specifically: 50% non-fibrous material and construction debris; 40% glass and other fibers; 9.2% cellulose; and 0.8% of the extremely toxic carcinogen asbestos, as well as detectable amounts of lead, and mercury. There were also unprecedented levels of dioxin and PAHs from the fires which burned for three months. Many of the dispersed substances (asbestos, crystalline silica, lead, cadmium, polycyclic aromatic hydrocarbons) are carcinogenic; other substances can trigger kidney, heart, liver and nervous system deterioration. This was well known by the EPA at the time of collapse.

Naturally, Ms Whitman and her merry bunch of lying sicko's deny that they knew of the danger that the dust posed to rescue workers. However according to the *Union of Concerned Scientist*s website:

News reports suggest that the EPA was not fully forthcoming about the air quality at ground zero. EPA scientist Cate Jenkins argues that the agency plainly lied in its public declarations. Jenkins told CBS News in September 2006 that the EPA knew "this dust was highly caustic, in some cases as caustic and alkaline as Drano." In September 2006, CNN reported that an October 5, 2001 letter from the EPA to the New York City Health Department warned of threats to worker safety from exposure to hazardous materials. Yet this knowledge failed to affect the EPA's unworried public statements.

The EPA's September 18th, 2001 news release stated that: "*EPA's primary concern is to ensure that rescue workers and the public are not being exposed to elevated levels of potentially hazardous contaminants in the dust and debris.*"
Yet despite this, a 2006 study by Mount Sinai Hospital in New York found that "*seven out of ten World Trade Center rescue and wreckage workers had new or worsened lung problems after the attacks*".

Moreover, The New York City Department of Health has a database of 71,000 people exposed to dust and debris at Ground Zero — a database created in response to hundreds of people's complaints of breathing and lung problems. *"The health of these individuals may have been saved if not for the government's willingness to place politics above sound science in the aftermath of the 2001 World Trade Center attacks"*.*

Furthermore, according to Reuters, some estimates put the overall death toll from 9/11-related illness at more than 1,000. Reuters further reported that; *"At least 20,000 ground zero workers are being treated across the country and 40,000 are being monitored by the World Trade Centre Health Program"*.

And yet a further study conducted in 2010 by the New York Fire Department Medical Office concluded that of the 5000 WTC rescue workers taking part in the study:

All had impaired lung functions with an average impairment of 10 percent. The study found the impairments presented itself in the first year after the attack with little or no improvements in the ensuing six years. 30 to 40 percent of workers were reporting persistent symptoms and 1000 of the group studied were on "permanent respiratory disability". Dr. Prezant noted the medications that are being given ease symptoms but are not a cure.

So, did the EPA know? Yes, of course they did.

In fact the twin towers had long ago failed the safety standard for Asbestos levels in a workplace and the daunting task of removing the killer insulation to bring the towers up to safety standards was not thought to be cost effective. However, to not remove the Asbestos would have meant that the Towers would have had to be closed down.

Indeed, it was because of this asbestos dilemma that the moderately wealthy, Larry Silverstein was allowed to buy the WTC lease at a bargain basement price. Larry *'I didn't know 9/11 was going to happen, honest Guv'* Silverstein then insured the buildings to the hilt.

And when the towers came down, along with WTC 7, Silverstein was catapulted overnight from the ranks of the moderately wealthy to the ranks of the super rich... Silverstein, is as you would imagine, a particularly unpleasant, snake in the grass type character.

Meanwhile, further down the American East Coast another of the seedy little men behind the 9/11 attacks was determined to see himself portrayed as a hero. Donald *'I make your flesh crawl'* Rumsfeld - in a public display every bit as sick as that staged by 'Wanker' Bush - was filmed carrying small pieces of aircraft debris from the Pentagon lawn.

However, this moronic toad of a man - no doubt blinded by his desire to be seen as someone other than a Cunt - did not possess the brains to realize that in doing so he was leaving himself wide open for criticism.

You see, for starters had the attacks really have been committed by Islamic extremists, then the little wannabe - in his capacity as the US Defence Secretary - would have immediately been taken to a place of safety.

Moreover, in his quest to be seen as a hero, the daft prat was actually committing a crime punishable by imprisonment. I am of course referring to the extremely serious offence of destroying a crime scene – an offence which was also committed at the WTC incidentally.

And anyway, ask yourself what the rush was to move this extremely dubious in origin, plane crash debris in the first place? I mean what threat or danger did these small pieces of wreckage pose to anyone? Absolutely None at all.

Indeed it was done merely to make this power crazed imbecile look good. Unfortunately, It will take a lot more than that you horrible little man.

Course, I don't doubt for a moment that this anniversary will be used as an excuse by the main stream media to subtly whip up hatred towards Muslims worldwide.

Moreover, I also expect to hear plenty of corrupt, self serving politicians scaring gullible people throughout the world into believing that the only way to keep them safe from the very [un] real likelihood of another terrorist attack is by them giving up their freedom and civil liberties.

These are the exact same gullible people who continue to cling to the highly improbable, nay impossible scenario that has become the American government's official version of events.

In fact I personally find it unbelievable that millions of people across the world still believe that four planes were hijacked by Muslim extremists, all of whom were armed to the teeth with an extremely dangerous plastic handled, Stanley knife each.

And then, having successfully taken over the planes they proceed to fly two of them into the WTC twin towers - resulting in their collapse.

The third plane we are told is steered - *in a manoeuvre impossible for any 757 pilot to perform* – into the Pentagon building, despite none of the hijackers being able to fly for shit.

Meanwhile the fourth plane - *amidst a display of all American heroism* - crash lands in a Pennsylvanian field, as a direct result of the hostages attempting to overpower the hijackers.

Personally, I believe that the fact that people still buy into the above nonsense is an affront to the memory of the alleged 2977 people who died on that day.

Likewise, it is also an affront to the memory of those who have died since as a direct result of their involvement in 9/11.

After all, it is scientifically impossible for Jet fuel to burn anywhere near the heat temperature needed to make steel melt - or even warp enough to trigger a collapse. And in fact, the black smoke seen coming from the towers was testament to the low temperature of the fires inside the buildings.

You see, all of the jet fuel was burnt up in a massive fireball on impact for crying out loud.
And if, as the official government version of events concludes, the towers then collapsed due to a combination of the impact damage and heat from the subsequent fires, then we need to rewrite all the laws of physics being as the towers came down at freefall speed.

Indeed, the only way... And I will repeat that for the hard of learning... THE ONLY WAY that the towers could have come down at freefall speed is via a controlled demolition.
Still, perhaps Osama Bin Laden was a demolition expert in his spare time... But then again, perhaps not.

Now, those of you paying attention may have noticed that I inserted the word *'Alleged'* before stating the official death toll earlier on in this article. I did so because the evidence actually points to the official death toll being nowhere near that figure of 2977.

Indeed, you have to question why, if the hype afforded to Bin Laden was true - *which it isn't* – he chose to go to all that trouble just to cause 3000 deaths. After all, had he waited a couple of hours more there would have been around 50,000 people slaving away in the trade centre. But, as the FBI's 'most wanted' posters prove, Bin Laden didn't do it. Even the FBI couldn't muster the front to apportion the blame onto Mr Bin Laden.

Course, the American Government sponsored terrorist attack actually took place at that time in the morning for very good reason. That reason was to specifically ensure that there would be the minimum number of deaths possible, while at the same time ensuring that the body count was still sufficiently high enough to outrage the public into allowing the American Government to go on a Middle Eastern pillage.

Now, understand this: The desire for a relatively low body count in comparison to what it could have been was not down to the government wanting to save the lives of American citizens. On the contrary, had they thought that they could have gotten away with it; the death toll would have been substantially higher. However, the less bodies that there were meant the less grieving families there would be to ask awkward questions.

Of the alleged 2977 people who died that day, 411 of them were supposedly from the emergency services... That is 411 Firemen, Policemen, and Paramedics, who were deliberately murdered by their own Government. There is however a dispute over that number.

That dispute comes along with the other 2566 people allegedly killed that day - including the hijackers. You see, at least 5 of the 19 hijackers are still alive and somewhat bemused to learn that - to this day - they are still officially listed amongst those who did die on September 11th 2001.

Of the remaining 2958 civilian and emergency service workers reportedly killed, a rather strange anomaly has cropped up surrounding their identity. You see, in the days and weeks following 9/11, 'relatives' of those who supposedly died took to pinning up photographs of their deceased loved ones at Ground Zero.

However, someone was paying more attention to these photographs than the government would have liked because it soon became obvious that a lot of them were photoshopped repeats of other 'victims' photographs.

In other words, someone – the government – had taken the photographs of people who had really died on that day, copied the photos, added a different background, reversed the images and changed the skin tones of the people in the copied photos. The photos and their copies were then pinned up at Ground Zero (a suitable distance apart from each other obviously) with the doctored photos pinned up under different names.

Worse still, some of these photos were photoshopped up to 3 or 4 times. (see photo 11 opposite)

It is therefore impossible to put an accurate figure on the total number of people who died in the towers on 9/11.

However, having said that, had only one person died in the attacks then that would still have been one too many. Indeed, the horror and suffering that those poor people must have gone through while waiting to die is unimaginable.

Then there are the plane passengers... Or lack of them since the seats on all four planes were massively undersold that day... Coincidence?

The Photo Wall

I mean a Boeing 757 can carry between 200 & 289 passengers and crew. Now take a look at the numbers supposedly on the four doomed airliners:

American Flight 11 had 87 passengers and crew plus five hijackers.
United Flight 175 had 60 passengers and crew plus five hijackers.
American Flight 77 had 59 passengers and crew plus five hijackers.
United Flight 93 had 40 passengers and crew plus four hijackers.

Strange then how the hijackers knew that they could manage with a man less on flight 93 which just so happened to be the flight with the least number of passengers.
So once again I ask you; coincidence?

However, there is evidence to suggest that Flight 93, the plane that supposedly crashed into a field following a hostage revolt, actually landed at Cleveland's Hopkins International airport where it was hidden in a secluded hanger while 'the passengers' were evacuated.

Donald Rumsfeld was also actually caught on video saying that flight 93 had been shot down. The alleged impact site is certainly unique if flight 93 really did crash land there since the debris, spread over miles, is like no other impact site seen before.

However, having said that the site is very consistent with what you would expect to see had the plane been blown to smithereens in mid flight.

Certainly, the reported phone conversations from flight 93 between alleged passengers and their loved ones at home are fake. You see, it was impossible to make cell phone calls from aeroplanes in 2001. The evidence therefore points to an empty jet liner having been shot down over Pennsylvania.

Course, it goes without saying that the alleged on board hostage revolt made for good propaganda. Bravo.

In regards to Flight 77, the plane that supposedly crashed into the pentagon; Believe that, and you will believe anything.
I mean, the impact site doesn't support the claim in anyway, shape or form. Furthermore, the mid-air turn allegedly made by flight 77 in order for it to have hit the pentagon building where it supposedly did, is impossible to make in a 757.

And you may also wish to consider this fact; the Pentagon has more CCTV cameras trained on it than any other building in the world. To date, the American Government has only released CCTV footage from one. That footage certainly does not show a plane hitting the building.

Yet in order to end the many conspiracies theories surrounding exactly what it was that hit the Pentagon, all the government need do is release a decent bit of CCTV footage showing the plane hitting the building. The fact that they haven't speaks volumes.

There is however much witness testimony - *totally ignored by the 'Mickey Mouse' 9/11 commission report obviously* - to say that a incredibly low flying 757, flew over the pentagon seconds before a Cruise missile slammed into the building. Therefore, going on the evidence available, I would suggest to you that no plane crashed into the Pentagon and as such; that obviously means no passengers died.

Flights 93 and 77 therefore reduce the death toll by a further 108. Similarly, there is much evidence to suggest that the two planes, American Flight 11 and United Flight 175 were in reality, unmanned remote controlled spy planes. And again, if that is true then the death toll is reduced by a further 167.

The evidence suggests that nowhere near the official number of deaths occured in the Twin Towers

The evidence suggests that Flight 93 was shot down in mid air. Check out the crash site and compare it to others.

Can you see a Massive Jumbo Jet in the CCTV footage. No, neither can anyone else.

Nevertheless, the fact remains that no matter how many people died on September the 11th 2001, they were all killed by the same scumbags who were supposedly elected to protect them.
That the people responsible for those who died 11 years ago are still breathing fresh air, never mind living in a manner that we can only dream about, is breathtaking in the extreme.

Amongst their ranks are people such as the Bush family, Dick Cheney, Donald Rumsfeld, Condoleezza Rice, Tony Blair, the Clintons, Rudolph Giuliani, Barack Obama, Henry Kissinger and Larry Silverstein to name but a few. May their souls one day rot in hell.

Evil Beyond Belief

George H Bush

George W Bush

Jeb Bush

Barak Obama

Bill Clinton

Hilary Clinton

Dick 'Ed' Cheney

Donald Duck

"Rudy" Giuliani

Tony 'B' Liar

Larry Silverstein

Condoleezza Rice

Unfortunately, these

abominations will continue to cause suffering, pain, and misery throughout the world as long as we allow them too. All those of you who refuse to speak out, or refuse to see the wood for the trees are accomplices to these psychopaths. For that tag alone, you should hang your heads in shame.

Today, on this 11th anniversary of what is probably the blackest day in American history, it is right that we remember those innocent victims of September the 11th 2001.
Those people - how ever many that may be - were deliberately murdered by their own government for nothing more than greed and power. May all those innocent victims forever rest in peace.

It is also right that today we pay respect to those who have since died following the American governments deliberate withholding of information regarding the dangers of working at Ground Zero.
They too were murdered by their own Government. May those poor souls also forever rest in peace.

And finally, it is also right that we pay our respects today to all of the armed service personnel and countless hundreds of thousands of innocent men, women and children who have died in the so called war on terror... An illegal war, brought into force as a direct result of the false flag operation orchestrated by the American government... A act of terrorism which has come to be known as 9/11.

May all of the countless victims, regardless of Race, creed or colour forever rest in peace.

*The following is taken from an RT News article:

GOVERNMENT FINALLY ADMITS THAT 9/11 TOXINS CAUSED CANCERS

RT – *The US government has decided to recognize around 50 different types of cancer that victims of the 9/11 terrorist attacks have been diagnosed with after more than a decade-long wait that has left hundreds dead without proper care or diagnosis.*

Civilians and first responders that survived the September 11, 2001 attacks but developed cases of varying cancers in the aftermath will now be covered by a government-administered health care program that will provide them with complimentary check-ups and screenings. The decision will apply to survivors of both crashes at the World Trade Center in New York City and the Pentagon in Washington, DC.

The National Institute for Occupational Safety made the announcement Monday, adding dozens of diseases — including cancers of the breast, bladder and lung, colorectal cancer, leukemias, melanoma and childhood cancers — to an already substantial list of diseases that are covered.

"The publication of this final rule marks an important step in the effort to provide needed treatment and care to 9/11 responders and survivors through the WTC Health Program," NIOSH director Dr. John Howard said in a statement this week.

In a separate address, New York City Mayor Michael Bloomberg said, "We have urged from the very beginning that the decision whether or not to include cancer be based on science." For several years, however, many victims and physicians have made countless claims that the effects of the attacks in NYC and DC did in fact contribute to developing debilitating diseases.

Thank you!

Thank you for buying this book and taking the time to read it this far.

More information on what I write and to keep in touch, simply go to www.chrisspivey.org

Just sayin'.

Printed in Great Britain
by Amazon